ANGEL LUST

An erotic
novel of
time travel

PERRY BRASS

Belhue Press

Belhue Press, Second Printing
Copyright ©2000 by Perry Brass

Published in the United State of America by:
Belhue Press
2501 Palisade Ave., Suite A1
Riverdale
Bronx, NY 10463
Electronic mail address: belhuepress@earthlink.net

Cover and overall book design by M. Fitzhugh
Cover photo by John Phillips

ISBN 1-892149-00-1
LIBRARY OF CONGRESS CATALOGUE NUMBER: 99-95215

There isn't any death

There isn't any death
but only constant life
lingering in the cells and the marrow
and the eyes of the world,

and how private
is this vision, this spinning
filament of grasses

and gentle seeds that blow,
and birds that fly back
on their way to the sun,

that often we miss the evidence
of turbulence and glow
of after-peace and still dusks

when the winds seep in
to the joints of rocks and tree trunks,
when the branches

whistle like coyotes
and the clouds skidding through
the distance make remarks

about ages and ages,
and lifetimes that repeat
themselves forever down below.

Perry Brass
from *Sex-charge*, 1991, Belhue Press

For the angels who have come before me, and who knew how many of us would come after. For Marc Collins, who called me his angel, for Jack Nichols and the many angels of Walt Whitman, and all the angels of light on earth who recognize themselves on sight. And of course for Hugh, my angel.

With great thanks to Patrick Merla, Mimi, John Phillips, and John Alvord.

Other books by Perry Brass:

Sex-charge (poetry)

Mirage, a science fiction novel

Circles, the sequel to *Mirage*

Out There: *Stories of Private Desires. Horror. And The Afterlife.*

Albert or The Book of Man, the third book in the *Mirage* series

***Works* and Other "Smoky George" Stories**, <u>Expanded Edition</u>

The Harvest , a "science/politico" novel

The Lover of My Soul, *A Search for Ecstasy and Wisdom*
    (poetry and other collected writings)

How to Survive Your <u>Own</u> Gay Life ,
    An Adult Guide to Love, Sex and Relationships

Chapter 1

For a moment, the dead of the night just stopped. Silent. Tense. The laughter jammed back into my throat. It was decision time that second, know what I mean? I looked at him, then turned around. Then looked back at him. He still had that funny, funky, unshaved, hunky-goofy, what's-next, "I don't get it" look on his face. I looked at his wide shoulders, his strong neck, the tar-black wavy hair, his eyes so deep and inky they glittered. I got a bit shaken. (Do I laugh; throw up some beer; or just show him what I want?) A storm began to whip up around us, as the sky belched up clouds like a load of wet laundry soaked in charcoal. After leaving Casa Julio—a couple of neons and 25-watt light bulbs, smelling of boiled hot dogs, beer, and pee on the Brooklyn waterfront—we had pushed out into Niko's beat up yellow Mustang. Niko Stamos was drunk from beer and a line of schnapps I had bought him.

"Where you wanna go?" he asked. The ripped back seat was decorated with McDonald's wrappers, cracked little plastic ketchups, dirty newspapers, and Happy Meal toys. I didn't hesitate when I told him his house.

"*Skata*—shit!" He shook his head. "It's too late."

I told him we'd be quiet and he smiled, and I grabbed his crotch, something I had not done before. We pretended to be even drunker than we were; always good. He unzipped his jeans and his cock flopped out. It was half hard and dark and silky and I touched the fat swelling head as it emerged from the soft pod of his foreskin. He was juicy with precum. I started to really shake. I wanted to suck him right there. He laughed to knock a hole in the car's quiet. "Fun," he said. "This is gonna be fun." It began to rain and for a moment all we were was the dirty inside of his car that smelled of motor lube oil, Mickey D's ketchup, and him, that wild dick-and-ass, guy-smell gushing straight out of him.

Uncontrollable sex, sure, it can be inevitable. Why fight it? You want your mouth where you want your mouth: It was happening. Lightning flashed like a slice of mirror over the black East River—a wriggling snake

now swallowing all of New York. I was happy. The snake could have it, this city without any eyes that only looked at you.

I had him. I pulled his jeans and white undershorts down—hard to do since he was behind the wheel—and he let me. The rain unleashed itself outside: coming down in climactic sheets and falls. He got up slightly and I squeezed in under his funky bare ass and started to suck at his balls, getting his own savage, distinct, young working man's asshole smell in my nostrils—it shot straight down into my lungs, until there was nothing left of me but that smell and his balls, soft and furry with black hairs slick from his sweat and the salt left over from early morning piss stains. I squeezed around more and licked the whole fat length of his dick. The entire sweet tube of it. "That's real nice, man," he said. "Nice. We done started this magic and I'm readin' it!"

He rubbed his hands through my springy dark blond hair. It was short, with about a two-inch brush cut on top, so dark and thick that sometimes at night it appeared like glowing steel, cool, metallic, pricked with light. I could feel his big fingers raking their way through it, then he lowered them down towards my mouth and jerked himself while I managed to suck him and still lick several of his stained salty fingers, wrapped around his cock like a school of Mediterranean sea horses.

"I can't last like this," he said and told me to stop. Satisfied for a minute, I got back up and he left his warm meat flopping out, while he started the car. He put it into reverse then turned it around in the small lot next to the bar. Debris all around, left over after a too-late banquet of the human mess: more McDonald's crap, cut-up tires, car fenders, rusting oil barrels, soggy bits of old magazines, the color shredded like fallen confetti. Everything. Then more rain. More lightning. Suddenly I could see his face—totally now, nothing to hide—in the lightning's quicksilver strobe: some deep pits from kidhood acne, the large, handsome Greek nose (I wanted to gently suck that, too), his lips, softly chiseled, fine and warm. We pushed out of the tight lot. Brooklyn started to roll behind us in the rain, saying good-bye to us in an eerie quiet, except for a few Land Rovers loaded with stadium-boom stereos. YO MUTHA IS A MUTHA-FUKKER, EAT THAT KILL THAT EAT THAT blasted away in the distance, reverbing into itself, echo into echo, finally disappearing beyond the last lingering rim of my hearing.

The final whisper of this roar started to sound strangely holy as it rolled back with the storm into some distant, long ago speck of me (which was, see, where I was going: I can't stop, I'm afraid . . . the story of who I am) and we rode across the old steel Kosciusko Bridge in the slashing rain into Queens, where he lived; into Astoria, a Greek city-state out of the Peloponnisos. Store signs in Greek. Bakeries, cafes. Stores gated up on Broadway, then over to Thirtieth Avenue, more of the same. Then off to a side street of little houses

like tin soldiers on guard, painted in Greek colors. Pink, orange, green, red. I could see this even in the darkness. It was close to two in the morning. Way too late; things were just happening.

"We'll be there in a minute," he said. "I better buckle myself up again before we get out." I told him I wished he could just walk out like that, buck naked. "Not in Astoria," he said. Then he looked at me and asked, "How'd you know this about me?"

"What d'you mean?" I asked, all dumb blond.

"You know? About me. *Skata*! I can't even talk about it. I was kinda lost. I was gonna kill myself once, you know?" His face dropped. "How'd you know?" I just looked at him. "You got some kinda funny brain in your head, like you knew me already? But you didn't . . . did you?"

"It's okay," I said. "Don't worry. You don't have to know everything. Right?" He smiled at me. It was a smile with a kind of dumb *smart* in it. A bit of that genius wordless (worldless?) people have when they know they don't have to talk anymore, even when all the *smart* people keep on yakking. "Besides," I said. "Like you told me, you got people to take care of. I understand that, taking care. But sometimes we all feel like we're on the edge, don't we, just looking down?"

"When there's nothing down there?"

"Yeah," I said.

"Man, am I drunk. How'd I ever do this fuckin' drive?"

I smiled. "I wouldn't let anything bad happen." Then I added (seriously): "Niko, I knew you the first moment I looked at you."

"*Je-zus*, Tommy! You're a buddy. You're younger than me, but you know a lot." He grinned. His face looked silly, positively, greedily silly with this soft vulnerable animal warmth in it: a sad, lost beauty . . . from way out, past anything you ever see in the "sell-it-buy-it" world. I wanted to eat him right there. Just suck his sweet lips till they . . . "You ever do crack?" he asked me.

"No," I said, dropping back to earth. "You?"

"Yeah. I dunnit. I'm not proud of it, but it can be real good shit. I wish I could go out some place, and do crack with you."

"Why?"

"'Cause then you forget about everything but sex. You could suck a wolf on crack."

"It sounds"—I wanted to say, too far out. Farther out than even I came from. Of course that was impossible. I—I didn't need drugs. I was *the* drug. More potent, more mysterious even than this night, turning too quick into morning. Sometimes I had to forget some of it, just to appear normal. "Sounds nutty."

He nodded his head. "I was lucky. I ain't got hooked. I got friends   11

who're hooked. Nice guys. Their lives become *skata*. Sad shit. Some in jail. A few dead." He stopped the car and his mouth hit mine. He belched right into my throat, then apologized. "Hurts talking about it," he explained. Then started the car again.

"Why'd they get into it?"

He shrugged his shoulders. "You know." I guess I did.

We found his street. Nice residential homes, all sleeping soundly under glowing yellow street lights. The rain had stopped. He parked the car. Put himself completely back together in his jeans. "It's all work," he said. "And your family. And nobody knows you. Just a couple of your buddies. And they don't know you none either. But they do. Or they think they do. Know what I mean?"

I nodded my head, and we got out the car, and he locked it, and we headed up the stairs to his house. He put his forefinger to my lips. We'd be very quiet. He lived with his parents—they had the front bedroom—and his son who was three. He had told me about him. "Joy of my life. Why else go on?" I agreed. He worked in a factory that made upholstered daybeds. Roll out sofa-sleepers. It was the world to him, the men he worked with, from every country. They all had a story: it was like being on a boat, except the boat never went anywhere.

We took our shoes off on the mustard-colored nylon carpet in the hallway. The house was immaculate. It smelled of pine cleaner and lemon oil and cloves, with a whiff of garlic, rosemary, and mint. There was something, I didn't know—maybe medieval about it. Certainly not of this time; I was in heaven. Bingo! The cock works, especially when you don't ask it questions.

I glanced at the pictures on the walls: cracked family photos from the old country, newer ones of holiday gatherings. Pictures of little girls. Little boys. Always separate. A faint light in the big aqua Formica kitchen burned all night; another dim night-light, from the hall bath across from his parents' closed bedroom, did the same thing.

We held our breath on tiptoe. He motioned for me to follow him down the narrow hall into a side room. Its door had been closed, but left slightly ajar. He opened it carefully. "Paul," he whispered to me. The little boy was sleeping in a kid's cot, with just a blue sheet and a thin blanket over him. On a plastic side table a small lamp glowed, its shade a brightly painted circus parade. The dark shadows of a lion, two elephants, and a trio of cha-cha bears on hind legs loomed across the room, cast by this single dreamy eye of light.

I felt suddenly guilty; a bit of an intruder. The boy's room was so still and peaceful, after blowing full-scale out from Casa Julio. I looked around at his toys and kid things, while the circus eye guarded him watchfully. Little outfits, games, stuffed bears, and fluffy beanie creatures. "He likes animals,"

(or *he*, is the marker a "he") have a name?

I could not say, but only knew that we were now curled around the same flowering thing, gathered in a pulling of Time. An immense pulling as mysterious and revealing as the furled tip of the boy's silken foreskin, opening in the darkness of my mouth . . . within that glowing, circus-watched room.

I gave the boy back to Niko, who drew his briefs back up and gently put him back into his bed. "He's gonna have nice dreams," Niko Stamos whispered, smiling. "No nightmares. No monsters. None of that *Star Wars* shit. I can tell. I can see it." He closed his eyes, and I wondered what he was thinking: always the unknowable question, even for beings like us. Then he kissed the little boy and put him back into his bed, and we tiptoed out.

His own room was further down at the end of the hall. It had always been his, he said, after he closed the door and we quickly dropped both our jackets on the bare floor. After his wife Angela had left him with the kid and he moved back in with his parents, he took back his room. His mother was happy. She thought Angela was only a whore, a *putana*, as they say all over the Mediterranean; real *skata*, shit.

There was no light in the room, except for a streetlight outside behind the drawn window shade. Niko lay down on the narrow bed, not much bigger than Paul's, and pulled me to him. His fat tongue went into my ear and he said, "My father used to kiss me like I kissed Paul. I ain't supposed to know. Some think the boys just forget. But it's tradition, they been doing it in Greece since Socrates and the old dudes. It's why us Hellenes are so smart— we're hell of a smart guys, you know? 'Cause the daddies kiss the little dicks of their boys."

He took off his T-shirt. He had the muscular body of a young gladiator; bulked-up forearms and biceps. Beautiful chest sprinkled with sugar-sweet black silky hair that glittered like spun glass even in the dark. The hair got very thick between his two small pointed nipples. They were like little coffee beans, but soft and ready for my mouth. I reached over and kissed them. I could feel Niko's cock mushrooming under his tight jeans.

"Yeah, baby," he whispered softly. "You sure know what you're doin'." I thought I was going to cream right there. "Wanna cigarette?" he asked.

I told him no, but he lit one anyway and smoked it for a moment and then unlaced his work boots. He shucked them off and then bent over and took his socks off. I leaned over, unbuckled his belt and lowered his jeans. They came off next.

Now all he wore were his clean white Jockey shorts, making a kind of bluish, silver glow in the dark with his cock bulging under the silver-white cotton. I ran my hand over the big bulge. His tight hairy stomach trembled. He wanted it: I knew. *Me*. And just the two of us together, in this moment of intense isolated desire.

14

Suddenly I could really smell his body. Whiffs of motor oil, olive oil, some mild still fresh-smelling bathroom soap (Ivory? Lux?); then the more intense scents of his rough feet and hairy hands. Then his hair, with an "herbal" shampoo; even some kind of barbershoppy hair tonic. And finally his own basic smell: sweat, skin, the whole sexy, raw man. "So how come you picked me?" he asked, taking another drag from the cig. "Hey!" he interrupted himself. "Why don't you get naked yourself?"

I started to strip off my T-shirt, and he grabbed it and pulled it off me. "You're so blond!" he noticed. "You remind me of a girl I knew once. She had hair just like you. But it came out of a bottle. Ya know?"—he paused, then said—"I'm drunk enough to wanna lick you, too."

He pulled me to him, then brought his mouth to my chest. I was hard in my jeans, and he fondled it, then unzipped me and pulled my dick out. I did not wear underwear. My dick was not as long as his, but fat. I am cut. "I don't suck boys," he announced seriously. "But right now, Tommy, I could suck you!"

I unbuckled my jeans and lowered them, while he lowered his head to my crotch and licked the soft, swelling mushrooming head of my cock. I was getting very hot. He started to dribble saliva all over me, and used some of it to jerk me with. I had to hold back to keep from exploding in his mouth. I drew away from him for a minute and then took off my sneakers, socks, and jeans. It felt nice to be totally buck naked there with him. I pulled off his Jockeys. We lay for a while just holding on to each other's dicks and kissing. I thought I was going to start creaming all over the air, all over myself, even *in* myself. You must know how that is, right?

"You wanna answer my question?" he asked.

"About?"

"Why you picked on me? One day I got out and there's you, and we end up eatin' a hot dog in front of the factory, with you lookin' at me. So what happened?" He paused, then looked directly into my eyes. I knew he could see very little there. But I was looking into his, and all I could see was want and hope . . . with desire, nakedly trailing behind them.

"Chance," I lied. "Accident." I kissed him with my mouth open, getting my tongue deep down into his mouth.

"Wow, can you kiss!" I nodded my head. "You're wrong. It ain't no accident. You'd been following me. But why? You thought I was . . ." He paused again, then said it: "*Gay?*"

"I didn't think anything really. I just knew," I paused, then said: "that we'd mean something to each other. Get it?" He nodded his handsome head. "It's attraction, that's all. It could happen anyplace." I knew I was lying, but then I stopped lying: "I also thought." I stopped, not sure I could say this. Sometimes words were harder than sex. Anyway, why not say it? "I thought,

15

Niko, you were sad. Like you were calling out something to me. Understand?"

"Sad?" He looked seriously at me. I had gotten to him.

"Yeah. Sad. There was something sad, I could feel it." My face was now at his. "You were missing something. I saw that."

"You did?"

"Yeah. So I wanted to do something for you."

"Yeah," he sighed. "I am sad. You knew. Boy!" His eyes filled with tears. "My wife went off with another guy. We had an arranged marriage, like they do in Greece, I was so lonely in it. I think we never really liked each other. It didn't work. At least I got Paul. I was happy when I fucked her and she got big and we got the little boy. I'd never been so happy. I guess I was only playin' at something, 'cause I wasn't cut out to be a husband. I knew that. But I was scared, you don't know how much that bothers me."

"Scared of what?"

"Bein' just a *malaka*. That's Greek for a jerk-off, a guy who can't get it up when he needs it. When you been fed one line all your life, and you fuck that up—and I was sure I did, no matter what people said—it was like eatin' *skata* for a year. After we broke up, my parents insisted I keep the kid. 'Sure! Let her be a *putana*,' Mama said. 'We get Paul.' But that didn't make me feel a lot better, even if he was what I really wanted."

I looked at him, watching the words flow softly out of his mouth, without judging any of them. The flow stopped. He hesitated, then said: "This is crazy, but . . . I don't believe in homosexuality."

"What do you mean?"

"It's just not something I believe in. I believe in Christ Almighty, the family, the home, but homosexuality just don't seem real to me. This *gay* business, once you get outta bed, just blows away. You're just two guys then, strangers on the street again. Know what I mean? It ain't real to me."

I nodded my head. I did understand, and didn't want words like "gay" or "homosexuality," or any words at all, to get between us. Certainly not then, not when what I felt was beyond most words. And was, certainly, beyond those words.

It's funny the way a word like *homosexuality*, so "scientific," precise, as if it actually described anything that human beings ever really did—or felt—could get in the way of so much. No wonder the stupid fundamentalists liked to throw it at you and then watch people skitter away, like it was a bomb. The oldest bomb.

The word came out of him like a road block: an indictment. It made no sense to me. I guess it was the old *sin* crap. Did man invent sin, or God? And if God did, then why was sin, which came from Him (or *It*) such a bugaboo? At least this sin, the "gay" one, was; though it's always been around (and

around and *around*), believe me.

But he was right. I'd picked him: I had roamed over to him. And now with everything standing between us disappearing, I wanted no road blocks, but only one road . . . right there. "Do you believe in angels?" I asked.

"Angels? You mean like nice guys with wings?"

"Sometimes angels can be nice. But not always. Some angels are demons, too. Some do the bad work, as well as the good."

"Then what are they?"

"Spirits. Part of the spiritual nature of the world. It has that, you know, a spiritual nature as well as a physical one."

"You're losing me, man."

"Okay, let me put it like this. Angels are like warmth when you're cold. You start to rub your hands together; you seek warmth naturally, sometimes without even knowing it. But the truth is, we have no more heat or warmth than anyone else."

"*We*? Are you saying *you're*—"

I shook my head quickly; why let that out? I did not want to spook him before I got to the good parts—like sucking his dick. Not that *that* was the only thing I wanted; there were other things, I admit it. Still, why was *I* being such a . . . I think he said the word was *malaka*? I couldn't tell him the truth. No way. It's part of angelhood: you don't let it out, at least casually. "No. I didn't mean to say that. I mean, anyway, don't worry about it. It's—"

"Oh, I see." He nodded his head. "So, maybe, I just sought *you* out, even without knowing it. Is that what you're sayin'? And this angel stuff, it's like you're talkin' in symbols. Right?" He stopped, then shook his head. "Man, symbols or not, that stuff is freakin' me." He smiled and shook his head. "I dunno if I'm ready for it."

I kissed him again. I liked the way his mouth tasted, kind of spearminty and tobaccoey; salty and young. Some men just have a taste that drives you crazy. This one did. "Forget it," I said. "What I meant to say is that some people know about you, even before you know they know. You don't have to say anything. It all travels between us."

He smiled. "I like that. I just don't want people to think I'm a *pousti*, a cocksucker. It bothers 'em."

"But you really . . . do like to suck cock, don't you?"

He hesitated. I knew I had caught him in a lie, but sometimes we find the truth unbearably heavy, until we find some personal way to lift it. His dark eyes closed; then he opened them. "I like to do a lotta things," he slowly admitted. "Anyway, I don't judge books by their covers."

He did not say anything else after that. He lifted me up and kneeled over me and put my dick into his mouth. He was good at licking and sucking me, at caressing my balls and softly playing with my ass. He ran his fingers into

17

it, and parted my cheeks. I got real hard and then maneuvered him down onto the bed, so that I was fucking his mouth for a while; then we switched around and I sucked him for a while and was happy. Happiness is not something people can take away from you that fast: it's just there.

Then we started going at it together, sixty-nining with one another, doing it at once. I stroked the soles of his feet while I sucked him, and sometimes took his cock out of my mouth and sucked on his toes that were dark and hairy and nicely made. He liked that a lot. He had my whole cock down into his throat and was playing me with all the skill he had at this. Then suddenly, he drew away from me and we pulled out. "You *knew* I was sad?" he asked. "Like I was missing something? Lookin' for it? Or maybe what we're talking about is not a 'it' but a 'him.' Is that what you mean?"

I nodded.

"You're right. I been so lonely, I feel like a hungry dog."

The words fell out of him. Suddenly he started crying for real, as if a huge emotional force he had been hammering down had started to push its way back up, all the way through him. It was uncontrollable, natural, and beautiful; like his beautiful sweet *schlong*—a real New York word for a big dick: a little peter just never makes it as a *schlong*—that went limp while he cried. It got hard again as I kissed the tears off his cheeks. It was a pure, real hard-on that comes from closeness itself, when the naked, physical part of the brain opens itself up to tenderness.

Maybe it was just too late at night. He was drunk and his feelings were coming out too quickly: he had ripped the mask finally off his face and I got to see him whole; beautiful; truly amazing to me. We couldn't stop kissing one another, and I began to dissolve into him as I knew I would.

It was a moment beginning in overwhelming sexual lust, that somehow turned another bend in that river of Life that pours through you. You're never sure where that river begins, and you end; and for that moment, I disappeared completely while I explored his whole body, every part of it, like some vast, virgin territory that went all the way back through Time itself. I explored it as that territory circled and then returned to me; there, in that little dark room that had been his since childhood.

Soft, slow music started to play inside us; bells, strings, off in the distance, making a circle vibrating around us. Until the music joined us together and our breathing became one breathing and we had our cocks back in one another's mouth, and we were making music that way, too.

Sometimes together; and sometimes separately. Sometimes him over me, pushing his dick into me, with me gratefully accepting it. And sometimes the other way. He was getting close, I knew—ready to release any second—I wanted his semen, that liquid life force of his, all over, on my chest, face, in my face, in my mouth. All over. To taste it, run it over my tongue and lick it,

and wash it down with my own saliva. I wanted it. The music. The him part. The smell, the life of him made liquid.

But I also wanted this to last and not be over. I kept freezing us both from climaxing, using techniques of my body as well as my mind: walking over the fields of Heaven; squeezing my dick on its head, pulling at my balls, counting distant markers on those fields that revealed Time, shining at me. Ten, fifty, a hundred, a thousand. A million. Years, breath, your own life . . . now you're soft again.

You're in a cloud, a garden, walking with him. I knew he was getting softer, then pulling back, then getting harder again. I'd come back to him. To this Greek gladiator with his beautiful body, his chest wet with coal-black hair, his cock warm then hot and so very nice—that all I wanted to do was get it back into my mouth. But before I could do that, he said: "Man, you know I'm not into getting fucked, but—"

"But what?" I asked. We were now sitting up, legs locked around each other.

"I like a finger up my butt. My wife used to do it sometimes, if I got her in the right mood."

I was in the right mood. I used some lubricating lotion by the bed and a little spit and stuck my index finger up him. He squirmed a bit, then I used the index and the middle. "Slow," he warned. "Just real slow and nice."

I did that, and he began to go all gooey and loose on me, his cock getting even harder, so hard and hot that I knew he was not going to last more than a minute like this. I pulled out of his ass, and then gently squeezed the head of his dick. "You know about that?" he asked.

I nodded, and then as he came down I sucked him a bit more, just along the shaft, finally licking the fat dark head that was juicy with precum. I liked the taste of it. It reminded me of salty wine or maybe rainwater. Yes, right then I remembered that: it came to me as a vision. Distant, distinct. Not really a memory, but an image. Going out in those stony fields, almost a thousand years ago—and watching little crooked rows of root vegetables . . . as the sky opened up, and I saw myself at an early age, as I once was.

He started to pet and stroke me on my stomach, chest, and shoulders. We could not stop touching one another and I liked that. I released myself to him, to that warm, intense, touching experience. And I started feeling this glowing, weightless, definitely familiar sensation in my back.

I was levitating. Without Niko knowing it, or even seeing it. I was slowly rising up from the bed even though, physically, I was still in it. I could see him now completely: I was floating directly over him. He smiled.

His face was close, yet distant as some moon . . . he had that celestial, innocent smile that I wanted to recapture, to hold from another time. My presence above him intensified. I became a ball of sexual energy, my hands

We were slick, newly born, covered in these primal roots. Back. Back . . . as the child and I mutually satisfied one another, wrapping our hands around thighs, until the water and flesh between us dissolved, and I knew I had returned farther: to the womb, to the very belly of my birth, as Niko's hot jet shot into my mouth—exploding in me and on me, in great, eye-filling star bursts of cosmic spurts.

"Wowww!" Niko said. "Ain't never had sex like that with nobody. Boy or girl." He was still wrapped around me. We were both naked and we must have dozed off for a moment. I looked around.

"Where's the little boy?" I asked.

"What boy?" He looked at me shocked. "What're you talkin' about?"

"Paul."

"*Paul*? He's asleep. He better be. He ain't in here. Gee—did you? Don't tell me; did you see him?"

"Didn't you?"

"No. He just sleeps through the night."

"While I was sucking you, did you see him?"

Niko smiled. "No way. That is real *malaka*, but—"

"What?"

"There was this moment when I felt like I was about three years old. Funny. All tiny and light."

I nodded my head. "I brought you back," I told him. "To being that young. I was having sex with you at—well, that age."

"How'd you do that? Man, this is nuts!"

"I can't explain, Niko. Don't ask me any more, okay?"

"Man, you're crazier than crack. I ain't even sure I wanna get you on that shit!"

I smiled and said: "I don't think you're going to have to worry about that." I got up and told him I should get out of there. He shrugged, and asked me why. "My folks are cool," he told me. "They never talk about anything they don't want t' know about."

I told him I thought that was helpful.

"It's the Hellene way; not American, but Greek." He smiled. "Why don't you stay here, unless you gotta go someplace else?"

I did, there was someplace I needed to go back to. But for the moment, I wanted to stay there. We snuggled, face to face, on the narrow bed with one of my hands on his firm hairy butt and the other on his resting cock. I felt strangely home free now: I had found him. I couldn't explain it, and he would never know what that meant to me. It was like something he could not talk to his parents about. I had to hold it all inside me.

We settled into a kind of mutual relaxation. He whispered a few things to

me. Mostly, I remember, "Don't worry. I'm gonna take care of you, really"; then a short while later I fell asleep with my face cooled by the soft black hairs on his chest. Some got into my mouth and brushed my eyelids. It made no difference. I didn't want to think about anything else; there was a big road ahead and behind me, but who wants to think about that? I slept there in Niko Stamos's arms for an hour or two, the dark pasture of hair on his forearms around me; then I woke up while he slept.

Something had pushed me out of sleep. I was no longer in control of myself; I thought I had been, but what was the use? These things were bigger than I could be. There's only Fate; I knew that.

I got out of the bed and sank down on my knees on the wooden floor. The cold crawled through me, but I could not get back into bed with Niko. I knew that. He was who I thought he was; but I could not at that moment return to his bed.

I became frightened. No matter who I was—or what—no matter how long I had spent walking carefully through the blowing fields of Time, there were still things I could not control. Had I transgressed? Had I gone against the will of my lord, the one knight to whom I had pledged fealty and my submission?

"My lord," I said quietly, "I know I cannot control my lust for this beautiful Greek man. I have missed him so much," then I realized that my lord would know this. He knew the whole story, but did he still disapprove, back where he is, almost a thousand years later?

I would have to seek the answer. I would have to go back and join myself, Tommy Angelo, to what I had been before: if only to witness it, as I had to. For I can go back, I can watch, I can be told, and I can tell; but do as I will, I cannot change what must be or has been. That is the eternal Law of Angels; and of our travel, I swear, over Time's mysterious bridge. Believe me, it humbles us, too.

"My lord," I sobbed, finally giving vent to how unworthy I felt. "Were not angels once clothed in lust, as well as in love?"

Then I prayed softly: "Bertrand, my lord, remember me. I am drawn to this troubled man as I was drawn to him before. For his sake, I have come to shed peace on him, for I know that he wanders and wanders, as I do, too. And, also, that he is looking for me, as I was for him. But only *you*, Bertrand, can make me whole again with myself. Amen."

I looked up at Niko's face now sleeping soundly, but turned towards me. He seemed at such peace. He had returned to his own handsome innocence there in the land of dreams, where angels are real, if you know how to dream of them. But my own peace? Where was that? Despite going through the

silent gates of death, I could not control my own unquenchable desire. I, Thomas, was Desire.

Just as I could not control my own unquenchable desire to know myself.

This desire would be the life and the death of me over and over again. Tears suddenly flowed from my eyes. I remembered then a prayer that I had brought with me from so many years back. Another life? We all have them. We know it. It is the truth. The truth behind the thin veil on which we exist: the veil of violence, greed, and vanity. But at some moment, this veil will be ripped apart by Existence: by the reality of Truth.

Then all those lies and untruths will be shredded, only to be made whole again in the vast material of the human soul. I began the prayer, and then, as far as my own soul was concerned, I disappeared once I had finished the last word.

My lord, my knight, I prayed.
My sheltering angel,
take me once more by your side,
kiss me with your wine-sweet lips,
spread your strong hands over me
and bring me calm and peace.
Take me across the woods of Time
that can never hold us apart
and let me lie atop your chest,
surrounded by your loving arms.

Chapter 2

My Christian and born name was Thomas Jebson. This was what I was known by and how I knew myself. I was the son of Jeb, a poor pig farmer, and for most of those years I bore a churlish life of filth and rags, sunrise to sunset. My story begins in a time of real trouble, thereabouts some thousand years after the death of Our Lord, the Son of God, the crucified Jesus Christ. A new era had begun. We were in England, eleven years after the Normans and their hated king, William, our conqueror (the beast, sometimes known as William the Bastard!) had come across over the black waters, and brought their strange and superior ways to us.

War. Darkness. Burning. Chaining us to that weary stony land through the constant fee—they called it the *feud*—and the villainy of serfdom. We were very poor. We lived in the North Midland Country, at the foothills of mountains, not far from Scotland; but, verily, I had never laid eyes on the vales of the Scots. See, I had been Nowhere; that was the only country I knew. Just Nowhere. But I dreamed about other places, I did, even as my poor family and I lived in the damp smoke of ignorance, bringing in pathetically little light.

I was a *cniht*, a churl, or serf, youth in my sixteenth year, though in those times not so young. Boys oft married at thirteen, girls at twelve. By the age of twenty-one, often we were spent. Dead.

I came from Oakum, a broken little settlement some path off (but it could have been, really, a hundred years away) from the fortress of a Norman baron. I had never seen him. I was not even permitted to look at his face. But his shadow rose like the vulture's own wing over our folk. We cowered at his name. It was whispered among us only as Odred, the Dreaded One, whose eyes were like ice and who could not be looked upon directly. He was Norman through and through. His ways were foreign, his customs hateful to us; he was a landlord of King William, the Conqueror. He had the Word, the Law, and even the greatness of God on his side.

This was said as the Truth.

We were not to question it.

I was of good height: medium tall, not too short, but not too big either. Our people being farmers did not grow so tall as sailors, who had the good breath of the sea in their lungs. I was fair and blond, too; with the good, sturdy honest features of the Danemen as well as the Saxons; smooth-limbed and somewhat muscular, not yet stooped from hard labor in the field. Longish and streaked, flaxen hair I had, reaching almost to the shoulders, as the Saxons like a man's fine hair; the Normans, all *passing snell*—so very warlike—clipped theirs round like sheeps'.

Years back, six generations or so, I had been told, our people had come out on the big ships, from the great fishing kingdoms of Deniscland, called Denmark by some. It was from them that I got my long blond hair, though I have dark eyes that sometimes appear green, but sometimes, as my mother has said, they look like the old lost precious stuff, amber, when the moon hits them. "Amber," she said with me on her knees, "with the sea's own drops of emeralds in them." She knew to talk this way, she did.

The *Dene*, the Danes, mixed with the old earth-tilling Saxons here and made good, honest people. Strong; smart; still a snatch of roving in their blood. They were not to be tied down. All this was whispered to me by my mother, Grett, a still youngish woman who looked more Dane, wheaten-haired, long-limbed, and blue-eyed, than Saxon English, who get darker and stocky; their menfolk hairier.

I was, I was told, of upright, gentle appearance. My nature (and I want you to believe my story) was not seen oft amongst our neighbors in the pig-muck settlement into which (by God's wishes) I had found myself birthed. Dear Grett, a poor farmer's woman but of true goodness and grace amongst the meanness of Oakum, was accused of birthing me a bastard. The village hags whispered that my seed had come not from Jeb's stringy loins. He was an old churl, now in his fifty-fifth year. Lies! Jeb was a peaceful shy soul, bearing a mind of his own. I knew he was mine own *foter*. Quickly Grett would turn from such words, and had no mind for churlish talk.

So we lived most alone on the leafy verge of the village, only amongst ourselves with a few pigs and some stringy chickens, who were both companion to us as well as meat for eating. On a farm sometimes even your feathered and four-footed friends can end up in the stew pot! That is the way—we thank 'em. Mostly though we ate root and grain; turnip, carrot, barley, oat. That sort of thing.

I grew up quickly but wounded at heart by our low station. I thirsted for something other, beyond the old sow grunting by our hut with her brood and the laying hen pecking dirt around her. There was another world beyond this; that of the deep forest and the far places. I knew it was there. I glimpsed at it

from time to time, when I sneaked past the hard gaze of the folk about us, as they spied at me on my walks alone.

It was with this yearning that I ventured out one day by myself, along the barren ground past everything I knew. I cannot tell you the fear in my heart, though it was in the turn of fall when the sky became bright, all blue and clear again, as fresh as a newly plucked apple. By myself I had ventured out in hope of seeing once more a handsome nobleman whose own young face and manner had delighted me at the very break of that day. This peaceful-looking knight on horse, his appearance, his sweet and unexpected smile, had drawn me to him in a way I cannot explain, except to say that it was like—how do I put it?—the first excitement of young love itself.

I had been up already, even before light. And there he was, one of three horsemen, going around for I knew not what, clopping quickly but cautiously towards me. His other companions cantered on, but he stopped, leaning in his fine saddle in my direction. We only looked at one another, he on horse and me on the ground, my eyes fearing even to look at him.

Then, suddenly, as the sun began to split the early morning darkness, he smiled at me directly. Our eyes were drawn so close that it felt as if angels themselves had spoken. And what said they? I cannot tell you, but I found myself all stone in my place, my mouth gaping at the miracle of him. He appeared golden. I thought I might lose all of my upright pride and cry.

Being only a lad, without enough sense to tell me otherwise, I knew then that I longed for this strong young noble's kiss, for his lips on my face. That is the truth, so help me. . . . And I promised myself right there that if he would but claim me in friendship, I would follow him no matter what. Even barefoot through the snow, through an icy wind; or a wet storm from the easterly direction of the sea, from where Grett's old people had come.

Through any dark place. Yes. I said that to myself.

I was now his, as a good dog is drawn to his Master. I cannot say it any other way, except . . . yes, I do confess, as we are drawn to the Blood of Jesus Christ with His pale chaste limbs on the Cross. So, I was drawn that way. And I imagined then the stranger's own finely hosed feet, suddenly unshod, exactly like the heaven-bound feet of the Savior, all naked and white, which we humbly beg to kiss for ever and ever. Amen.

I felt thus, in all my simplicity and youth.

Now there I was, following his horse on my own two aching feet, clad only in the woolen slippers Grett had sewn for me; we were too poor for good leather shoes. But there was no ache in my heart. I remembered the face that drew me to him, but knew not his name. I knew only that each step I took was filled with danger; but so it had to be, as I had decided to follow him. Why he had come to us, I did not know. I knew only that on that very morning, before the rooster's first crow, he and two companions had turned

their mounts by the pig ruts on the outskirts of Oakum. And a moment later, they were gone.

Disappeared into air. As if I had only imagined them, though I knew this not to be so. This youngest one, "my knight," I will call him, had ridden harder to catch up to them; then all I saw was their dust. Perhaps the three had been lost or were trying not to be seen by our *seigneur*, Odred, and his bad knights, who were known to kill foreigners of any sort, even those of fine character.

That morning when I saw them, I was first about from our hut, to hoe pig muck and tend the chickens. Living by the verge, sometimes we saw strangers riding through; a bit later the Norman horsemen would race by and question us. They would pull Jeb out from his work. He would try to evade their grillings, but if threatened would admit, "I did see one o' two." Then he would point these snapping dogs in the wrong direction, hoping thus that good strangers might be safe.

But often to our grief at *aefen*, sunset, our eyes would be stung by black bonfire smoke blowing from the fields over by the woods. Smoke holding the belly-turning stench of a burning corpse. Grett would clutch me to her and sob; Jeb would cast his gray, balding head down. "'Nother done," he'd say again. "'Nother soul lost to the Norman worms. When will it end?"

We would go into the hut, hoping to disappear from the smell and the sight. "You must leave," Grett warned me in the dark silence, while Jeb looked away. She was already starting to stoop and wrinkle a bit from worry, though herself she had no more than sixteen years on me. "No matter what," she begged, "leave. One day these monsters will come and kill us, too."

Why, I asked. I was so simple. Protected, maybe.

Her voice lowered in fear though we three were alone. "We are not like they, our neighbors, who are only churls and know it. Jeb has his good wits about him, and I—I come from other people. The Norsemen. We were fine once. Princes, even, remember that. But with such dolts as live around us, we must pretend ever to be something we are not. We are poor, but still we can think. We can see. We can know what is right."

It was true. The neighbors were ignorant. They spread evil gossip about us: I was a bastard. My mother a witch. Jeb a fool and a cuckold. The farmer folk would do anything for a copper farthing or a boiled pig's foot thrown to them, tossed off by the rich. They had little shyness about pointing *Seigneur*'s, the Baron Odred's, men to any worthy strangers who might become their victims. To these poor folk, all gnarled and twisted by toil, by fear, it was but the local rich robbing passing ones; with the churls hoping they might catch a few coins left from a cut purse along the way.

Ignorance, I came to see, loves murder. And even with a smile will point a way to it.

For this reason, and not wanting to involve my parents in any danger in regard to these strangers, I did not say a word to them and left their sleep inside the hut undisturbed. I had hoped these strange knights, no matter what they were doing, would not be seen; and no one would question me.

I had wished to call out and warn them, but instead stayed locked in bashfulness. What could I say? I was ignorant and, truth be told, I could hardly breathe, so smitten was I by the one who had stopped for me. On his great black stallion, he had smiled with those sky-blue eyes set in a warm face. And for that moment, our eyes had rested gratefully on each other, making me wonder later if he might also have been as shy as I; and so, not given to words.

I thought my heart would stop; then he was off.

Though I could not read or write and had only sufficient number-learning to count pigs, I was enchanted by this man as if by magic. Truly moved was I in my heart and, yes—I will say it; Jesus, condemn me not for this!—in my groin as well. I know I was young, my mind fixed there as the young are set to be. But there, between the legs, it was as if a twinge of lightning had snapped into that place where the little men live inside you. The small demons and faeries, it is said, who swim in a man's own life-breathing sperm and bring his cock to full alert, when the time comes.

At least, that is what some menfolk said.

Since this is the sort of private thing I would tell you only upon my knees, I must relay now some secret knowledge to you. There are, I swear by Mary Herself, men called "faeries" or "faerie magicians," who dwell deep in our own woods. Deep in their forest lands they appear at night. But every now and then, they could be seen by us, at dusk, at early evening time, in those grassy, blowing regions where the deep forests parted and made their first bow to the meadows.

Perhaps you have heard of them, these men, but high-born types, it was said, did not admit of knowing them. Or they pretended they existed only in tale or rumor. But I want you to know that this is not so. Very much, they do *live.*

In hard times one or two would appear near our huts. They were poor and in rags, and would ask us for food; us, only poor farmers grubbing for a root or some grain, in rags ourselves. We had only a little millet or barley. A carrot; a scrawny chicken. The pigs we must sell cheap to the Norman barons, who carried them off as a tax. Some of the faeries, the forest men, did speak about our Lord Jesus, who loved the animals. He loved children, He loved all of that; a good Savior He was.

But (and this you must keep quiet) other foresters whispered about the ancient secret Saxon faerie gods, the *Ealdweard*, who were worshipped in

the Ealdcraeft, and who—this is the worst blasphemy, but true—never disappeared. . . .

For this, the honest forest men could be burned at the fires of the stake. It was a sadness to me, a heartbreak. So they must speak only so to men with whom they felt trust. Young as I was, I was one; I am pleased to say this, though I kept totally hush about it. You cannot imagine the shame involved, the fear, the Norman eyes around us.

Yes, I must keep hush.

Still, I was certain with all my years that what they spoke about quietly was the truth, and by holding back part of our story—the part about the olde religion, the Ealdcraeft—we were only learning half the truth. And many lies. Some of us wanted to hear both, the Christian and the Saxon, stories. These, too, must be said, if truth were not to be forgotten.

For the tales of the Eotens, the giants who lived once amongst us, tell us much. They tell us about the life force in the forests and on the good Earth. And of this great force, all men, I believe, are a part. The force is in them, in their most secret places and their hearts. It comes all the way from their heads down to their toes. Their whole bodies, in truth, have this force.

And there is one other thing about these old Faerie gods: the *Ealdwulder* still possess magic. A most powerful magic, invoked through secret rituals guarded from the evil *seigneurs* who had come to stay around us. A magic both good . . . and feared.

I, Thomas Jebson, knew of this magic, though out of the woods it was forbidden to speak of it. What kind of magic? To know, you must believe in the magic of the night; the magic of the deep grasses; of the brain, the soul . . . and, yes, the magic of the little men in our under parts, the places covered by the codpiece and the breechcloth. The little spirits, we say, of the *tarse*, the cock (for every man possesses a friendly, though sometimes spiteful little knave who lives there, inside this organ of his). And there are also, I know, the spirits of the two balls and the arsehole. I have sought out these spirits, and I know that these little men must be reached for, and petted, and stroked if you want their magic to spill out and work for you.

To do this, I saw the forest magicians paint their faces with green and blue berry stains and brush themselves with crushed, fragrant leaves. They wrapped vines around their bare chests and waists, then danced naked in circles, holding each other by their cocks, or stroking the testicles warm under them. In this way, the little men inside the big men were invited out. They lingered amongst us. And brought magic, power. Lightning, heat.

And light, like the fireflies' glow itself.

Deep in the vine-hung bellies of the forest, where the wild stag and boar still hide, you can sometimes hear the drum, flute, and sounds of these forbidden dances. And perhaps, if you wander by innocently in the dark, you

can come face to face with these painted men. Then, if you show no fear or foolishness, they may even allow you into their dances.

They did this with me, seeing that at heart I wished to be one of them. They took me in hand, deeper and deeper through the tangled, vine-bound floors of the forest. And there I found in the dark, dark shadows, men knowing each other in the closest and most loving ways. I was surprised—yes, shocked. I did not know this could happen, for such things were not spoken of openly in any way, especially now with the Norman brigands about us.

There, the foresters made close bonds of affection, and spoke in a manner of such truthfulness that their words must never leave the wood, or they would be silenced with their own blood: the blood of the blameless, who knew the truth . . . in a violent world.

These men stink of leaves, grass, stag hide, unwashed manliness and secret lusts. That is their way, as they lead you deeper through the twisting vines, the deep groves and the ancient mazes of trees where they dwell and sleep. Some village men would whisper about them and venture out if they spoke in the meadows, as I said, close by the forests. Old Jeb was once amongst them and he, still aching with fear and his old work-worn limbs, took me with him. But then, quickly enough, he ran off as the sun began to sink.

I, curious, and always mindful to leave the bounds of village life, stayed on. One of these same men, big-chested and bearded, verily a powerful magician, hearty and playful, came up to me and took me in his giant hand so that at my age I knew of these things and there, with them, in the great, leafy groin of the forest itself, I spent the night.

Yes, there I was inducted secretly into their magic. And I would have stayed on, tarried; nay, even lived with them forever. . . .

But for fear of my parents (especially old Jeb), I did not. I chose to keep this night to myself. And I returned to the village, to my misery and disappointment, and did not stay behind those deep curtains of leafy woods with the faeries.

The faerie magicians call their rites *holtenweir*, "forest magic." They perform them with lust and merriment to invoke the ancient spirits of the woods, the *weir* of the mistletoe and ivy, which they twine around their own exposed private parts, and these they offer in the shadows to prayerful mouths and fingers. In this manner, the men of the olde ways, the Ealdcraeft, pair off or gather in small groups for their own communion.

In these dark cloisters of nature, they call on the Green Man, the Goatboy, the Earth Goddess, the Sky Lord and all the Ealdcraeft. They blow on the sacred fleshy horn, the cock itself, licking, caressing, holding, and openly sucking it. They pray that the good spirits of the tarse will guard them from the flames and daggers of the conquering barons, who do evil to

31

foresters.

The rich in their stone fortresses abominated these rites, and burned much of our land to push this magic deeper into the woods and farther away from them. They instructed the priests and churchmen to preach against the Ealdcraeft. "Hear! Hear! These woodmen are servants of the Devil, the *Yfel One*," the fat churchmen preached. "Satan himself, who crawls from the greenwoods at night with cloven hooves and head horns—who holds in his teeth virgins and young innocent boys—that very Satan, they serve!"

I had heard such lies scare women and children, but I ignored them. I nodded my young head while the shaved priests and their toadies prattled on. Sometimes I became convinced that the priests were actually secretly excited by their own words; and that even the respectable rich secretly yearned to practice everything that the shaved heads preached against.

"The *Yfel One* will bugger young men in their arseholes! He will turn them into the Devil's messengers! He rapes the virgin and turns her into his own daughter! He does so at night, in the midst of fire and brimstone. His vile minions are all around us! You will know them by their horns and their big stiff phalluses that never lie down. Yes, always stiff, my friends! Always looking for any place they can find! And they go into the holts, the forests, at night to do these things. And though they are men, they are witches, too, and followers of *Yvel*!"

I must tell you, I did not believe this idiocy, even though I, too, was ignorant and could not read or write. Jeb and Grett, too, heard these stories, and like me they nodded. But we knew who the real devils were: the barons who burned our farming settlements and paraded through the charred ruins on their big warhorses. They also burned many of us at the stake, as believers in the Evil One. They frightened most into silence, but not I.

(At least, in this telling, I will not be silent to you!)

Their lying words only increased my desire to flee Oakum. In my dreams, I saw myself on such a journey. I would take off on a great horse, in fine clothes, for a place where safely I could learn to read and write, if only my name. How happy I would be; imagine, I thought, what my name would look like on fine vellum in beautiful script, like I had seen in the church, in the big books we were not allowed to read.

That my name might be written down would preserve it forever. I would be like the heroes of stories, in the Bible and such, as my name would then be in script and very fine.

It would be sad to leave my parents, but neither could I live nearby in the forests, like the forest faerie men, their hidden lives always in danger. If I did thus, my capture would mean humiliation to my parents—and perhaps their deaths. But leave I must, I knew this, and hoped that at some point I would find a way out. That something good would come to me and allow my own

strength to take me from the settlement and the ignorance around me.

But I would need help; after all, I was only an ignorant farmer's *cniht*, and there was danger on every side of me, from the sword, the burning stake, robbers on the road, and every sort of roving demon and animal that came forth in the night. Of this, I was certain. If God truly were to honor my request, I would have to seek out a nobleman and offer myself to him humbly in every way and serve him gladly with my heart.

To him I would truly offer my willing body and soul. I would pledge submission to him, and in return ask only for his protection and kindness.

With that in mind, I set out to seek this noble young personage who had smiled at me and given me such happiness with his eyes. I was not sure even if he spoke our language, but his smile, direct and natural as that early morning's light, lit the way for me.

I convinced myself I had to see him again and, if necessary, though I had never done anything of this sort, I would walk at least ten days to find him. That was the time that I decided upon; though, in truth, ten days then seemed like an eternity to me. Beyond that, more I could barely imagine. I was sixteen, but as you can see, I had a mind of my own, believe me.

I returned to our small hut and quickly formed a lie in my mind. I was not used to going against the truth to my parents, but knew that for their sakes as well as mine this falsehood had to be done. I blew into my cold hands and did not look into his face, as I told old Jeb that I was going out to do work on Amos's, a distant neighbor's, land. I might stay, if needed, for ten days. Jeb only nodded. Amos, I said, would pay me with a basket of turnips, a rucksack of carrots, and two good young hen chickens. His chickens were the best about. Jeb suddenly smiled; we were poor and could use all that. Two of Amos's big brown hogs were ready for butchering and his fall wheat for cutting; this would take days, I knew. I would sleep in his barn, bigger than our hut, with his watch dog, the fat sow pigs, and two cows for warmth. Amos, a prosperous churl, did sometimes watch out for the local knights and was not much to be trusted, but as long as I did no talking, everything would be safe.

My father sat up from his straw bed with Grett. As men of the farm did in sleep, he was naked, mostly bones. "Be careful, son," Grett warned wearily. "May Jesus go with you and bless you with goodness and count you as one of His sons. But remember, like I tell you, the less you say—" I nodded my head. Jeb only smiled, lifted his hand, and bid me a good day and God's fortune.

I packed a small round of barley bread and a bit of oats in a little pocket sack. I took a little jug of water and was about to leave the hut, when I saw another horse gallop by. I hid my victuals and with my face to the ground came out towards the rider, a harsh knave I knew as Mars, a vile brigand of

the Baron Odred.

"Seen two strangers?" Mars asked. His face was scarred and bony, his teeth pitted like an old horse's. He stank like a privy hole.

"On my Faith, no," I answered, swallowing hard. 'Twas true. I had not seen two strangers, but *three*. I looked down at the ground, without facing him. Surely, he could not kill me for reporting such truth. Nay, I had seen three strangers!

"Must 'a come afore cock crow!" He spat out a wad of mouth gunk on the dirt, only two fingers' length from my feet. My stomach flipped over within my belly, then his brown spittle sank into the dirt, its own natural partner. "You lie, boy, and I aim to thrust my sword right up your arse, till I cut that pretty hair with its point! Understand?"

I nodded my head and did not take my face from the ground till I heard his horse gallop off. Then I did look up, and saw Mars gathering speed in the opposite direction of the three men. I smiled and watched his dust disappear. I hoped, as naturally I would, that he might disappear forever with it.

Then, without another word, I hurried into the direction the stranger and his two companions had taken a short time before. I did not look back at Jeb's hut. I was afraid he or Grett might come out and say something to me. Even though Jeb slept starkers naked, he might come out bare as a rabbit. It was his custom; near his hut he felt free to do so. He would let forth a stream of yellow piss right there by the pigs, and even finger himself gladly with me looking. He would only wink and say, "If it feels this good, the Lord won't mind."

I knew I would miss them, miss my old man and mom. But I had to get away. Somehow, if things went well, I would get word back to them. Or I might come back dressed as a gentleman's groom, in splendid clothes, with silk and green hose and good stuff like that. That had always been a wish of mine, to have green hose. Every boy has a wish, you know.

Soon the sun was above me, but I knew how to follow its course and so determine my direction. The land around me was charred; the road, if it could be called so, was merely stamped dust, like a place where the Devil had used his tail to beat the earth down. It made for slow walking. I followed this and hoped with all my might that the young stranger and his two friends had not changed their course.

Some time later, about when the sun had already risen well past noon, the land mercifully did change. It was no longer gray and brown. There was grass, bright meadow, and good shrub about. Never in my life had I been so far away, embarking so on this "adventure," a going out. That was it: I was going . . . out. I felt good, walking was fine. I sang to myself and forgot my fears. I walked and walked, holding on to the direction of the strangers, while the earth became even greener, the rich hue of bright copper as it turns in the

rain and the sunny green of young eyes in smiling faces. It was all that, this new land, as I went farther through it.

I came to some good trees, pleasant fields of them in the softly rolling ground. I smelled fragrant herbs, a sign of fresh water, and soon noticed a brook flowing through the herbage. I hurried over. I knelt, drinking like a thirsty puppy, getting water on my face and up my nose, then slicking my blond hair with it. I took off my wool shoes and soaked my tired bare feet. I would have stripped and washed my whole unclothed self, except that the day was approaching coolness and, like any soul, I feared the quick death brought on by evil humours. This going about was all so new to me. Yet, so far, I felt no regret, a good sign I was sure.

Then the sun, without any warning, as I sat by the brook, fell into the darkening West. The old Sun himself had deserted me, without even a wink. I looked around me and realized that soon enough I would have no guide for direction. All manner of thought came up to me.

Suppose the Yvel One *should* get me on my quest, and, as the wandering priests warned, shove his green tarse, that long and pestilent piss-piece of his, right up my tender arsehole? Or make me suck his rod, all slimy and reeking of sulfur and the black dung of swamp dragons? *Ughh*! I shivered as the dark, gathering cold shot through me.

Still, I was determined. No matter how much I feared, I would not be deterred. I would find this handsome stranger whom I followed, who would make me his own slave if necessary, to protect me.

I would keep on for another day and then another and another. For ten days I would do this, until surely Jesus Christ Our Lord would agree to it and our paths would cross. Then I would kneel at his well-shod, knightly feet and beseech him to allow me to join him. This, I swore to myself I would do.

Then as I had to, following practical matters, I sought a place to sleep. I spotted such shelter on a distant knoll, a little hill some way before me. There, as only a smudge before my eyes, was the shape of a leafy holt, a small grove of bushes and herbs, crowned by a clump of low trees. From the distance where I saw it, it seemed like a place kind faeries had made solely for me. There was a pale ring of stars above it, faint twinkling lights, glowing like a magic cobweb in the purple dusk. Surely this was a sign from God Himself.

I trudged up to it, while from up above a half-moon presented itself, white as new snow, in a clear cloudless sky. The moon's light in the gathering darkness made the low arms of the small trees appear twice as black, affording me the shelter that I needed. A screeching wind began to whistle through my long pale hair. My lower body shook with chill. Still I pushed more distance behind me, and walked on towards the mysterious shelter that I sought.

I reached the trees and crouched under them, then drank from my jug. Water trickled down my throat, spilling onto my dry lips, but quenching me. I bit off a chunk of the hard barley bread, and crunched some of the oats in my mouth. I felt somewhat better. Then I realized that I had not emptied my gut all day, and, though alone, I found a gully off to itself to squat; and, there, did so.

Leaving a goodly stump of shit, I felt better. Since I had been taught decent ways by my parents (certainly amongst the coarse pig people about us), I scooped some dirt over my turd to lessen its odor, and also cleaned my little hindmost with green leaves, even dousing a bit of water from my jug on them. I did not want to smell bad to this young noble. On a close-by hill, I found sprigs of yellow wild chamomile and lemony bay, and rubbed my groin and arsehole with their crushed fragrance. This, too, was not something most done by our kind. But Grett had told me that the Lord looks well on clean people, and I had learned to value such things.

Doing this, I felt so good that I gathered handfuls of soft, fresh herbs on the hillside, as I let my nose take in the sweet-smelling breeze. Then, removing my dusty shoes, my tunic and breeches, I rubbed my arms, chest, legs, face, and loins with them. I was completely naked. I forgot every fear and looked up at the stars, clearer now and more distinct in the almost black sky.

I wanted to leap among them and dance for sheer joy.

My young skin—bare, smooth, willowy, but strong—felt happy. Warm all over despite the cool air. I thought again about the young nobleman on his horse. His intense blue eyes. His strong dark capable hands. The wide, firm set of his shoulders and his deep chest. Thinking of this brought heat to my loins, just as when I had danced in the faerie men's magic circle. I knew then that I had been drawn to him in a very similar way—I could not explain it, but it was there.

In that circle, the good men had touched me in the name of the *Ealdweard*, the olde gods. They had taken me with their warmth and sweetness, made stronger by many surges of good-natured affection.

They were bearded, naturally older than I, and had knelt big, strong, and naked in front of me, taking turns stroking and fondling my young cock. They made it hard and big, sucking it as an offering to the green holten spirits who came forth out of the dark. Finally, with my back arching, they sucked down the rich white liquor shooting forth from me. They told me it was fine, good as the precious, tiny eggs of the quail or any of the Irish monks' "noble distillations" that their own tongues had ever before tasted.

"Be proud!" they said, hugging and kissing me. "Stand up straight, Tom. Be not afraid of the rich folk who fear this forest."

"The rich are fools!" their leader, Richard, as I learned his name was, roared. "And when they die, they go down to a Hell filled with fools just like

them. Yes, there they are, kindling for the Devil!"

I returned to the little coppice of trees and lay down naked under it, on my worn clothes and my tattered cloak. Then, for the joy of it and to feel less alone, I began to touch my nether parts. These had been dubbed by our local priests (who forgot that, under their musty robes, they were as naked as I) with such names as, "the backdoor to filth and shit!"—thus they cast the arsehole. The good groin they dubbed, "that black hairy hallway to hideous Hell!"

But my favorite name was for the male feature itself—or, as we say, the tarse. "The sly Devil's old walking stick," they called that!

It was my favorite because, like old Jeb, I, too, liked to take mine out and walk with it. Sometimes I let it swing out, totally naked, in the forest, where I felt at home. There I could finger my young stick as I wanted, letting it flop along or get hard, and also letting the tall grasses and gentle leaves tickle my bare downy thighs and blond arsehole. Fingering my stick felt good. Since no one else was there, I licked my fingers and used some spit to pleasure myself and please the knob's warm emerging head. It was all throbbing, good and pink. I also touched my soft young balls. They felt ready, warm, and friendly as I stroked them with my hands, both to please myself and to ward off the fears that would come to a *knabe*, a youth, in this darkness.

Thus I forgot the dangers around me. My heart began to gallop, as I lay there alone, a boy fiddling with his own lust. But, alas, this feeling could not go on. While fingering my stick, a new blast of cold—this one very *raw*—blew hard against me. The night, now complete, fell like a great black pall, pressing in all about me, even heavier than I had expected, out in this wilderness.

Was this terror real, or something only in my own young poor mind? I could not tell. The mind was that of a farmer's lad, reasserting itself, with all its ignorant fears.

Even more afraid, I looked around into the moon-pierced blackness. I heard distant, unseen animals cry. Wolves? Dragons? Who knew what waited out there, as I lay with only the leafy branches above me blotting out the stars, and all manner of barons and devils in the dark, sniffing like a pack of dogs at my trail?

For comfort and warmth, I rolled myself, still naked, into a ball of young flesh, clutching my knees to my chest, as my hair tickled my shoulders. Even fearful as I was, I must confess that I resumed fingering the Devil's own stick; I did this to bring some warmth into my anxious cold hands, which soon enough spread through my body. I was now totally hard, and if I had continued would soon be at the point of making the little men push semen out the hole.

I smiled. Those little men knew what they were doing!

This felt so enjoyable that I wondered how even the Devil, who preferred meanness to any delight, could enjoy such a thing. He was the *Yvel One*. He was said to produce vileness and pestilence. Yet, were it not the goodly rich, followers of the priests and their sort, who burned our forests and trampled our farms to keep that very Devil away?

I thought about these things which now filled my mind as my tarse filled my hands. I felt once more less frightened. Presently I released my grip upon my tool. Even though I was young and energetic, I was also greatly tired; and soon, clutching my cloak about me, I fell into a sleep. With that came this dream—the handsome young nobleman showed himself and befriended me. He taught me the magic, forbidden art of reading, that the priests said none of our kind can learn. We were not to know what the sacred letters said about Jesus Christ. Only the rich and the priests could know firsthand the Word of God.

This they preached was true, even as the coarse men who roamed the forests and gleefully groped and sucked each other laughed. What a laugh! The laugh of a big, throbbing cock! Like a church organ! Like thunder! Like the beating hooves of stags! Or horses!

Yes, very *bigggg* horses!

That laugh—I could hear their laughter rolling in my dream—and that made me feel better. Then the laughing stopped. I saw once more the face of the young nobleman. His genuine smile; his piercing blue eyes; and all my ignorant yearnings towards him came out—with no one to hold them back. I yearned nakedly for him, as I had not done ever before. I crawled towards him, my youthful body strangely hot to the point of fever. I reached out towards him there, in the dew-soaked, frigid night air; and with a shock, woke up.

A razor-sharp breeze whistled over me.

I opened my tired eyes and heard in the vast, barren silence about me, the thunderous clack of horse hooves, faraway, racing in the distance. I got up, cold, unclothed.

Walking out on bare feet and straining my eyes, I saw in the farthest distance, like a needle pricking the darkness, the tiny roaming eyes of torches. They were there, at the very lip of the horizon, burning, too, into my own eyes.

Murderers! Fire! The black charring of our forests.

My blood sank to my feet; my hands froze. Once more brigands would burn the land and put to sword those who dared oppose them. They would burn the woods, rounding up anyone they called heretical. They were near; they would find me. I knew it.

How could I, alone, save myself? I wondered that as I watched the

torches disappear in the black distance.

I went back to the shelter of the trees, pulling my tattered cloak over my cold self, and, heartbroken, sobbed. Never had I felt so alone, so unaided, so in need of mercy. I knew nothing of fighting, of armed war; but, choking back the tears, thought that, perhaps, by some miracle, at daybreak I might leave this place, unharmed.

Before sunrise I would resume again my quest in the stranger's direction. I clenched my eyes and stopped crying. Cold, more I was sure then from fear than the temperature itself, ran through my limbs, shriveling my pale, young "walking stick" until it became merely a small button of loose flesh with a shy hood closing over its head. Fear had gouged great holes into my frightened soul. I began to pray. First to Jesus, then, still shivering, I asked help from the ancient Ealdcraeft in whose forbidden rituals I myself had joined. I prayed and prayed until finally the prayers must have worked. I felt less alone, less aware of my loneliness, as if something else were there with me.

I cannot say what it was. But hugging my rough knees to my chest and rocking back and forth slowly, I became united again with the last shred of peace and goodness left inside me. Something was, indeed, glowing around me, this I knew. Perhaps it was only my desire to be united with the strange knight whose presence, I knew, was glowing around me.

The wind had stopped, and the night itself felt warm.

In my mind I walked once more, innocent, stripped to the waist in the glowing fields of a warm spring, with the old Sun himself kissing my bare, slightly freckled shoulders from above. I felt warm, peaceful, and indeed moved to tears with gratitude. There, within me, was the love that I possessed; I would find *him*—I knew this—the young stranger, and give him this very love. I convinced myself of this, as clutching my cloak, I held my naked limbs to myself and listened to the quiet of the night. . . .

It was a most gentle sound to my ears.

But too quickly the quiet was punctured by the beating of a horse's hooves. Distant, but distinct; rushing towards my direction. The sound approached in the dark, before the horse did. It hit me like thunder. It pulled my guts into a knot.

I got up slowly, edging my way out beyond the shielding trees. I had to determine which fiend was out there, looking to find and kill me. I had expected to see the stranger again with his two noble friends. I had not anticipated one lone horseman, galloping up the hill towards me.

But now a lone warrior rode up in full armor to that knoll where I had tried to hide my naked self. I stood transfixed as he came upon me, rising up ever bigger, until the glint and shine of his dark armor sparkled in the starry, silver moonlight before me.

Such . . . amazement! It allowed me no time to reclothe. I watched, 39

stunned, as if a dream were galloping towards me from out of my sleep; though it was more like watching my own approaching death, as he appeared before me, fully armored, helmeted, outfitted, shining like a single star in heaven, from which he seemed to ride. I felt tiny as a mouse; this, despite the fact that in a few years I might have risen to his full match in height or weight. But I was unarmed, only a young churl, smudged with dirt from travel, accustomed only to rags when rightly dressed.

Soon, he was close before me, seated arrogantly on his horse, a few paces beyond my small mound of trees. His black stallion unable to contain its fire, stomped over the ground, making noises like a dragon or some creature from realms that I had not seen but could imagine. Afraid but somewhat curious (like a cornered dog), I peered over at this creature of war and saw that his black leather saddle was skirted and overhung with banners of various signs whose meanings I could not understand. Embroidered in silver and scarlet against white and black, two banners were topped with a device of four five-pointed stars in a diamond over a triangle. The bottom star was smaller. There were other signs strange to me.

Among these signs I noticed two animals (billy goats? rams?) *rampant*; that is (do I, an unlearned *cniht*, use this word right?), as if each were dancing on a single hind hoof, with a lone horn growing from the top of each beast's head. They faced one another and right above, where the two horns almost met, a thin silver cross (made upside down), glowed against the black, like it was falling from heaven.

I felt stupid. I could not decipher this thing—and even more, on this clear fall night I was caught naked—a condition hated by the church sorts and goodly rich types. Soon enough, this knight, who looked so aloof on his horse, might kill me. Suddenly I wondered if I did not, in truth, as an idiot churl, deserve such a fate.

The knight began to lean forward a bit on his high horse, to pet the beast's neck and shoulders. He spoke some words. I tried hard to listen which, was all I could do, as I was too dumbstruck to move. The horse, calmer, settled down. He lowered his huge head, dropping gobs of hot white snot from his nose onto the cooler ground. A slight wind whipped up. I began to tremble from cold, goose bumps rippled across my bare shoulders and smooth stomach. I thought I should clothe myself, but was afraid to move.

His rider talked gently to the horse, as if I were not there. This made me feel better. Perhaps he would find no offense with me. Being a foreigner, he might restart his night ride and only report later that he had found a young man all alone, naked, on a hilltop. ("*Naked*? Is that the custom of that country?" I could imagine well-bred laughter.)

But the horseman did not ride off. He stayed.

And I became aware that from within his black-plumed helmet, his eyes

were on me; I felt frozen in his stare. His gloved hand reached towards his sword's scabbard and then, with some effort—perhaps he was fatigued; it is hard to say—he dismounted.

As he did this, his armor's metal clinking cut through both the silence around me and the loud beating of my heart. I became afraid that I might just pee on my own cold feet; I was that frightened. For by all that was called right in Jesus's own land, this knight's razor-edged sword could push its way directly into my bare chest. Without any problems, as a noble in the land of William the Conqueror, he could kill me and leave me dead there.

To my young, burning shame, a warm trickle of piss moistened the dirt at my feet, as he approached. I looked up, humiliated. What could this creature in black armor think of me, even before slaying me; that I was no better than a dog? A pig? Something to just cut and leave?

With this in mind, I knew that I had to show all my spirit. I had to scoop it up from my heart and show it to him. I had to show this knight that I was not without some fineness of my own. Where I got this idea, I knew not; but I could not die like one of Jeb's pigs. I swallowed hard and, leaving a piss mark behind me, stepped towards him. Then, stark naked and my hair tangled from sleeping on the ground, I presented myself to him.

Each moment seemed like an eternity, as he gazed at me from under his black helmet, plumed in glistening raven feathers that caught each ray of moonlight. Sword in hand, he was now in front of me, trees behind us, and we soon met one another in the way of strangers in an unnamed place. Who could say what would happen; or even, if he felt moved to murder me, if he might report it?

In silence, I prostrated myself before him, lowering my forehead to the dirt. I stayed there, and thought, if this black knight is going to kill me, let him respect me and do so now. With speed. No delay. But let him see that I will neither whimper, nor beg for mercy.

For I was proud, too.

I could hear his horse, cantering, coming up towards us. My heart approached bursting. I looked up and saw the rider take his shining sword from its scabbard, and lift it up towards me. He could do it now. A wordless murder . . . my knees shook. I tried to control myself.

Then, without a word, he brought me to my feet and gravely handed me the sword.

Who could forget such a moment? If I lived for a thousand years . . . I would not. His blade was heavy. Pure steel—of the type I believed Frankish nobles used.

I felt weak, but grabbed it by its grip and then stood with him in front of me, as he took me into his arms and ran his black-gloved hands through my pale hair and then embraced my naked thighs.

41

"*Toujour*," he whispered. "*Toujour*, I sought you." Then cupping my chin, he bade me look into his dark, helmeted face and drew his visor up, so that I now looked directly into his amazing blue eyes.

He was the knight whom I had sought, and now he had given me, Thomas Jebson, a *cniht*, his sword. The immensity of this—its true meaning—escaped me at the moment, so happy was I not only to be alive . . . but to find him.

My gladness was overwhelming. "But I have been seeking you," I told him, the words leaping from my throat.

He nodded silently to me. He knew . . . yes, knew!

My walk now seemed to make sense, but how and why did we find each other in this way? It could only mean that God's own mercy had brought us together. I handed him back his heavy blade, then took his other hand. There were tears in my eyes that I had to blink back. But I managed to remove his fine black gauntlet, then brought his strong fingers to my lips and kissed each one.

I pressed his wrist, sprinkled with the black hair of his forearms, to my mouth, pouring my love upon it. I became lost in this, in kissing his noble wrist, then his upturned palm which he cupped to my face. Finally, mysteriously—I had expected no such thing—he brought my lips to his. As a young man, kissing one only a few years older, I kissed him gratefully.

"You are innocent," he said. "A *jeune homme* of God. I altered my plans and came back for you."

I nodded, trying to understand what he said; then, filled with such a depth of feelings upon this mysterious meeting, I fell to my knees and clutched his armored legs. That he had said this to me—young and ignorant as I was—moved me so much.

He looked down at me. "You must rise," he commanded, and I did as he said. "By what are you appelled?"

I looked at him blankly.

He laughed and cocked his head. "I shalt talk plainer. Thou art Saxon, though blond. Your name?"

"Thomas Jebson . . . son of a pig farmer. That is all."

"Sufficient, Thomas Jebson. If it pleases thou, it satisfies me. A goodly, honest name. *Gentil*. I am called Bertrand. I am a young knight, a *jeune homme* myself, but from far away. Thou may think me older, but in many ways I am not. That is why among my insignia is the *unicorn*, beloved of the innocent Virgin. For me, the unicorn dances with his friend and brings new life between them in the form of the fallen Cross."

I nodded my head. Now I understood. He went on, "And, *ausi*, I have four stars over the Mountain, for the Trinity and my own soul. I come from a place called the Land at the End of the Mountain."

"Where is that?" I asked. "I have been nowhere. I know nothing. Not to

read. Nor write. Truly nothing, sir."

He smiled again and kissed me softly on my cheek, which I took naturally, as naturally as his first kiss. "My young friend, you will learn one day these things! Me, I am from very far away. Days on boat and horseback. Please do not ask me about my origins. They are not as yet for you to know. But I have sworn myself to protect you and other good souls like you. That is why I have come back for you. I wandered, looked, left my two *confrères* for you. Please know that."

I listened to what he spoke, and had to catch my tears; they were collecting within my throat. "Sir," I began, shivering with this new, immeasurable love for him, just as before I had shivered from the wind and my own fear. "If it is good for you, sir, let me follow you as your vassal and liege slave. You may strike me dead, if that is your will. I know that. Or take my body as your own willing tool, or whatever else my noble Sir desires."

Bertrand nodded his head solemnly. He bowed slightly to me. "*Content*, enough. You will see that I desire nothing other than such a bond from you, and your sincerity. And I shall give you nothing more than my protection and *honneur*."

Honor! I had wanted only green hose to wear. Never had I believed it possible that any son of Jeb would have honor as well! And this *honor* from a knight whose Frankish accent I could not place, but who still did not seem like a hated Norman. His manners were too beautiful, as he was; and his sleek black hair too long to be a Norman's, as it was almost as long as mine.

He smiled weakly, and began to yawn. "I am tired, Thomas. My *confrères* are off on their own, and I am alone. May I be permitted to spend the night in this place with you?"

I told him that would be my greatest wish. The two of us could face the dangers of the night certainly better than I could alone—and I would prove my loyalty and use to him as quickly as I could.

"*Bon*!" he cried, his blue eyes twinkling. "Directly you may prove yourself to me, my young *monsieur*, by helping me out of this armor!"

I was pleased then beyond words, as he instructed my awkward fingers in the hinges, knots, and buckles of the armored joints whose workings protected him. Each dark plate, I saw as it came off, was expertly made. Outside they were engraved with figures of men at war. But inside one plate, in secret, next to his heart, was cut a design that I quickly recognized, despite what some may feel was its strangeness.

There the men were in all sorts of "interesting" positions. And they were openly, freely naked. Some of them strode about hard, big, with their cocks fully ready, while others were seen accepting them; for they were making forbidden, masculine love—in the ways I knew so well of the forest. Trees and leaves were engraved about them, but without hiding anything.

With his young, muscular but darkly hairy chest bared in the cool night air, Sir Bertrand pointed this out to me and asked, "Does something of this nature frighten you, Thomas?"

I told him no; though I had not so many years, I, too, had knowledge of these ways as they were practiced in the old forests. I knew of them, though most Saxons would no longer speak of such things.

"Then you are not dishonored," he asked. "By a scene such as this?"

I told him definitely no. Then I told him, as I felt I should, that I would follow him anywhere; barefoot, if need be. "Through the steaming pits of Hell," I swore. "Through any freezing night. If only you will keep me as your vassal, and allow me to sleep with your dogs."

He shook his head and smiled. There was no need for that, he promised. He would want to sleep close to me, if only for the warmth. He would have me sleep not with his dogs, but next to him. In his own chamber. Soon I had helped him strip even more, his boots, even down to the breechcloth that covered his private parts, and saw that though young, he was indeed remarkable beneath it all—all sinew, muscle, flesh, and perfect form; his strong, horse-riding thighs were like marble columns, but dark and already hairy; and his shoulders muscular and as wide as the beams of a church. I could not help looking at him. Then he turned from me and untied his breechpiece covering, and shyly cast it onto the ground so that now he was even barefoot, and as completely naked as I was.

I smiled as I watched him from the back, hoping that he would not see my pleasure as this sight, for his back was broad and handsome, too. I noticed that he kept his visage away from me, as if in some kind of embarrassment. Then he turned back towards me.

His eyes were on the ground, but the heavy bounty of his breechcloth was now unashamedly erect in the cool air. He could not hide its great size or stiffness. It stood out straight as his sword and almost as broad. I realized then that he was, perhaps, only six years my senior; and that was all. So in age, he might have been only a little over twenty-one, or twenty-two. And I realized, then, that in such matters, this knight could also be bashful.

He looked up at me, his eyes distant and blue, and he smiled. Then he whispered to me gently, "I gladly share myself with you, Thomas Jebson, *mon jeune homme*, in the ways of the forest men you have told me about. The secret ways. And if you will take me as I am, I will say no more."

I nodded. He had asked acceptance from *me*! Such a thing seemed impossible, but I was so unversed in the ways of gentle folk. For a moment I knew not what to say, then I said, "You have a goodly tarse, Sir Bertrand. I am grateful for your company. Believe me, sir."

I could say no more. The words had left me.

He closed his eyes. How beautiful he looked. The curling, raven locks of

his hair flowing softly from his head. His big chest, scarred in several places; I guessed from the sword or the joust. His two large, slightly bumpy red nipples. The muscular, strong, goodness of his arse. His large cock, that jumped nervously with each beat of his pulse. I took in the whole form of him. His voice lowered. He seemed almost shamefaced; I could see that. Perhaps knights were like that, a bit solemn.

"*Bon*," he said. "You, too, young Thomas . . . are most favoured in my eyes. I kouth it so. I have long dreamed that I would find a *garçon* like you. We will take each other with love deep inside us."

"Yes, sir," I said quietly, "I am pleased." Then, as I noticed that he was now shaking slightly and perhaps not too sure what to do, I knelt down before him and sweetly kissed the warm fat shaft, then the head of his swollen rod. I slid the silky sheath of its foreskin back to reveal its sweet pink flesh. I kissed, licked, and sucked it, giving thus all my attentions to this noble man, who would henceforth be called my master and lordly knight, and who, despite his own youth, would be many other things to me, some of which I could not, at that moment, know.

He moaned softly with increasing pleasure as his boy vassal took the full shaft of his member, longer than the length of my hand even, into his willing mouth. Its stiffness and heat increased, I swear, and my lord's pleasure climbed in peaks and tremors towards his satisfaction. His strong hands raked through the long blonde strands of my hair, stroking and touching me, my face, and my throat; sometimes gripping me, as his pleasure increased, to the point of choking me.

This, I fear, only excited me more. I began to moan and even cry as I knew the warm liquor of his sperm would soon pour down my gullet. I tasted my own salty tears on the finely veined skin of his swelling organ, as it jerked and rammed all the way into the back of my throat. I yearned for his completion and begged for it, with each stroke of my mouth on his thick shaft. I was breathing as hard as he, and fingered myself below so that the ol' Devil's walking stick became long and hard enough to bear weight, as my own excitement mirrored my mysterious rider's.

Then with no warning at all, the young naked knight pulled his member from my mouth. I could not hide the surprise on my face. Had I displeased him? What had I done? I was afraid he was going to slap me, rebuke me for . . . what? Being too eager? But instead, in the full hot flush of his desire, he pulled me to him and kissed me.

His mouth lingered at my lips. He pushed his tongue all the way down my dumbstruck throat that had wanted his cock, taking my breath away. I panted. I was taken with him. I feared my heart would burst. There was now light glimmering in the darkness on this hill, as his pale, beautiful face came towards me with this unexpected, though gratefully accepted affection.

45

Chapter 3

Then with no explanation, he withdrew from me and stood slightly aside, looking white as the moon despite his dark hair, next to my churlish sunburnt skin. He was all white fire and flowing raven locks, his eyes intensely watching me, looking at every part of me. The tremble that I noticed before resumed. What had I done? What had produced this displeasure, this trembling rage? I wanted to kiss him again and again. I yearned for him, his lips, his hands, his chest and tarse, for his body next to me in any way he chose.

Finally I could bear the silence no longer. "Have I provoked my lord?" I asked.

He closed his eyes again. I missed their blueness.

"Provoked? Do you think I am *unpleased*?"

"I know not what . . . ," I answered.

"Thomas, you have no idea how happy I am at *présent*!" He began to laugh, then suddenly kicked me lightly with his bare toes in one thigh and then on my arse. He laughed more and more, but I could not comprehend the nature of his joke. Was this his noble humor? Was it so much above me that I could not understand it, as his station was so much higher than mine—a churl—now his vassal? "You, Thomas, displease *moi*!" he laughed until he had to hold on to his sides.

"Yes, sir," I said. "Have I displeased you?"

I approached him, my head down. I was afraid he might restrap his armor himself and leave me in this small grove, naked, alone again. I would have to find my way back alone to Oakum. I might be killed on the way. But why would I care, if he left me?

I clung to him, and he gently slapped my face as one might a spoiled child and then my firm round ass as I begged for his attention, for his member down my throat again or any place he cared to lavish me with it. He pulled me to him, and held my face in his noble tender hands.

"Thomas, you do not know what *you* are to me," he whispered. "Thou art   47

more than thou wilt ever, ever kouth. Please permit me to speak plainly. You have taken away my lonely state, the condition always of a wandering knight. You are the gentle simple light of morning that I have sought, as I shall be the full moon that you seek. I kouth this to be true."

"Then you will do with me for your pleasure?" I asked.

A smile lit up his solemn face. "I shall, *cher* Thomas. I shall spray my golden piss on you, drag you through hills and brambles. Let you sleep with my hunting dogs. But only if we both want this!" I smiled and nodded my head at him.

He went on. "But I shall never forsake you. And you will be happy. I will give you the love of the angels that you so deserve. I will gladly kill for you, if need be. For I am yours as much as you are mine, young *monsieur* Jebson. This I swear with my knightly oath. And you will never go hungry, cold, or without drink." He paused, then licked his lips. "And, speaking of drink, have we a libation? I certainly could use some beverage at *présent*."

I nodded my head, retrieved my small jug, and he grabbed it. He drank eagerly, dribbling water down his broad chest so that it glistened in the black hair there. I wanted to lick these drops off, but quickly he threw the empty jug on the ground and then beamed openly at me. "Thank you, Thomas. Your water has helped your lord. He is grateful!"

"You are welcome, sir," I said, but noticed that Sir Bertrand had not shared any of this last bit of water with me, as I thought a noble would. The ways of knights, I was to learn, were difficult.

He must have seen some flicker of doubt on my face. He pulled me to him and then kissed me lightly on the cheek again. Was he only toying with me, as if I were a child? I did not want that, and asked him to stick his tool once more down my throat, or he could do with me in any manner that he pleased. He could even use his tarse to bugger my tight young arsehole; old Jeb had told me with a wink that some sporting knaves, once they unhitched their breechcloths, did such things. I was serious and filled with desire for the knight.

I waited. He only smiled and toyed with me more, pushing me this way and that, looking at me in the clear starlight from my backside and then my front.

I wondered what all this meant, as he gazed at me; I knew that I was not of his noble level. In the distance I heard the faint cries of a wolf. It must have been crying at the clear crescent moon, which seemed as far away from it as Bertrand was from me. I was only a churl; and he a knight. He could leave me, kill me; both; make me do his bidding, and I would be only too happy that he had once tarried with me, for some sport out in the wilderness.

The wolf's cry ceased.

48   Then Bertrand stopped smiling and began to kiss me in places I had not

dreamed I would so be kissed, with his warm manly lips on my brow, my tender nipples stiffened by the cool air around them, and my stomach salted by sweat from the road. I whispered my loyalty to him; I could barely breathe. I was sure he would leave there after every kiss, that his words had been only the fine words of a knight to a serf; that he might, indeed, only command me to re-armor him and, then, using my naked back as a hoist, remount his fine black horse and disappear.

I waited for this to happen, but he knelt, and in full command of himself, kissed my tarse, the thick, fleshy cock of a churl, quite as full and willing as his, but still only a peasant's. He kissed it and ran his firm tongue down its thick-veined shaft, lapping at it gently as he would milk or water, even though I still felt unwashed and crude compared to him. "Do you like that?" he whispered.

"Verily, lord," I replied.

He proceeded to form his mouth manfully to suck my cock, making me harder and hotter than I had ever been or knew myself possible to be. To my surprise, he seemed to delight in pleasing me as much as I had delighted in doing so to him. And as he did this, I wondered how such a man could do this. That he could place his gentle mouth on my lowly tool; young, smooth, and hot as it was. And then bring me to such heights of ecstasy, while he fingered himself, merging his own swelling desires with my throbbing rushes.

Soon enough he had brought us both to that edge where the stars themselves came down to explode; that very trembling, ecstatic place. The one that the priests back home feared most of all, saying that this was where the Devil himself grabbed his tail and beat time in a circle.

There Bertrand truly forgot himself, so that my noble lord sucked me happily and greedily, and brought me to a total, rushing satisfaction that knocked at the very door of Heaven. He smiled, then pressed his jerking member to my lips, and I did the same to him, tasting the thick rushing joy of his semen in a white, silverish liquor of manly juice. We lay then under the little grove of trees in one another's arms.

"You, Thomas," he whispered, "shall no longer be any man's serf, but for my eyes alone—just as I glimpsed at you earlier this morning. Please let me tell you that I am *votre ange*, your angel, a bringer of the Light amidst the Dark, just as you in ages hence will be mine." I nodded my head and listened, but had almost no idea of what he really said.

Bertrand went on, "I will share my soul with you and protect you as I would myself, Thomas Jebson. I swear this, friend and companion to me for all eternity." He smiled, then added: "And you will sleep not with my dogs, I assure this. But with me, wrapped in furs, silks, and *très riche* stuff from every place."

We slept then in the dark, under my tattered cloak, with the stars out there way above us and his fine armor nearby. But we woke often through the night to please each other. He seemed to have an endless lust, and sucked and stroked my tarse until I was sore with pleasure. Then, briefly before daybreak, we heard very distant horses galloping towards us. We were still half asleep, in each other's arms. "The Norman barons of this land!" Bertrand cried, shaking his head. "Corrupt, evil. They are seeking me and my *confrères*."

"Why, my lord?"

"Because I am good. Not corrupt, as they are. And also, I am young. They detest that. They will use any lie and deception against us. I tarried here too long, taken by your simple kindness and youth. I must re-arm myself, and you must help me. Then I will take you on my mount, Fire, and, as I promised, keep you safe."

I nodded my head and swiftly re-armed him, then I redressed myself and he got back on his horse. He pulled me up to him, and I clung to him on his saddle. He pushed himself forward in the seat, so that there might be room for me behind him. At first Fire, feeling the extra weight, would not gallop. He reared back, cantered a bit, then came to a stop. Then Bertrand leaned forward and said something that I could not understand into one of the steed's black ears. After this, the horse took off.

I asked him what he said.

"It was in my language, Thomas. I said, 'Fire, we're either off from here quickly or we'll eat *you* tonight!'"

"Smart boy!" I said. Then I wrapped my arms around Bertrand's armor as tightly as I could as we sped off, away from the approaching storm of warbound horses. Halfway past the break of day, we were safe from them. The air was clear. We were in a high green thicket, next to a stream. There the great horse again slowed down. We were off the road, on a grassy path. Fire put his head down and quietly began to eat.

Even as strong as he was, the heavily saddled stallion could not carry both Sir Bertrand in full armor and myself and speed away. Before us was another hillside filled with trees. I begged the young knight to leave me there; without me, he could gallop on. I would find my way back into a forest—and from there?

From there I had no idea. I would do something, somehow. But I wanted Bertrand to be safe. That was how I felt about him already.

He refused. "*Non*," he replied. "They will burn the whole land to find me. And kill you. They will torture you. They will track us both."

He turned around to me and kissed me, holding my face next to his, burying my lips in his mouth. I thought my heart would break.

"Besides," he added, "I can *not* leave you, Thomas. You have my oath;

have faith. I am protected by Sir Garet du Fontayne and Sir Ansel, my two *confrères*. With God's love that brought me to you, they kouth that I am in this region. If I do not come back soon enough from my ride, surely they will follow."

I nodded my head and hoped that what Sir Bertrand said was true. God's love indeed had brought him to me; it would protect us, also. I had to have faith. Bertrand's appearance to me that night was too mysterious to be accidental. Verily, something else was here . . . but what?

"Sir Garet and Sir Ansel," Bertrand continued, "are familiar with the brigands who reside about here. *Regardèz*, I am not afraid of fighting one-on-one, but I fear that they will never fight fair. By *droit*, if I kill their leader, they should leave us. But they do not fight this way, these Normans!"

We both got off Fire, and Bertrand led him to the top of the hill. The sun quickly rose. We sat while the horse grazed and Bertrand brought water from the stream over to him. I felt suddenly tired, then in the distance saw again the dust of galloping horses. But whose dust, I asked myself? I felt as if my whole life were suspended in thin air. Or as if Sir Bertrand of the Land at the End of the Mountain held it, indeed, in one black-gloved hand.

"We must go quickly," he ordered. He jumped back on Fire and hoisted me up. He turned the horse away from the dust, and we rode off as fast as we could, pacing the horse with the two of us on him. Now without any question, my fears all left me. We could ride through deserts, mountains, rivers. We could freeze. But since I had found Sir Bertrand, the young knight I sought, it seemed that nothing could be worse than being separated from him. Our destinies were now one, making even death itself look innocent.

Yes, even death itself.

EVEN DEATH ITSELF. . . . the words raged at me. They fell like a sudden cold rain. And at that moment I returned, with a shock that came instant and freezing.

That warm wave of Time that had carried me, rolling me back, farther back . . . that had taken me all the way to the beginning of the Second Millennium, to the England of young Thomas and the knight Sir Bertrand . . . had stopped. And the bridge, all light, all crystal, all substance without substance, that I had to take; the cold bridge back to Niko's room . . . had come flashing down, in front of me.

I was again on the wooden floor of his room, kneeling, when Niko's eyes opened. "You're a strange dude," he murmured. "You ain't no usual *pousti* at all."

I nodded my head: If only he knew. I got up and went for my clothes. "I've got to leave," I said in a rush.

"Why, babe? Stay. Mama'll make breakfast for us. Ever had a Greek

breakfast? You won't eat for a week!"

I told him I'd better go. He asked me if he'd see me again. I told him I'd come by the factory where he worked. He got up and fumbled around for a pen and paper. He found the back of a slip from Macy's, and wrote his telephone number on it. Then he held me in his arms and kissed me. He put on a pair of boxers, and led me down the long hallway to the door. "Know how to get out of here?" he whispered. "Maybe I should just drive you back into Manhattan."

I smiled. That was good of him, but no. I kissed him good-bye again briefly at the door and then walked out into the cool morning light. The air was fresh after the storm the night before, and I enjoyed being in a strange place, just walking and having my head completely clear after everything that I had experienced in one way or another.

Time. Time short; Time eternal . . . elliptical . . . came rushing back to me, there in Niko Stamos's tiny room. But it would do that, always; for Time means very little to me.

Really.

The nice thing about New York is that you can always get someplace, no matter what time is. It was Saturday, about six in the morning. I had to return to the master of my life. I knew that. Oh, I had been drawn to Niko, there's no lie about that. Why? Besides his own Greek handsomeness—and the raw, yearning, delicious power of him—we, too, had had a history of our own: I knew that. It went back. It did.

But how could he know this? Who could know? When queer men meet, is there something else guiding them? Perhaps, but only angels know.

About angels: people think about these ancient mythical beings, in whom, deep at heart, they want to believe—okay, I mean *us*, we angels— anyway, they think we have wings. Big old pigeon-feathered flight equipment. And that we look like something painted on stained glass windows, or in old oil paintings and on Easter cards. We look all kind of holy-rolly; and never anything else.

Wrong.

We can look like a lot of things. The expression "angelic," meaning nice, innocent, cute, sweet—does not, in any way, describe what angels physically look like, or, spiritually, are. We are, folks, more real and bigger than "cute." We're a force; a spiritual force. We exist the way hurricanes exist. And earthquakes, and a drop of mountain water. Even a drop of mountain water on the planet Jupiter. So we don't need wings to carry us anyplace.

Especially if we can find a cab.

Luckily, I did so quickly enough in the morning light of Astoria, where men were already gathering in the diners along Broadway and some of the side streets. The driver asked where to? and I told him the address of my loft

on Lower Park Avenue. "You been out partying all night," he asked. I thought he was Greek, but it turned out he was Russian. Handsome, maybe twenty-eight. He did something to me, and I was too . . . well, just say I was too happy to be myself, Tommy Angelo, once more to resist. The awkward little thing that Time had brought me back to—and I'd once been—Thomas Jebson, had long ago disappeared. My balls stirred looking at him. I could have blown him in the backseat; I knew it.

That energy. That coarse, pure, uncontainable windstorm of lust, that never died in me, was still whipping up and pouring out . . . even after my night with Niko. It filled every space around me like an electrical field.

I looked over at his driver's I.D. and told Boris I had been. *Partying*. He looked back at me through his mirror. He smiled. All teeth, dimples, radiance . . . I liked that. "You must be . . . how you say? *Pooped*?"

"Not totally." I answered.

"Sometime," he said, still smiling back at me, "You never get *too* much fun."

I nodded my head; then asked him if he'd like to park the cab for a while and join me in the back.

Chapter 4

He found a side street, next to a small, run-down park in God-knows-where, not too far from the Queens side of the Midtown Tunnel. Everything out there stretched into a kind of blur—squatty tenements, bigger apartments; low humming noise—that happens when you're in a part of New York that you don't know. I smiled. He parked the cab. There was no one around. The neighborhood was just poor enough that no cop was going to stick his neck in to bother us.

Boris got in the back with me—I watched him get out; he was about ten pounds overweight, too much Russian cooking, I guessed—and I unzipped his dark polyester pants and sucked him off completely. Getting all of him right into my mouth. He tasted great. Gushes, just reams of jism right there. Hot, wild. The whole thing took about seven minutes. He had a great wonderful thick dick with a foreskin like an inner tube. Big, hairy balls. The foreskin drew up. The head was beautiful, clean, and a deep, slightly dark pink underneath.

He was all sex—pure flashes; lightning—I liked that. *Me?* I was running on . . . well, call it "angelic energy." Was I even there with him—who knows, maybe I was still with Bertrand? I wasn't sure, but when it was over and I saw the look of warm Slavic contentment on his morning-shadowed face, I knew I'd done the right thing.

What a rare feeling: when you're too worn out to censor yourself, and only want more. He offered not to charge me for the trip, but I told him the pleasure was as much mine as his. All I asked was to ride in the front seat with him.

He smoked a dark Russian cigarette, and offered me one. To be sociable I took it, but hardly did more than drag it out the passenger-side window as he drove. He asked me all sorts of questions about myself. What did I do for a living—I told him I was an "unlicensed massage therapist," another word for a whore, I guess. Was I married? No. Yes. Maybe. It all depended on your definition of marriage, or Time, or . . . anything else. Did I like girls, too? Yes, I told him, if they had dicks like he had. He told me he was married— 55

"But divorced now. She no give me what . . . you do. A man can like a lot, yes?"

I nodded my head. Yes. A man *can* like a lot.

He told me he was from Odessa. "Nice city, was very pretty once." Then he asked me where I was from. By then we were back in Manhattan, not too far from the white loft building where I lived with Bert. I hesitated, then said, softly, "Everyplace. . . ."

"I know," he said, nodding seriously. "I comed from all place, too."

A moment later, on Lower Park, he stopped. We both shrugged shoulders at the same time. I took out a twenty-dollar bill and leaned over and put it into his blue shirt pocket.

He smiled, nodded his head, and kind of blushed through his beard stubble. "T'anks. I not forget."

I kissed him slowly on his mouth, which tasted of Russian tobacco, last night's vodka (maybe), whatever; but great. I wanted to rip his shirt off and go at his chest, but . . . I had things to do.

"All places," I told him. "I'm from all places, and times."

A sliver of early morning light, like a pair of silvery wings, eased its way in from a high northeast window in our ninth-floor loft, above Union Square. The light greeted me as I unlocked the door and walked in. The loft had belonged to a photographer named Ray Lang before we took it over. The space was bleached to a pale, pine color, wide, and open. The changing light of the city did beautiful things to it; I just wasn't sure this morning that it was going to do something beautiful for me.

I opened the door to our bedroom cubicle, a private space that had been carved out in the back, away from the main business area of the loft. It was still dark in there. A sleep-hazed voice asked, "That you?" I answered: "Uh huh," then went into the tiled bathroom. I took off my T-shirt and jeans. Before dropping them, I gave a quick sniff. All at once: oily factory floors, greasy Julio's in Brooklyn, dribbled beer, a little lick of piss; one more schnapps, grotty crotch sweat; old cigarette smoke, and then the broken, foam-rubber upholstery of a truly filthy yellow Mustang. I thought about sniffing the underarms of the shirt a bit more, but I was too tired. I showered and managed to stand up, vaguely awake, while I did it.

The warm jet of water hit me gratefully, but I wished that I were in a huge tub. One big enough for several elephants and those shy, beautiful Indian boys who used to service maharajahs. I wished a few of them were in there, too; naked, with me.

It was a nice dream, one of those brief waking fantasies you have somewhere between drifts of reality consciousness. I dried myself, brushed some of the night and Niko Stamos off my teeth, and then went back to the sleeping area.

Bert Knight, the man I lived with . . . well, let's just say, *more* than any other man . . . pulled me to him in the dark. He was big and dark and hairy now—kind of a bear, you could say—and his naked, sexy, clean-crotch, warm smell felt great to me. I kissed him full on the mouth, getting my tongue down his throat. "Tommy," he said. "You're like that little battery-driven rabbit: you just keep on going!"

"And *going*." I reached down to his dick. It was hot and hard for me. I got down in the dark under the light covers and just took him into my mouth. Bert made precum like some kind of instant coffee; it was always available. A nice before-breakfast treat. Then he did the same thing for me, but the exhaustion finally hit me and I knew that any second I was going to flake off into that sea of darkness that sleep often meant for me. I don't think I dream like other people. Dreams were just replaying things that had happened to me—and sometimes I wasn't sure I wanted to replay them.

But while Bert had my dick in his mouth, I realized that I was back on the elevator in the factory building where Niko worked. I had found *him*. The question was, would he ever know it? I was replaying that moment now with Bert. The nerves, the flickering lights. Bert was licking and sucking my dick, and . . . I was just smiling again as I saw Niko's beautiful Greek face. "I have a son," he said seriously, that moment when we met.

Then, I don't remember anything else.

I slept for a couple of hours more, I'm not sure how long, but managed to open my eyes and saw Bert's half-dreaming features turned towards me. I edged over to him in the warm bed and definitely did not want to get up. "You been out there, nourishing the troops again?" he asked, only half-awake, but smiling.

I nodded yes. "Not troops. But a couple o' officers, sir."

"I keep forgetting," Bert whispered, nudging my cheeks with his soft graying beard, "how easily moved to comfort others you are, my little Tommy." He paused and looked away, as if he were trying to hide the intensity of what he needed to say next. "Any troops in particular?"

I was afraid of this, but how could I lie? Anyone can get jealous, no matter how long they've been around. Bert proved it. "One," I said, my palms suddenly wetter than I had anticipated.

"I see. So, he pops up again?"

"Maybe," I smiled. "Or maybe not."

He pulled me to him. "I should have let him die, back then when I had the chance. What's he look like this time?"

"About the same."

"You bring the old lovers and tricks back; how do you do it?" he asked.

There was nothing to be jealous of, I said. As for letting him die, "You   57

didn't," I told him. "I guess that's why I'm always with you."

"Shit!" he answered, then kissed me once more. "Okay. But just remember: I'm the one in charge here." I smiled at him: sure. "That's the way it'll always be."

"Yes, *sir*," I said, emphasizing the "sir." "You are in charge. But sometimes the Devil just makes me do it."

"Sure. Him and his ol' walking stick!" His eyes met mine. "Any chance of a decent cup of coffee?" He pulled me towards him for another warm wet kiss. His mouth suddenly tasted even better than his cock, which always tasted good in my book.

His dark beard stroked my cheeks and neck as his softer lips found my mouth. He was all sable-black hair with drifts of silvery gray every now and then. Sable silkiness covered his big, broad chest, his still-tight stomach, his muscular tennis-player thighs; and, of course, surrounded his thick cock, which rested like a beached sea lion on our blue sheets. Any second it might swim playfully towards me—something that obviously never bothered me.

His dick still kept its usual morning half-erection, as we both emerged from sleep. I had to give it one more sweet kiss and a little swing with my tongue. Some crotch hair in my face, but isn't that nice? Burt never approved of shaved crotches. "What's the use of shaving there?" he asked. "Half the fun of being down there is getting lost in that stuff, right?"

I got up and found a white terry cloth robe, some rubber flipflops, and brailled my way to the kitchen. It was towards the back of the loft, away from our sleeping area. I found a canister of Cuban-style coffee, flipped a measuring spoonful of it into our Panasonic coffee machine, and then went back to Bert, dropped the robe, and stuck my cock right into his face. He smiled dreamily, and began licking it, slurping his tongue down into my balls. I slid back into bed and brushed aside the down duvet, while he still had a lot of my dick and a part of one of my balls in his mouth. Then I managed to get a fistful of Bert's growing "daddy" in my hand. Even though in various lives we have been close to the same age, in this one he was the older angel. I called his *schlong* "Daddy" and he called mine "Junior." Sometimes it was "Boy's Toy."

Frankly, I enjoyed the present arrangement, but wondered if at some other point we might reverse action; just as then, in the heat of the moment (slightly hungover, tired, wired, horny, too dumb to know better) we got on equal footing. Before I could say, "Stop that and let me just suck you for a while," we were eating each other simultaneously and enjoying the holy daylights out of it.

As the light really did start to come in, we both came. Bert's cum tasted wonderful. Breakfast of champions. Lemony-salty. I have no idea how he did

it, but then he always smelled nice, too—just a kind of natural, fleshy, male,

new leather smell. Don't ask me how he did that, either. It was not a 10+ orgasm for either of us. No screaming revelations of Immortality.

But it was hunky-wonderful anyway.

Funny, if you can call anything that has to do with immortal life "funny," but sometimes that did happen. In the vast reach of orgasm, we saw ourselves as we had been before: we glimpsed our own physical bodies emerging through Time.

Physical, real, reaching *forward* to us, here in this moment.

We had been together . . . forever; there was no longer any question in my mind about that. Together through almost endless transitions, epochs, and physical states of ourselves. Together through a consciousness made physical, of what we are; a consciousness that is, in its pure self, "angelic."

Angels are neither born nor made, but at some point recognize themselves. This recognition, truly, becomes *us*; it gives us the power to do what must be done. (Though the ultimate Power is not ours.) Only in knowing ourselves do we become what we are. We start off as "ordinary" people. We have parents, we are born, and we "die." That is, we go through the physical transition of death—but we know death for what it is: only a momentary transition, part of a journey, the directional curve of energy we take as part of the God-Substance Itself.

The first time I met Bert in this lifetime, everything was revealed to me. He *knew* me, and then, amazingly enough, I *knew* him. It seemed to happen in an instant. It was like taking all your clothes off in front of someone, another man, say, and you know that you've never felt so happy. So joyous and comfortable and turned on . . . all at once.

Sometimes in the middle of sex, both of us would start traveling at the same time towards the same place: a world of an Age gone for most humans for close to a thousand years. But there we were, wandering back, meeting again for (what seemed like . . .) the first time, as we experienced once more that incredible hot energy of the two of us coming together.

("How are you *appelled*?" he had asked me; I had asked him to speak plainer. I was just the son of a farmer . . . many of his words were foreign to me. Many words have changed. The word "gay" did not mean what it means now. Now, here we were in a loft on Lower Park. So, had we come a long way, baby? Or had we not?)

But, you may ask, how after all these lives (and deaths) did the two of you end up here, doing the jobs you do? The answer is simply . . . necessity. The Mother of Most Answers. We do what we do—and have done what we have done—because, well, this particular life, the one we are currently visiting, requires it.

Bert edited and published a gay magazine called *InQuire*. It was mostly a   59

New York affair, but distributed all over the country. *InQuire* published some serious writers, some queeny gossip fluff, some arty pictures, some pure crotch-shot porn; and it managed to make a slight profit despite the fact that Bert did *not* screw the writers and photographers who worked for him. At least, not screw them out of money. Sometimes we both screwed them. We liked sharing sex with other men. We had a fairly "open" relationship, that is, it was open to some wandering. (*Some*? Maybe I'm just fooling myself!) Many relationships—gay and otherwise—are like this, but few are genuinely "open" about it.

I know that possessiveness, in reality, is a personality trait that some men have, and no matter how "honest," "open," or "contemporary" they try to be, the old-fashioned desire to possess another human being remains with them. Bert Knight has that trait, though the gracious Mr. Knight does do a little celestial wandering himself. Men find him irresistible—it is this power he has that I can barely fathom. Even those who are not into "daddy types" find themselves impossibly drawn into his big arms and chest. There is something warm and comforting—essentially male—about him. He is kind of like . . . well, *God*, I guess; God, at least, as the Power is so often imagined in those terms.

And people, I mean *humans* as a group, often do imagine God like that— as having some "Bert Knightliness" to Him (the Great Daddy: warm, Jovian, comforting, strong). They visualize their own distant image of God this way; but the true Substance of God is so much more than that, that the "God the Father-Daddy" presence merely exists as one of Its faces.

This I know . . . as humbly, I have been allowed into the Substance. I have known It . . . partaken of It in Its angelic Splendor. And I can bear witness that even the "Great Daddiness" of one angel (one Bert Knight, as he is temporarily physicalized), is tossed away like so many ashes before the Splendor of *It*.

The Substantial Consciousness—without outer consciousness; all that *Is*, as It *is*.

(Which, of course, does not relieve the daily questions of us, such as—)

To keep our incredibly greedy landlord off our backs, Bert also did some interior work—he could do anything with his hands, as well as his mouth and other parts of him—and, finally, just in case you thought things might get a little too angelic and boring with us, he ran a massage service. I'm afraid you got that right: we could be whores, too.

Of this, I was the main attraction. Known "professionally" as Tommy Angelo, a striking-looking, Italian youth but with blond hair. (Northern Italian certainly) To be honest, I am not really Italian at this point, though in my various lineages there have been some strikingly handsome men of this background.

Bert and I actually came up with the Angelo moniker. My legal name was Thomas Smith, fairly white bread, from the hinterlands. It made us wonder who would take out his wallet and dial a back-of-the-gay-zine ad for . . a "Tom Smith?" Even one with obvious attractions? In this world as most of us know, you gotta have a gimmick: so I became Tommy Angelo, just like Bert became Bert Knight.

In our gay world, sometimes you have to invent a part of your identity. You have to see yourself in a different way than those around you may see you. You are not simply "single," but paired with another man. You are not only a son, but the "father" of your own gay self. It's true that I had a real father, a mother, and, for a while, a childhood, though none of that seems that real to me. That recent past life certainly doesn't mean as much to me as my own "real" life now: that life you're finding out about here.

I think this is true of many gay men, angelic or not. They have a real life—apart from their lives in the "normal" world—and it begins at certain times; with certain people. Just as mine does. But mine goes back for a thousand years: and it continues forward. For reasons that even I do not understand, we're here. Then, out of some Plan that is larger than myself, we—the angels who know each other—meet. The ancient realities of ourselves come awake, they bloom; and we become the angels that we are.

Between those moments of intense knowing, we return not to the dead, but to that vast pool from where all Life comes, that . . . is the intricate moving pattern which makes the great "carpet." In this pattern, Time is a containable dimension; just as physical life is.

Angelo.

Tommy *Angelo*. Okay, so you thought angels had wings and didn't work as whores. Okay, "unlicensed massage therapists." Truth is, we needed the money—even two strange birds like us have to pay Gil Levenberg, our landlord, who's been out to evict us for the last five years, after we took over the lease from Ray Lang, the fashion-and-naked-boy photographer. Ray split New York for Key West, where he bought an old shrimp boat and now runs Nude Cruises, which kind of speaks for itself.

Ray still shoots butt shots, but at present his models are mostly unprofessional locals. That has opened up the manscape a lot. "Less attitude," he told us. "More genuine dick. These guys will do anything to see themselves in pictures." From time to time, he comes back and visits. Mostly smirking and shaking his head. He has suggested that we kill Levenberg, and the thought had crossed our minds. Lofts like ours have become high-end yuppy fiefdoms. They show up in the *New York Times* "Style Section"; acres of buffed polished floors, no furniture, a few scattered potted palms imported at great expense from the Ivory Coast, where the annual income is sixty-seven dollars a year. The idea that hardworking gay people should also have a place to live

is no longer in fashion, unless of course we are talking about gay investment bankers. (We are not two of *them*, believe me.)

Ray's loft had been "rent stabilized" (or as Levenberg put it, "commandeered under Soviet management"), which means that our esteemed land baron will do anything up to (and, probably, including) bombing us out, to get it back on the "open market." Meaning, open to anyone except us.

But that's just a New York detail, and I must have been hungover and slightly weak-willed from too much (too good) "good morning" sex to have started off with it. Why we ended up in Ray Lang's loft and what we're doing there, is another story. It's a story as old as we are. To understand it, you have to believe—as I do—in "heroes." By *heroes* I don't mean something out of a Tarzan epic, but the idea that men can follow one another past the closed doors of Time. What I'm saying is that we don't just evaporate. But we do have this amazing, subtle influence on each other, that can penetrate the boundaries of our own "unique" life spans.

It means that there is something about us that can carry on from generation to generation, from age to age. In short, it's possible that we can know each other, as I have known Bert, forever. How we recognize this knowledge, though—well, I guess in the long run, that is up to you.

He is the hero of my life; the man I have chosen to submit myself to. (Now don't start barfing . . . you, too, would do it if you could. If you could find *him*.) And, in all this time, one thing I have learned: heroism can be as addictive as heroin.

It is, I believe, a central part of the life quest of any gay man, as this quest is seen, in all of its naked realization, on earth.

Now, let me 'splain, Ricky.

I'll begin, for argument's sake, to say that every one of us, at some point, has a yearning, a questioning, a drive to get to that *light* at the end of the tunnel we call "existence."

You wake up. Now, you're conscious of who you are.

Your place in the world. Your name. Your size. Your body; how it works. (There's this little peepee; you eat; you make doody. Anyway—) Then there's your mind. It's puzzled, there's all this stuff to stick in it. Then what? You keep following that distant light through the tunnel, long or short as, Time-wise, it can be. Until you find yourself at last, free . . . and rolling somewhere, deep, in those ancient primal grasses where your own spirit is finally released and joined to . . .

The Answer.

To *what*?

. . . .

Scary, isn't it? (But then, perhaps, you were one of those just too afraid to ask the question. The Question is too forbidding. Too . . . but try it, if you

will: how about . . . *who are you? where are you going? And, what will you find, once you get there?*)

In the end, it all becomes the same Question.

So? You had expected, naturally, two *angels* . . . to have no cocks. No balls. And those cute little wings? Sorry, Lucy. Don't be shocked, or disappointed: angels don't look like we just jumped out of a pigeon coop. Nor like Brad Pitt, fresh from his personal trainer; although that can happen . . . but physically, when we're physical, angels can be anything. Real beauties. As well as dorks. Slobs. *Schlemiels*, and beer-bellied good ol' boys. You never can tell. We can be appealing or outwardly revolting. Depending, I guess, on what boat you're floating on at what time.

And, sometimes, let's get this out of the closet: our behavior can be *un*angelic. I mean, like, we can get violent, hostile, bitchy, and horny. And, I should add, get authentically pissed off. (Just as, at other moments, we can be charitable, warm, compassionate, and kind—as any human creature should be.)

So what is *angelic* about angels?

Aside from the fact that Time to us can be as travelable as any three-dimensional space and we can, when necessary, go straight back through it, we are simply pure *spirit*.

Naked, transparent: it shimmers directly through us. And there are moments when we will allow you to see it.

This spirit is as real to us as your face is to you. It is our real identity; it is the last big Question that comes with its own Answer. And it survives past death, even though we are, by every definition, alive. With a beating heart and breath, eyes, hands, feet. Muscles. Cock. Balls. Belly. Nipples. Ass. And the spirit, too, is sexual. We can't deny it. It is part of the angelic life force; part of the spirit-form itself that moves and animates us, that embraces the world and, also, heals.

That is eternal and real.

Now, this is something many geeks in the "religion business" fear and loathe. They're too busy condemning you ever to *heal* you. They are too busy cutting your cock off to see the real spirit inside you, the one that *needs* to come out and that we, angels, are there for. But we are a real force of this spirit itself. We know it, and are it. And as I said, we are as *real* as a hurricane. As real as destiny itself, floating through Eternity. We're there. And no matter how we appear, we understand you.

(We do.)

So, finally, what are angels? Just say: a thread of naked spirit diving into and through the depths of this vastness we call Time; a piece of that complete energy we can barely imagine, that is eternity. (Before, by the way, you got to buy *Eternity* on the street floor at Bloomingdale's; when it became the name of just another perfume.)

63

I was sharing eternity with Bert, my other half (?) and *hero*. And finally, if you get right down to it . . . sharing eternity with myself: Thomas. Tommy Angelo. Tom. All of us wandering around a name, carrying something *angelic*.

So Bert had become that "other half" to me, a warm, sweet piece of my very self, though at the moment he was on the crapper, while I was getting coffee, some cereal and orange juice, and putting them on the small oak table by the kitchen. The toilet flushed loudly. Loft plumbing is famous for not being very subtle. Water ran a bit in the tiny bathroom sink. He came out. "Sometimes you just gotta clear away the last day before you start the next," he said, and smiled.

He wore a blue-and-white terry cloth shaving wrap knotted around his trim waist, his favorite cover-up around the house when we were alone. He scratched his dark naked chest, and a single white hair, like a downy feather, fell from it. "Must be molting," he joked.

"We have any clients this afternoon?" I asked, hoping no.

He shrugged. "Somebody called last night. He's staying over at the Raleigh House on Central Park West. He says he knows you, but I don't really remember the name."

"A repeater?"

"Might be. He might have used another name before. They do that." Bert chuckled. "Then they forget what name they used, like we're supposed to remember."

"I prefer repeat business. At least, that way you know they're not cops."

"Yeah, most of the time. He said he'd call us back to confirm. We could use the money. Anyway I've got to get the next issue out. I've got writers coming by with disks at noon. You want to go to the gym? I'll beep you if he calls back with a definite appointment."

I could use the gym. He went to the door and got the *Times* our super, a kid named Johnny Zeppolini, brought up for us. Back at the table, he opened it. The usual news. Misery. War. Poor people shot on the streets in the Bronx or Brooklyn. The new (or old) super rich trading companies and the human beings who came with them. "Just like the old days," Bert observed. "The defended and the defenseless. Feudalism in all its glory, returns."

"Without the human side," I agreed. "Now it's all computers. So people are much more efficient at screwing each other."

He shot me a funny look. "Come on, you know they weren't all that bad at screwing each other back then either." He shrugged his big shoulders. "And they could come up with some pretty inventive ways to do it. Of course, not everyone's lucky enough to find someone like you." I nodded to him. "Thanks for your cute little dick in my face this morning."

"Wait a second. It's not all *that* little."

"Sure, kid. But it was still a nice way to wake up! And just when I was

having this close-to-wet dream."

I smiled. "About what?"

"Oh, finding this young knave in the dark naked. I call that great service! You know, you don't do that enough anymore."

"Should I do it now?"

"Daddy'll tell you when *he* wants it." Bert Knight smiled.

"That was certainly one meeting that will never leave us," I said.

"Never."

He was right; it never did. It seemed that no matter how many times we'd come back, there was always that first meeting, that moment in the middle of the eleventh century, in the early years of the Second Millennium—me at sixteen, frightened but still kind of snot-nosed, offering everything of myself to him; to be his vassal and liege slave. For him, my young, handsome knight *erect*, or errant. Me kneeling before him, and then him taking me and giving me so much more.

"What were you thinking about?" Bert asked. "You looked like you were really far away."

"Not that far. Just kneeling at your feet, getting your dick in my—"

"Good boy. Keep that thought."

I was always horny for him, could hardly keep my hands off him, no matter how many times we had cum. Maybe it was the sense of control he had, that he had refined now through a thousand years. Coming with him (coming to what?) was like having light poured down me, a light that came directly out of Bert's wondrous (and I should say, godly) cock. Sometimes I had to control myself just to get through the day. I looked at him, he smiled and then we both smiled. He pretty much knew exactly what I was thinking; he knew it all the time. We dug back into the papers again. Bert liked to look at the "Business Day" section. It's where "the real news of the day is," he said.

Bert put the paper down, then suddenly looked up at me. "Something strange is going on here. It makes me wonder what the real story is."

"What?" I was ready for some toast. I usually liked a slice after my Sugar Frosted Flakes. I put two slices of bread into the toaster and got some orange marmalade out of the refrigerator.

"There's an interesting piece about gay businesses in New York."

"What's strange about that?"

"Well, first, it's not something the *Times* usually covers. Gay businesses aren't their regular beat, you know? What do they care? They leave stuff like that to fallen royalty like us, at *InQuire*—which makes me think that maybe we should be covering this story."

My toast popped up. I went over, pulled it out, then scraped some butter onto it. Next should come the marmalade, but Bert stopped me with a hand

on my wrist. I looked up at him. "Tommy, do you want to know about this story, or not?"

"Okay," I gave up. The toast could wait. Who cares about warm toast? I had dealt with worse things in the past: Cold toast. Freezing feet. Once almost being burned at the stake, but—

"It seems," Bert explained to me, "That a lot of gay businesses in New York are being bought up by one man. Part of a syndicate. You know, a lot of slimy invisible money people backing him. Speaking of slimy, our Mayor's making it hard for sex businesses. That's no secret. They're all going under. So this syndicate figures that if sex as a business goes under, then maybe other businesses will do okay."

"That's what the *Times* says?" I asked. Now I could finish the toast. I handed Bert a slice with marmalade. He took it and chewed it happily while he read.

"This is nice." He meant the toast. "Thanks. Naw—see—the *Times* never says anything that smart. They always cover the money trail as best they can. It could lead somehow back to them and their big advertisers. So you have to read in between the lines, where the real story is."

"And you figured this out?" He nodded to me, and I realized he was right. Bert usually is. Angels are not always known for their great sense, which is probably why the world's so screwed up; but Bert is smart. He'd learned a lot over the last . . . anyway, a long time. "What's the name of this guy?" I asked, finishing the last of my toast. It was good and I wolfed it down. Bad of me.

"Funny name," he said, wrinkling his forehead. "Alan Hubris."

"Doesn't ring any bells." I started off towards the bathroom.

Bert nodded his head. "Something tells me it will. Something tells me that we and Mr. Hubris may end up seeing something of each other." I smiled briefly. It was time for me to disappear into the john. "Maybe," Bert called to me, "I should consider writing a piece about Mr. Hubris for *InQuire*. Knowledge is power, right?"

"Always has been," I called back from the bathroom, winked quickly, then shut the door.

Chapter 5

I was on Sixth Avenue at the Bed, Bath, and Beyond in Chelsea when my beeper went off. I had stopped there on the way to the gym to pick up some vanilla-scented massage oil with a little coconut in it. It's amazing how you can get that stuff anyplace now, and a lot cheaper than in specialty shops. I needed a couple of new rubber dildos, too. "Tools of the trade," you can say, but they were *beyond* Bed, Bath, and Beyond. At least this year. I checked the number on my beeper.

It was my Mr. Knight. I use a beeper with a cell phone, because we don't like to give out the cell phone number. In this trade (unfortunately), there are customers who will get back at you. Especially if they find out how to play with your head while I'm playing with the rest of them. All right, I admit it: sometimes I become too attached to my clients, despite Bert's warnings and his always larger than life presence in my existence. Even angels have Achilles' heels. Or hells.

"It's definite," Bert said softly. "The client wants your golden hands all over him." He chuckled. "He says he remembers your body—he'll never forget it. I guess that means he just can't get enough of a good thing!" I smiled. Bert paused, then continued, "Do you remember this guy at all?"

"From the Raleigh?"

"Yeah. He says he knows you."

I asked his name. "Funny name. Knoedel."

"What?" I asked.

"Like 'girdle.' It's German. *K-nerdle*. He seems nice. He says he met you on another trip."

"Did he use the same name?"

"You might have met him at a party or someplace, and just set up an appointment."

"I don't remember the name, but I'll be good," I promised.

"Not *that* good. Take care of yourself, Tommy. Don't get so far in, you can't wade out."

"That depends on what he looks like."

"Tommy, how can you be an angel and such a whore at the same time?"

"All covers the same territory," I answered without thinking about it hard. "I'll give him his money's worth."

"That's important. Sorry about the 'whore' comment. You're my favorite whore anyway. If you have any problems, you know how to reach me."

"Sure," I said, then asked the usual questions: his room number. Payment? (Bert was able to take credit cards through the magazine; this time Mr. Knoedel used that method.) "I'll be nice," I promised, then hung up.

I had a couple of hours before my date at the Raleigh, so I walked over to the gym in Chelsea where I worked out. Luckily I have a workable body, tall with big runner's legs and a smooth, muscular chest. Wide swimmer's shoulders and the developed arms to go with them. The gym is a favorite of Chelsea boys, who're actually not favorites of mine. They're usually way too much into themselves. I've gotten down with a couple of them. It's been like hitting the sheets (or for that matter, the floor) with a shaved, tattooed window mannequin. Sometimes, under all those buffed muscles, you expect to find a little key in the back. Wind them up, they get hard. Wind down, they deflate.

The place was jumping. Crawling with good-looking, young gym bunnies. Lots of eye work and cruising, even some vague smiles, but not much other than that. I got to my locker, took off my clothes, put on a jock, some shorts, and a T-shirt, and then went up and did some reps with the free weights and machines. I never exercise a long time. I've found that doing serious, controlled movements is much better than just showing off, doing dozens of pointless, quick reps, while wasting a lot of time eyeing guys.

I was through in about forty minutes. This left me time for a steam. I went back down to my locker, stripped to just a towel, then went back out to the steam room. In front as usual was a lot of shifty eyeball action. Guys doing the old "now-you-see-it, now-you-don't" routine with their dicks and towels. But further back, there was real jerking and some actual sucking going on. The management pretends that this is against the rules, as if the queer guys who go there are not at all involved in exercising the truly wondrous muscles between their legs.

Yeah, sure, *really*.

I eased my way towards the back and sat down on the bench. A gorgeous black man, very dark, about twenty-six, looking like he had been carved out of solid mahogany, walked past me. He was completely naked and his nine-inch cock, that was paler than the rest of him and really inviting, bounced up and down in front of a nice pair of balls, waving itself like a flag at full mast. He waved it right past me, there under my nose. The head, as thick and appealing as a ripe plum, suddenly came to a full rest about two inches from

my mouth. He smiled; unusual for this place. I had to hold myself back. I wanted to thrust my tongue out at his dick. Instead, I reached out and patted his tight muscular rump, then smiled, too. He grinned at me, and sat down next to me on the bench.

I had my gym towel on. His dark warm hands started to meander over towards my crotch, stroking the tight folds of the towel. I could feel my cock starting to crowd the towel out, and a moment later, it poked out completely, tenting some towel over it. I brushed that aside, and let him stroke my thick, bare, fully hard dick.

He went down briefly on me, taking most of my shaft into his warm dark lips and mouth. He eased it down his throat; I had to stop him. I was getting very hot, very fast. I needed to unwrap my towel that was already sopping with steam. Anything else would have been rude, right? The back of the room was solid now with steam and I felt private enough. He started to suck my nipples, getting them equally hard, while his hand at the same time softly stroked my dick. I smiled, got down, and a moment later was all the way on him, swinging my mouth on his cock. He bent down and his tongue rolled into my ear, then down the back of my neck, licking a line of steamy sweat beads that rolled off it.

Soon we were all over each other in the steam, as slick beads of perspiration dropped all over us. I went crazy about his body—its dark, sweet creamy chocolatiness. The warm, fleshy, slightly sweaty taste of his meat, with just a slight ring of foreskin pushed up behind the pale, slightly purply swelling head. He reached for my left nipple, then bit lightly into the soft, thickening part of it that ended in a tiny knob like a little horn. *Zong.* Pure electricity shot right through me.

I had to be careful; the situation was getting much nicer than I'd expected; I had a massage appointment that was getting closer . . . and he had this really sweet face. Pure, warm and inviting. He got down and started expertly licking the pink head of my cock, then he gave the full shaft some real attention. A deep blanket of steam rolled in around us as he got most of the full eight-inch length of my organ down his warm throat.

He started sucked and licking me. Softly . . . nicely.

All I can say (in my defense, sir) is that I went into a . . . just call it an "angelic trance." Bouncing through the air; walking on an ocean of water with no land in sight. For a moment, I lost connection with real time . . . I was riding with Bertrand on the back of his horse, holding on to his armor.

I had my tongue in my liege lord's ear. I was kissing him and had lost myself in my complete devotion to him, as if I had found God in a human body. It was unfair, truly, that I could find myself so completely present in another human being, with hardly knowing who he was. But it was so that night, almost a millennium ago, in that wild darkness.

That wildness. . . and now, again, I lost the other guys around me in the gym with its boring rules, who either pretended this wasn't happening, or were watching it, kind of detached like it was a sporting event. Not exactly cheering, but not looking away either. Then, too quickly, I came back into the moment; and there I was: back in reality.

Which I enjoyed. His mouth on the sensitive ridges and silk of my cock. My hands on his beautiful dark chest, all smooth, sleek, and meaty in certain places, down to the coarse, black thicket of hairs at the southern tip of his stomach.

It would have been easy then to become pure sexual heat. To suck and fuck anything that came within my reach. And this beautiful black man definitely was. But we were at a gym, not a bathhouse. An actual gym, where some amount of butch decorum was expected.

I pulled his sweaty face off my cock. He got up, then I put my hand on his dick, and slid it slowly down to the dark, firm, nubby bag of his two balls. There was still a field of coarse curly black hair on it. I was glad. Too many guys shaved their balls nowadays. What a waste!

His cock was like a T-bone steak, and just as succulent. Boy, did I want to suck it. Who wouldn't when you get down to it? Who would not want to punch that button and go nuts with sex? All that crap we have about denying our sexuality; for the life of me, I still can't figure out who invented it. Ever since the dawn of Man (and Woman) sex has been this wondrous appetite that connected us both with the animals and the angels. But the truth of that is forgotten now.

So, before one more bullet-assed Chelsea clone popped up to give me a big "No-No!" in the steam room, I stopped myself. Several other guys found their way to the back. They all had those poured-out-of-a-Nautilus-machine bodies. Muscles on their frames tight as bullet casings; asses as tight, too. Too many tight-asses. What they needed was a good dildo up them. Eleven inches, at least. I had a rubber one like that for special clients; the ones who begged and pleaded for it, while I sucked their dongs and fucked them with my greased fist. When the fist just didn't work for them, they wanted a dildo. Sometimes they wanted both. (That's when they really cried about heaven, and I knew how to take them to it. . . .)

I smiled at the black guy who'd been nice. A gift from the holy spirit itself, I'd say. I asked his name ("Ernie," he said, shyly), told him I'd see him around ("Hope so," he said sweetly), then squeezed my way towards the front, where the steam got lighter and the cruising heavier, but (by any standards), less productive.

I showered, dressed, then got ready to go uptown to the Raleigh.

The Raleigh was an old luxury hotel on expensive Central Park South, built in the 1920s or early '30s. The lobby's walls and ceilings were carved with swirling, black Art Deco friezes, mostly Aztec-inspired geometric patterns, with gilded, handsomely muscular naked men tumbling about through them. The lobby men, who were also beautiful, golden-skinned Hispanics, wore dark blue uniforms with about four feet of gold braiding on each shoulder. Although these beauties seemed like a natural part of the decor, to my taste they were vastly overdressed.

I told them I was going up to Mr. Knoedel's room, and one of them winked at me and told me which elevator to take.

The room, actually a suite, was on the fourteenth floor with an immediate view of Central Park's changing fall trees, the fountains, the paths, and the little bridges. I could see all the way up to the Boat House; the rest evaporated into blue air. A tall, good-looking room service man carrying a tray was about to leave as Mr. Knoedel let me in.

"Tommy?" I smiled and shook his hand. "Would you like a drink? I just had a bottle of Scotch brought up."

I told him no. I couldn't drink and do what I did, no way. But if he wanted one, why not? The attendant, after being tipped, bowed and left. Knoedel locked the door quickly behind us. Then he poured himself a double with some ice from a small bar cabinet fridge.

He smiled nervously, as if he still weren't quite sure what to do with me. I tried hard not to let his nerves get to me. Nerves can be contagious. Before you know it, you're as uptight and fearful as the client; definitely not what I was there for. Knoedel was short, kind of square-faced and balding.

Certainly he was no Chelsea-boy type. Chunky—okay, pudgy. Middle-aged. Bland face hidden behind thick glasses; bloated body. He made me feel as if he'd lost being young a long time ago. Some men, especially gay men, remain boys forever. But not Mr. Knoedel. It was a nice face, though, more shy than jaded: this appealed to me. He wore a pair of dark trousers and a white button-down, kind of floppy business shirt, open at the neck. "It's business, business!" he said, shaking his head. "Sorry. I'm Chuck Knoedel." He looked at me like I should know him.

"I met you last year," he explained. I asked him how. "A bathhouse in midtown. I followed you all over, then you gave me your card. I figured if this were the only way to get to know you, why not?"

I shrugged my shoulders. Maybe it had been one of those evenings when Bert and I got bored and decided to see who was out there. I smiled at Knoedel and nodded my head. His pale watery eyes, barely recognizable as blue behind his thick, gold-rimmed glasses, brightened. "I never forgot," he said. "Glad you could come by. Sure you don't want a drink or something?"

I turned down the drink. Like I said, you can't be drunk in this business. 71

Then I told him I was glad he had asked for me. I did feel more at ease with him; the bathhouse story meant there was less chance of police entrapment. The New York cops have been famous for pulling this: posing as massage clients in order to sting sex workers. As if what we did, making worried, lonely businessmen like Chuck Knoedel feel happy, had no real purpose in life.

(Sorry, Mr. Mayor. Wrong number!)

I remembered Bert telling me that Knoedel was from L.A. I told him I had never been there. "But I guess I should go," I added. "It's the City of the Angels, isn't it?"

"It's all right," he said. "It's like any place: it depends on what kind of work you do."

"Everything does," I said to humor him, then smiled. "Why don't we start with a massage? Why don't you get your clothes off?"

"I will if you will," he said. "Your body drives me crazy. I remembered it from the bathhouse. I wanted to see what you had under that towel."

"Thanks," I told him. But the truth was I really could not remember meeting Knoedel. Not that I am that much of a slut, but in this business you end up giving your cards out to a large number of men. Mostly they end up in the garbage the next day, with a couple of Chinese take-out food cartons. "We'll do the massage on the bed. You have some towels we can put over it?"

"Sure," he said. "They're in the bath. I'll get some."

He came back shortly with two huge bath sheets and I threw them over the king-sized bed. Then he took off his thick glasses and stripped down to a white T-shirt and some blue cotton boxer shorts. He looked at me shyly, blinking, his mouth slightly open. I pulled his T-shirt over his head, which made him smile when the shirt cleared his face. He had a bit of fine ash-blond curly hair on his puffy chest, with some gray in it, and big, really sweet-looking nipples. I liked that. I pulled down his boxers, and his short fat cock was already hard. It kind of winked at me as I casually took it for a moment in my hand. He gasped.

I took off my polo shirt, sneakers, and jeans, but kept on the white bike pants I was wearing under them. They stretched against my crotch, making my dick look that much more inviting. I uncapped my new bottle of vanilla massage oil from B, B, & B and poured some on my palms. I asked him to lie down on the bed, face up, and I spread some oil on his soft chest, stroking his nipples with it until they got tweaky and hard. His dick started to twitch with excitement, but for the moment I did not touch that part.

The fun was knowing how much he wanted me to touch it.

I could see his mounting excitement as his equipment, shaped like a kid's torpedo, started to do quick little whirlies in the air, back and forth, all by

itself. His hands moved shyly over to my crotch, then started to press at my cock. He rubbed it inside the Lycra shorts until it stood out like a garden hose. "Why don't you take your shorts off?" he asked, almost panting.

"I will in a second, Chuck. But first I want you to get more comfortable. I just want to pay attention to you. Is that all right?"

He nodded and closed his eyes, while I worked on his shoulders, his stomach, then the area around his groin. He moaned and sighed and his cock jumped every time my fingers reached gently around his pubic area, stroking and cupping his loose balls and the soft skin of his scrotum.

"You're really good at this," he whispered. "I've been looking forward to it."

I nodded, then asked him to turn around on his stomach.

"That's not going to be easy," he said, trying to catch his breath. As tense as Mr. Knoedel was, he was just as easily turned on. The contradiction must have left him quite defensive; that I could tell.

"Relax a moment," I said softly. "Take a deep breath and let it fill your stomach, and then just let it go slowly."

He did that and his short, hard dick got a bit more pliable. The head of it jumped, like a little pink frog, then shrank back. I looked at him. He looked vulnerable, sweet; kind of pathetic, I thought. I tried hard not to suck him. I had that impulse; I usually work on impulses. Plum crazy, right?

He eased onto his stomach and then I started kneading his back, neck, and shoulders. His neck was stiff as a brick. "You're carrying a lot of tension here," I said, gently running the ridges of my fingers through his short, thinning hair—now more salt than pepper—and then down the back of his neck.

"Could be. Like I said, it's always business, business, then more business."

He groaned as I worked on that area more, using the palms of my hands, and even, lightly, my elbows. Then I traveled down his back to the cheeks of his ass. For a desk man, they were not too flabby; maybe he played squash sometimes. I played with them, kneaded then, stuck my fingers into them, and then slowly peeled off my Lycra bike pants and placed the fattened length of my dick carefully against the crack of his butt.

His hand reached up to my cock and he stroked it, guiding the bottom of the shaft somewhat deeper down into the crack, as he moaned. I told him to close his eyes. He did.

"This is nice," he sighed. "When you work for the kind of people I do, you can use any kind of relaxation you can get!"

I stroked and kneaded his ass some more, trying to keep my cock still in the crack. He responded to the firm touch of my fingers rippling over his butt, then my thumbs pressing in harder. Using my big shoulder muscles, I really went at it, alternately applying heavy and light pressure. I've learned

73

that the more muscles you use in a massage, the happier the client is—and the less tired you become. If you only use your fingers, wrists, and forearms, you'll wear yourself out in half an hour. He liked being taken care of this way. He had a kind of baby contentment, along with the pure sexual pleasure of it.

"What kind of people do you work for?" I asked. It seemed like a good time to do this: ask him about himself. Let him get it off his chest, if he wanted to. Every good whore is a therapist in his own way, and, I'm sure, probably vice versa.

He exhaled. His body became more relaxed. "Some real funny ones. Ever heard of someone," he paused, then finished, "named Alan Hubris?" He opened his eyes and turned towards me. I looked into his face.

I shook my head. "No." I decided to see what Chuck Knoedel would tell me. Sometimes clients drop amazing bits of information on me; things that Bert and I find quite useful. Bert had talked to me about a piece for *InQuire*, and now something was being tossed right into my lap. I decided that as soon as I finished with Mr. Knoedel, I'd call him. Some message (it appeared) was right there, in the massage.

"Maybe it's best you don't know him. It's bad enough that I do. Jeez, I shouldn't talk so much. Why bore you with this?"

"It's okay," I whispered. "My clients tell me everything. Part of the service. It never goes any further, but if this is causing you to be tense, sometimes it's best to—"

"Sure," he said, turning his face towards me and smiling. "Just get it off my chest—or my ass—right?"

I nodded.

"Well," Knoedel went on, "Alan's the front man for the actual people I work for. They formed what they call a 'blind syndicate.' So you don't know who else is in there. Mostly it's rich money guys. Big landlords. Wall Street types. Hubris is taking over most of New York's gay life: the baths, the bars, clubs. They'll scarf 'em up; yuppify 'em. Then, when things really come up, they'll close them down for the real estate value. Hubris and his money men take on stuff like that."

"Stuff the Mayor is trying to close down?"

He nodded his head, while I fingered his ass more. "Yeah, I'm ashamed to say that. It's a shitty situation, and I'm not even sure how I got myself into it. You see, the Mayor is trying to prove that he's a friend of the gay community. And he's using Alan Hubris as a kind of . . ."

"Shield?" I asked.

"Naw," Knoedel said. He turned around to me. He was serious now. "No, Hubris is more like, anyway, what they used to call a 'beard.' You know, like a false wife or girlfriend. Closet queens used to have 'beards' all the time.

Well, Hubris's a false front that the Mayor puts on for the gay community. When the right time—or wrong one—comes along, the Mayor'll just chop off his 'beard.'"

"I see."

He smiled. "I'm surprised they still let little guys like you operate. Like they haven't tried, you know, to close you down or put you in jail. They use AIDS as the big scare tactic now. But it's really about money, real estate, and power. Hubris'd be pissed that I'm telling you this; or even that I called you. He wants to take over the massage business, too. Everything. But I remembered your face and body from the baths—so, here we are."

"Good," I said and suddenly kissed him. His eyes closed for a moment. It was probably the first moment of affection he'd had since . . . who knows?

"That was nice," he said, opening his eyes. "I didn't think I'd get to talk to you like this; I mean get to trust you. The truth is, they just flew me in from L.A. to do the books. The money people back there flew me in: their finances, see, sometimes get weird. Anyway, they figure I'm not going to let anything out the bag to anyone. They know that I deal with enough crooks back in L.A. that they can trust me here."

I nodded my head, like I really knew what he was talking about. I've found with business people, who talk among themselves so much, that they automatically take it for granted that you're on their wavelength. Actually, I did want to know more, and I had a plan in mind. "Mind if I try something?" I asked. "I want you to get your mind off all this for a moment. Then, if you want to, we can talk later,."

"Sure," he said. "Try what you want."

At a certain point, I decided, I would get Chuck Knoedel to tell me everything. But first, I took out a thin, pliant length of black rubber hosing, and with it tied his wrists together softly behind his back.

"I use the same stuff to tie my cock," I said. Mr. Knoedel turned his head towards me and I tied the same kind of hosing around the base of my dick, so that it stood out, hard as a tire. I aimed the head seductively towards his mouth. His tongue went to it, but I made sure that only the tip of his tongue could taste the peach-round head of my cock. "Why don't you give me a little more of that?" he asked, smiling.

"In just a minute," I said, and then took a bandanna out of my pack and used to it to blindfold him. I asked him if he were all right with that.

"Sure," he said. "Normally, I'd get skittish, but I know you. Besides, something tells me that your friend Bert wouldn't send me anyone bad. You ever see him? He sounds so nice on the phone."

"I see him," I said grinning. "What did he tell you?"

"Not much. Just that you were good-looking, which is true. Young, and a nice guy. He said you'd know what to do with me. That's true, too. I never

75

told him who I work for, but he seemed to understand how much I needed something like this."

"Bert understands everything," I said. "He has a real angelic quality. You'll see, if you get to meet him."

"I'd like to one day. I'm going to count on it."

I turned him back on his back, and began massaging him again, this time working on his chest, but also licking his nipples every now and then, getting them very hard and even using my teeth gently on them. He moaned and his cock jumped like a rabbit every time I did it. I teased his face with my dick, running it under his nose, and then taking it away, making him squirm to get it, but his hands were bound behind his back.

"No fair," he said, and I untied them, then retied them again on his chest, so that he could reach his own cock and try to grab mine. He liked this a lot, even while I dragged my cock and balls on his hairy chest, then down to his crotch, and massaged his dick and mine together with my oily fingers. I thought he'd explode. He started to cry for my dick in his mouth, just moan for it. "Say 'please,'" I told him. "'Please give me your dick. Just put it in my mouth.'"

"All right, Tommy. I can do that," he said, smiling under his blindfold. "But I want the blindfold off."

"Not till I'm ready," I said.

"Okay. *Please*. Please give me your cock in my mouth."

"Who?"

I saw a smile go to his lips as he said, "Tommy, please give me your cock in my mouth."

I did that, and pushed my dick into his willing, waiting throat. He began to suck on me, lavishing me with his tongue. He was good at it and brought his bound hands up to my balls and massaged them, too, at times even licking my balls with the rubber hose around them. I admit, Mr. Knoedel was turning me on, not as much as Ernie at the steam room had, but still . . . . he knew what he was doing.

I pulled my cock out of his mouth and massaged him some more, working on his neck and chest, then started to stroke his dick. While I did this, he managed to untie the hosing around his wrists—frankly, he did not need to be Houdini to do this—and then he triumphantly untied his blindfold. When he did this, he grabbed my head and firmly pulled it down to his throbbing cock. I took his equipment in my mouth and softly licked the small head of it. At that moment, the phone rang.

"Jesus," he said. "I'd better answer that. It's probably Hubris."

He bounded off the bed naked and hurried into the living room for privacy. I could hear him talking from the bedroom, and eased forward, without him seeing me, to understand what he was saying. I also liked looking at him

as he talked business on the phone, naked. He seemed embarrassed by it. There was something about that that seemed kind of appealing and nice to me and, frankly, I wanted his cock back in my mouth. It had started to feel nice there. There was something about Mr. Knoedel that appealed to me. That seemed kind of earnest and good, despite his working for Alan Hubris.

Or was I just being a stupid angel?

I got off the bed and crawled on the thick beige wall-to-wall carpet towards him, so that he could not see what I was doing. His back was turned to me, and when I approached him I stuck my tongue into his ass for a moment, and he shook for a second from the surprise. He turned to me, and on my knees, I took his cock into my mouth. He pulled my head away and shook his head, then smiled. He continued talking and brushed his short, fat, hairy-balled dick against my cheeks, and then fed it again into my mouth.

"Okay," he said on the phone. "Whatever you want, sir."

He hung up and I got up at the same time. "It seems like the shit's happy," he said. "He just bought another club. This time on the East Side, in the high rent district. The Mayor's behind it; he's even gonna hang out there, though nobody's supposed to know it."

"Sounds interesting," I said. "So Hubris and the Mayor are really tight?"

Mr. Knoedel shook his head back and forth. "Thick as thieves in a bank vault. Let me tell you: there are some very funny trails here, and you have no idea where they end." Then his face dropped. "The bad news is, he wants another meeting with me in, maybe, an hour."

"An hour? You mean here?"

"Don't worry. No matter what, you'll get paid for the whole thing. He said he'd call me back, so we'll have a little more time to play. The worst thing that can happen is he'll just leave a message for me. I'll tell him I was in the shower."

"That sounds better," I said.

I got down and grabbed his ass cheeks and sucked him some more. This time I really gave myself over to him and enjoyed getting his dick in my face. Sucking men is so different from sucking boys; there's that power in it. It's always there. You want them just to let go in you; to give you all they have. Squirt some down your throat, and not hold back.

I brought him almost to the edge of coming, then he pulled out from me; making me, this time, want to beg him for it.

"I want your dick," I said softly, turning the tables I knew on myself. "Why not give it to me?"

"You'll get it," he said. "Boy, you're really something."

I got back up. For a second, I'd forgotten myself. *Who* was getting paid for this? It was an occupational hazard. Bert warned me not to get so involved with my work, but when your work involves so much pleasure . . .

well, what else can you do?

Most of the time what I wanted was to give my clients a sense of their own worth. I know you must think that's funny, coming from a "massage whore." But, in my own way, I am a healer. I know that. It is within the angel to heal the broken spirit; and many times sexual healing—really healing that broken, rejected spirit of men—is even more important than healing their bodies.

So many of our problems came from that feeling of worthlessness, which Chuck Knoedel certainly exhibited. I knew that. There was a quick knock at the door.

Mr. Knoedel looked panicked. "Expecting someone?" I asked.

He shook his head, and edged naked over to it. "Yes?" he asked, his voice as low as possible.

"Room service," a man answered. "From Mr. Hubris. A gift for you from him."

"One . . . one minute," Chuck squeezed out. Then he motioned to me with his hand. We walked away from the door. "Get in the bathroom, Tommy," he whispered. "Hubris doesn't know I've got anyone in here. Like I said, if he knew I did stuff like this he'd be pissed off. Hope you don't mind this. Just for a moment."

I dashed through the room, collecting all my stuff as best I could, stripped the bath sheets from the bed where I had been working, and then with Knoedel rushed into the bathroom.

Chuck pulled a big, white, hotel terry cloth robe off a hook behind the bathroom door and knotted the sash around his chunky waist. Then he shut the door, with me behind it.

The bathroom was big and white-tiled, with the same old Art Deco, Aztec geometric motif that I'd seen in the lobby. It was wonderfully luxurious, and actually bigger than some New York living rooms I'd been in. There was a bath *and* a stall shower. I decided to wait in the shower, just in case anything really funny happened. I wasn't sure, but having been in the massage business for a while, I knew that not everything about it was angelic. I could only hear a few words as they muffled through the distance between the front room of the suite, the bedroom, the heavy bathroom door, and then the shower stall where I hid. "Nice of Mr. Hubris," Chuck's voice, now a little calmer, said. "Nice. He knows I like this . . . that's the truth."

Then, about a minute later, all I heard—or, maybe thought I heard—was this voice, a man's, that sounded very dull and cold and distant. It cut all the way through, echoing among the cold tiles, where I stood.

It said, "You know he hates the truth."

After that, there was a complete, empty silence; eerie. I stayed in the shower, pressed up against the back tiles. I felt embarrassed to be there;

embarrassed, also, for Knoedel. The smoked, bubbly glass door stayed shut tight, with me behind it. Then the door to the bathroom popped open. Actually, it was more of a slam than a pop.

I didn't move.

From where I was, I could see nothing, but stayed jammed against the wall and held my breath. The silence continued; then, finally, about two minutes later, the door to the suite snapped closed. I knew that: I'm not sure how, but I knew that the last door had been closed.

I was still naked. I waited about a minute, then edged very carefully and quietly out of the bathroom.

I felt relieved, though my heart was still racing. I could see the thinning back of Chuck's head as he sat in a comfortable leather armchair in the sitting room. I went over to him, like I was going to surprise him, and put my hands on his shoulders. This time his shoulders did not feel so stiff. "Everything okay?" I asked.

Then I realized Chuck Knoedel was dead.

He had been left there in the chair, still in the terry cloth robe, strangled with a piece of cord or wire. The whole thing had been done so expertly, so horribly quickly, that I could not help but stare—his eyes were still open. With no glasses on, they were much more blue than I had thought. I closed them.

Then I realized I'd better get out of there. I ran back into the bathroom, jumped into my clothes, and gathered up everything I had—the vanilla oil, the black rubber hose, everything.

Luckily, my fingerprints weren't on any drink glasses. I used a wetwash cloth to go over whatever I had touched, including the taps in the sink that I had touched to wet the cloth with. I snuck out of the suite—there was no one in the hallways—and walked down several flights of emergency stairs. Then I took a self-service elevator on another floor. I knew that the good-looking Hispanic guys in the lobby could probably identify me, but had they been really observant enough to associate me with Knoedel? I was just another face; would they remember me? Hopefully, Chuck Knoedel had come in and out many times, and had had a number of visitors; sometimes faces got blurred that way.

There was still the room service guy with the Scotch, but he had been too interested in his tip, and hardly noticed me at all. Back on the street, I took out my cell phone and thought about calling Bert, then decided not to. Even angels are smart enough to know you don't say things on cell phones that you don't want half of heaven to hear.

Chapter 6

Back in the loft, Bert was still in the middle of work for *InQuire*, talking to a fairly unknown writer who published under the name Smoky George. Smoky was of medium height, lean, gray-haired, kind of Jewish-looking, fidgety, but dressed nicely in a pink polo shirt and jeans. Frankly, I couldn't tell how old he was; somewhere from the mid-twentieth century, I figured. After working, probably, so much by himself, writing those strange jerk-off stories that he cranked out, he didn't seem that comfortable with other people (did they ever come up to his fantasies?). Bert had been working with him for a while and, as usual, knew how to handle him.

"I liked some of your earlier pieces," Bert said, trying to be diplomatic. "But you're getting kind of mild lately. Can't we get a bit more kink in them? More *edge*?"

"Edge? What d'you want? Sex out in a cabin in a snowstorm with amputees? Dream sex with kids? How about the dead? You want to do the dead?"

"I said 'kinky,'" Bert insisted. "Not stomach-turning. It takes a lot to sell people nowadays. The old sex-and-romance jazz just doesn't do it. Not like back in your time."

"I see," Smoky said. "Sometimes I feel like Gutenberg, trying to sell movable type." He took a deep breath. He looked ready to faint. "I'll see what new perversion—or *diversion*—I can come up with. At a certain point, my brain goes blank. How about animals? I've been told some guys are getting into Vietnamese potbellied pigs."

"They aren't talking about *real* animals," Bert explained. "They're just looking for little porky types, who think they're pigs. You know, hair all over the place, cute little peckers . . . anyway, that's not a bad idea. 'Porker Sex.' Can we see something on that next week?" He smiled and shook Smoky's hand, which must have been the writer's cue to leave. There was still a photographer around with a stack of older butt shots for an upcoming "Daddy"

issue, and a totally bald designer in a plaid kilt; but Bert could see that I was upset.

He asked me if I were all right and why was I back so fast. "Weren't you supposed to have a full session with Knoedel?" I told him I had to see him in private. We went to the back of the loft, to our bedroom. I closed the door and began to speak.

"Remember that name we saw in the *Times*? Hubris? Alan Hubris. It seems Mr. Knoedel worked for him. He told me how thick things are getting with the Mayor, the real estate people, and gay businesses. It's quite a story for us, but—"

"A real story, you're not kidding! We could use that instead of the usual dry-asshole porn. This sounds like it's got real juice in it."

"There's a story, all right. Knoedel's dead. It happened while I was there. Somebody strangled him while I was in the john."

Bert looked at me. He started to laugh. "Not that big old dick of yours again?" That was not funny, I told him. Not funny at all.

"What am I going to do, Bert? The terrible thing is I liked him. He was a sweet guy, just in the middle of all this shit. But he's dead. He told me all about this Hubris character: there's nothing kosher here, believe me. They— the cops and Hubris—will be able to get to us. They'll trace him to here. Knoedel called here, right?"

Bert looked calm, amazingly so. He could do that while I was freaking out. He put his fingertips together. "They *can* trace him. But I'll just say he was interested in investing in the magazine. Happens all the time. I'm kind of surprised Hubris hasn't tried to buy me out, too."

"He would," I said. "If he could get to Gil Levenberg."

"Don't even talk about him. We got another letter from his lawyers, Gilhooley and Weinstein. This one says we're running an illegal business here. 'One used to promote deviant sexual practices.' I guess I'll have to stand on my First Amendment rights."

"You don't think he means the massage service?"

"We don't do that here," Bert said. "It's all takeout. Anyway, if we were paying full market rent—twice what we're paying now—he wouldn't say a word. He'd probably be one of your clients."

"They're all real estate sharks," I said. "Didn't you say it's the only business where you and the bank go in broke, and you come out a millionaire?"

Suddenly, Bert looked a little less cool. "Maybe the stakes are even higher than I thought. The question is what to do about you; suppose they try to nail you for this? Exactly what makes you think this guy Hubris did it? Maybe it could be somebody else."

I told him everything that Knoedel had told me: about the blind syndicate, the real estate, the Mayor. Knoedel had got a call from Hubris just

before the murder, probably just to make sure he was in the room. Then a room service man had come to the door and said he had a present from—who else?—Mr. Hubris.

So, Knoedel, thinking that I shouldn't be there, had put me in his big bathroom. Luckily I hid myself in the shower stall, with a smoked glass door. In the old days people wanted modesty when they were wet. No clear plastic for them. Whoever did it came into the bathroom, but did not look inside that glass door.

"You're lucky," Bert said. "Maybe I should go away with you. As long as they can't find you, the police can't question you. I'm frightened that whoever did this will try to kill us both."

"Or kill somebody else. Someone equally innocent." I sank down on the bed. "I feel like I'm losing something; that spirit that holds us together. Fear does it. It robs you of your soul, doesn't it?"

"I know." Bert sat down next to me and held me. "I'll never let anything happen to you, you know that." He started to kiss me. His mouth, warm and large, felt very nice. I just wanted his shirt off and to dig my hands through his big hairy chest. "Let me get rid of these people," he said, motioning out-side. I told him he'd better do what he had to do. Getting out the next issue of *InQuire* was important. We had to achieve some amount of "normalcy," no matter what.

"As far as I'm concerned," Bert decided, "you're just not here. You haven't been here for several days." He paused, lost in thought. Then he said: "Can you go where you were last night? He helped you once."

"That was a . . . ," I wanted to say "thousand years ago," but stopped. I had Niko's phone number. Suddenly now it did seem inevitable: I'd have to call him. There were no two ways about it. But where would all this take me? "I'll call him from downstairs," I said to Bert, "then I'll call you back."

Bert went back to work on the magazine, and I started to shower. I had a lot of that vanilla massage oil still on me, and I was tired of the smell of it. In the shower, I fell on my knees and prayed. It seemed like the only thing to do, as the warm water came down in a fine, dull spray over me. It brought me to a feeling of peacefulness within myself and I prayed to other angels to help me . . . and to Bertrand.

It may seem funny to pray to somebody who has been dead for close to a thousand years, give or take several decades, when his latest "form" was in the next room. But Bertrand had a distinction that Bert, I'm afraid, had lost; a clarity; a true, real, touchable nobility . . . it had somehow flaked off through various lifetimes, and to tell you the truth, I missed that.

"My lord," I said softly. "You must know that I'm in trouble now."

My eyes were closed, but I could feel the fine mist of the water running 83

in little dots on my face. Then I saw him. His handsome nobility; his young, dignified form—dark, hairy, all sinew and muscle. He was there with me in the shower stall. He pulled me up and held me. I felt for a moment blinded in his bodily warmth, breathing in his smell, feeling him . . .

. . . as the shiny, fragile, momentary bridge of Time appeared, and I left the shower, the loft, and Bert.

Bertrand and I were both naked, holding on to each other . . . now in a hidden finger of a river, where we had stopped at midday to bathe, with his full armor and black horse, Fire, waiting in a nearby patch of birch trees.

"It is *bon*, we are safe here," he said. "Hidden by the grass, the trees, the water. They cannot hurt us. They will not."

I smiled; now shy Thomas Jebson. "Tell me about yourself, my lord," I asked, as I kissed him in the cold river, holding on for warmth to his strong, slim waist, marked by its own landscape of thin scars and hard muscles.

"I come from Provençe, warm land of the troubadour. I miss *le Soleil*, the sun. Here it is cold; the people too cold. *Chanson* is *part d' votre vie*. Part of our life. Singing. Poetry. At heart, we are all poets. Many troubadours are like I am. Lovers of men, but in secret. In truth, we know each other. We see it in our eyes."

I looked into his. The sheer blueness of them, and the depth in his dark face. Never had I seen such a face. "Your people must be handsome," I told him.

"I did not know my mother, Beatrice. She died in childbirth. *Mon pére* was a *miles*, a knight like I. He is now gone on to be with *votre frere* Jesus. He died in a war in Burgundy. There is no end to war. I was raised by nuns and priests. As a *très petite garçon*, I saw *mon vie*—my life—was a miracle. I cannot say more to you; you must accept me as a *mystère*."

I asked him what that meant.

"*Oui*, a mystery, Thomas?" He smiled, flashing his white teeth. "It is something you walk into, without knowing. I give myself to others. I uphold truth and honor. All *mystères*, and miracles; in this age."

"Aye, sir, miracles," I said, kissing his firm stomach crossed with rippling veined muscles, getting great patches of his dark body hair into my mouth and joyously licking it. I sucked on one of his red nipples, pasted with hair from his chest. His cock got hard, and I went down in the cold river water to taste of that, too. His legs parted, and I crawled under them and stuck my tongue into his arse crack, like a fish exploring an underwater cave. His legs buckled. They shook.

Then, out of breath, I got back up. He smiled, drew back my blond hair, pulled me to him and kissed and kissed me. Then, without any warning, we heard his horse Fire make a low nervous sound. The horse pulled at the slim birch he was attached to. We could hear the tree shake, and also, at some dis-

tance, another horse's hooves.

"Shhh," Bertrand warned. "Come with me."

We left the river and, still hidden by the thick, tall grasses and weeds growing there, crawled up onto the bank. A lone man on horseback approached. He saw Fire, tethered and richly saddled, but without a rider. He dismounted. From where I hid, all I could see was that he was big and hulking, and had the short-cropped hair of the Normans. Still, there was something oddly familiar in the way he walked in his clunky old armor, a breastplate over his chest that had been dented in many places. Obviously, since he had been riding for a long time, he wore no leg pieces. He was a seasoned old knight—and he was now searching for us. That was only too obvious.

So we, caught naked, were forced to ambush him.

Bertrand pointed for me to stay hidden. Then using only fingertips and toeholds, staying as far down as he could, he crawled through the rocks and high grass by the river edge until, like a snake stalking a bird, he was behind the knight.

He jumped up, and grabbed him by the throat.

They were quickly on the ground, rolling over each other, neither of them free from the other's grip. But Bertrand was naked, and much faster than his opponent, so he could rear up and push him off balance, which he did many times. The other knight, clanging in his old armor breastplate, became more rattled and angry with each flip and roll Bertrand put him through.

"Who are you!" the knight demanded. "Claim yourself!"

"You kouth me and my friends, *monsieur*, but not like this," Bertrand answered. "And you come after me, I know."

"Not true!" the knight's voice rasped. "I come *as* a friend. By Mary, I do."

"*Pas!*" Bertrand spat out, and grabbed one of the knight's calves and tossed him on his armored stomach. He stayed there, like a turtle flipped on his back. "You are no friend!"

"Then you kouth more than I, sir knight," the older man replied. "Allow me to become naked myself. For I am at a disadvantage with you. In armor I am too slow. Are you a knight or a brigand?"

"*A votre désir*," Bertrand said, and he stood aside as the other knight unbuckled his breastplate, threw off his tunic, and took off his shoes. He was then barechested, but kept his breeches on.

"Now we shall see whose sport is better!" I heard the knight declare. Then I watched them, through my place in the grass, take up their fighting once more, grappling and rolling, tossing, jumping up, and attempting to hold and choke one another.

I was now closer to them myself, for in the midst of this, I had managed to crawl up to the very edge of their fight. I watched, unsure what I should

do, until the decision was made for me. At that point, the other knight was now winning, not by strength but by stealth. He had used his knees and feet to kick Bertrand in the stomach and head, and was pummeling him with his fists and then, while Bertrand was attempting to rise up from the ground, the knight revealed a small dagger that he had concealed all the while in his breech's right leg. He raised his right hand, aiming to use it, but not before I jumped on his back and yanked the grip of the blade clear from him.

I, only a churl, hesitated—to do more seemed impossible. I was too fearful. The knight screamed and cursed at me, and tried to throw me on the ground as I clung to him as best I could. He called me every filthy name he knew, tried to grab my hair, and was only a breath away from freeing himself when something—I kouth not what, perhaps boiling anger rising into my brain—made me ram the blade's point directly into the back of his neck. I pushed it through to the other side.

He fell, face down, only a foot from Bertrand's head.

"You saved me!" Bertrand cried, rolling up slowly, sore from being kicked and pummeled. "*Amour!* My dear friend and love!" Immediately he covered my face with kisses. "I want to fight fair." He shook his head, as if sorely disappointed. "Knighthood has become *merde* with these vermin!"

I shrugged my shoulders. What could I know of these things?

"We had best leave," Bertrand advised. "I will re-arm. You get dressed again. But let me kiss you once more."

He took me into his arms and kissed me in gratitude, though I was the one to be grateful—he had fought this strange knight for me, to protect me, and I knew it. I was still shaking, but happy that I had been able to kill him. I kouth not exactly what force allowed me to do it, but I was thankful.

Then I knelt and turned the dead knight over. And I saw that my familiarity with him was no mistake. The pitted face with the horse teeth; the huge shoulders. Of course I had never seen him half-naked like this, but I would know him anyplace. I got back up, pure white at that moment.

"What?" Bertrand asked. "We must hurry! His companions will be by soon. Dogs of this type never travel but in a pack."

"I kouth him."

"*Oui?*" Bertrand moved behind me and held me close to his chest. I pressed my back to his young strong body. He placed his tarse in the palm of my hand and I held it as I stood, looking at the revolting dead face below me. We had no time to make love as young men do, but I wanted that more than anything.

"He was a brigand who worked for Baron Odred," I said. "The local *seigneur.*"

"Ahh, I see. His name, kouth you?"

"Aye," I answered. "Mars."

Chapter 7

"So?" Niko said smiling. "You came back!"

"Yes," I said. His mother had let me in. She was a thin, wrinkled woman in dark clothes who looked careworn, but was probably not as old as she appeared.

"It's nice. I didn't think I'd see you again." He smiled and held me in his arms. We were back in his room, the door closed. His mother knocked on the door and he let go of me. She poked her face in and asked us if we wanted supper. Niko smiled and said yes. "I told you she was cool," he said after she left.

"I'm glad you were home," I told him. "And you could see me."

"What's this 'see you'? You think I got some big social life? Besides, you're what we Greeks call a *filos*, a friend." He pushed his hand through my hair and looked at me. I liked the way he did that, naturally, very sweet.

"*Filos*?" I repeated.

He nodded. "Yeah. The Greeks are famous for *filos*. We are *filo*-sophers."

We both laughed, then he kissed me. Niko was like that; open; real. I had sensed that the first moment I saw him—his real true openness—and that he had depths to him and some life that, probably, even he did not know.

He kissed me again and I asked him where Paul was. He said with one of his aunts, Niko's sister, who took the kid sometimes on weekends. "She has three kids, so one more doesn't bother her. They live out on Long Island. I just dropped him off an hour before you called. What do you want to do tonight?"

I had not thought that far ahead. All I knew was that I had to get lost for a while. I needed to call Bert, like I had said I would. It might be dangerous, but I decided to use the phone in Niko's room. He handed it to me, and Bert answered immediately. "No," he said, cryptically, "No one's come by for you."

"Does anyone know yet?" I asked, watching Niko watch me and smile as 87

I spoke. I stroked his dark neck. He made a noise like a purring cat.

"It's on cable news already. You can't keep a hotel murder quiet in New York. They just said Charles Knoedel, a businessman from L.A., was found dead. They want to turn it into a pick-up killing. New York doesn't like the idea of the locals killing visitors for the heck of it. Bad for tourism. They haven't said anything about Alan Hubris, or the Mayor's involvement. I know that's par for the course. We both know how the straight media is; you don't want to offend your best advertisers, or friends in high places."

"That doesn't help me," I said. "What should I do?"

"My advice: stay where you are. Is there some number where I can reach you?"

I told him he could still reach me on my cell phone, but I hated that. There was no telling who else was roaming out there, trying to find me as well. But frankly, I was so good at reading Bert's mind—and vice versa; we were so telepathic with one another—that I wondered if he would even need to reach me by phone.

"So why don't you just call me?" he asked. I told him I would. "If there's no one here at the loft for more than a couple of hours, then . . . we have trouble."

I hung up and turned to Niko. I was not sure how to say it, so I just blew right into it: "I need to stay here for a few days." I said, seriously.

He smiled. "So? That's cool. I been in trouble before—I ain't no angel. You probably figured that out. Just don't"—he smiled at me—"get my parents into anything. They're old and nice. My daddy loves the shit outta me, no matter how much I misbehave. So if you got trouble, I don't need to know what's wrong. Understand? But, hey, you're welcome here. You're my buddy, my *filos*. You read me even before I did! We sucked each other's dick. You can't get closer than that. What else I gotta know?"

He was right, and that only confirmed my basic feelings about him.

Supper was a huge Greek meal. We had *stifatho*, a wonderful rich stew with lamb and cloves, one of Mrs. Stamos's specialties; and also rice, artichokes, green beans, macaroni, salad, some dark Greek wine, and little nut cookies with powdered sugar, called *kourabiethes*, for dessert. They were served with strong black coffee made in a small copper pot. Afterwards, his father peeled several oranges and passed the sections around the table. I watched his old tanned hands as he carefully did this. Niko told me that was his way of welcoming guests.

His parents smiled at me, asked slow polite questions, but said almost nothing in English. They spoke to Niko in Greek and argued among themselves a bit, but that seemed natural to me. They did not know me, or how I had met their son. While I was eating, I thought about the first time I had seen

him. I sat next to him at the table and my hand went over to his crotch and he smiled slyly at me, with that funny detached, but very hot way that he had. He did this even though he was actually looking at his parents, or trying to.

He gave my hand a little squeeze, then under the table cloth unzipped his jeans and stuck my hand inside. I found his cock, and began playing with it. He smiled at me, and continued talking in Greek to his mother. She got up to go back into the kitchen, and I realized that I had better quit doing that fast— and I did.

But that only reminded me of meeting Niko . . . and in my mind there I was again, riding up in a big freight elevator. I was in Brooklyn. In the factory building by the river where he worked. It took balls for me to do that, but then balls are not something I lack. Judgment, maybe . . . sometimes.

But not balls.

The elevator was slow and creaky. Each time it passed the large windows of a factory floor I could see the distant evening lights twinkling outside. A long length of the East River passed through the lights, like a dark snake crawling at night through a jungle full of secrets. Secretly, I had been waiting for Niko himself to come into my life . . . for a long time.

Come in—or, possibly come back.

Out of boredom one day, leaving Bert in the loft (he was too busy with *InQuire*), I took the subway out to Brooklyn. I started looking at stores, houses, streets. But mostly at the men. There was still a kind of authentic working-classness there that had been lost in Manhattan, where everything was money. *Money New York*. The new city; spire upon spire of money. A whole city of money: and that's all.

The Mayor was a part of it. You could see it in his pinched face. The tight mouth. The dark angry eyes. But then so was the choking octopus of mega-corporations, the banks, the sky-high rents, and the new gay "lifestyle" of passing for what everyone else only wants to pass for.

Dead. Why not just *pass* for dead?

This half-dead-but-still-alive business had no appeal to me. I knew what living was about. I'd tasted life, swallowed it again and again—and there I was on the streets of Brooklyn. On a rotten overcast day with all these dark young men packed into skin-tight jeans, leather jackets, and tight white T-shirts, walking the streets with me. They ambled out of bodegas and key shops, jumped out of vans and the driver's seats of cabs; out of subway entrances and the small factories I saw around me.

This, I thought, is what New York must have been like a hundred years ago, filled with handsome immigrant men, walking together, strutting about, holding on to each other. The kind not yet spoiled by the total in-your-face greediness of living in the Big Town.

No, I wanted to look at their faces. Lick them with my eyes.

I ended up outside a factory that made upholstered furniture. Its crew of handsome, rough hardworking men was spilling out for lunch. The sight of them increased my appetite to no end. I was all excitement; every nerve ready to explode. All I could think about—was this thinking?—were those tight young dark stomachs, sprinkled with obsidian-black hair, leading down to a patch of even thicker, curlier black crotch hair, surrounding a thick waiting dick.

I reverted to that deeper, darker part of me: angel of pure lust, all-reaching spirit. I was ready. Uncoiled, thunderous. My cock and balls and heart reconnected to every lost piece of me, the parts we "normally" squash down. The dreams . . . the fantasies. The true life.

When that wild sex ride starts, my energy becomes endless. There was one thing now on my brain, and it was more than Bert could deal with; even more than I could. I knew I wouldn't sleep that night . . . and I knew, angel of lust that I am, that I would connect with one man.

As I saw those young men leaving the upholstery factory, I knew that one would release that powerful need with me. And suddenly, I imagined them all there, buck naked. Hairy. Dark. Wild and funky, fully erect. Holding me. Passing me among themselves. Kissing me with their warm meaty lips; their tongues. Saying nothing. Stripping off their T-shirts. Their work jeans, half-shredded at the knees and crotch; the kind whose zippers have a hard time staying up. Their ripped, funky briefs.

I could feel it happening. Them licking me, working their warm tongues over me. Down my chest with its nipples that end like little horns. Then to my belly. I have some hair, silky soft, pale there. They want to get their teeth into it. Lick it. Taste it—that hair and the skin under it.

They wanted to yank my Jockeys off, to slap my round young ass and lick the fat sweet head of my dick. They wanted my cock in their mouths like a piece of hard candy they could suck on for hours. They wanted all of that; I knew. And my cock was ready for them. Just as my mouth and ass were, because I wanted to do all this, too, to them.

Then suddenly in the middle of all this, Niko's eyes, dark as Greek wine, met mine. Accident? I don't think so. In truth, in the real story of life, I had known him. And he was the one pulling me to him, even if he did not know it.

His lean young face pulled me; his eyes spoke an entire library, thousands of volumes, of want. It's a library many men like this can't openly speak from, but their eyes read it. We looked at one another. I smiled, and he did, too.

I could feel tiny, blood-deep bubbles of excitement popping between us. My hands itched to roam over and unzip his tight jeans, the minute he looked at me. His eyes, dark and amazingly, frankly, ready, were like a hidden lake

that I was swimming naked in; and the smile in them did not stop, so I swam over more.

We started walking in the same direction. Looking at one another, sometimes directly, sometimes from the corners of our eyes. I was not sure what he was, but something—maybe just the pure handsomeness of him—told me he was Greek. He was of average height, about twenty-six or-seven, with a lean athletic body like a gymnast's, sprinkled with silky coal-black hairs on his muscular arms and chest. I could see the black hair at the top of his white T-shirt. He looked like a young gladiator. Or one of those fresh, naked young men painted on Greek urns.

What else could I say?

He grabbed a greasy hot dog from a street vendor at a corner and I did, too. There were other guys around, but we looked at one another and I smiled. Then we both nodded. We sat by the river and kind of looked each other over, then I cleared my throat and said, as casually as possible, "Nice day."

It wasn't, really. It was chilly and overcast. But who cared? Who gave a . . . ? Out of all the rocket-hot men who had come out of that factory, I'd been looking at him—sure, cruising him—and now I felt like this pure bit of heaven, of tempting maleness, had been dropped directly on me . . . and all I wanted was more of him.

He took out a cigarette, a Camel, and offered me one. Obviously he liked something about me, too. Nice. Who needed a lot of beating around the bush? All I knew was that I wanted to suck his dick. Whatever else came with that, I was ready for: and *probably*, I told my strange, horny self, it would be only too . . . definitely cosmic for me, like walking out into the wilderness once more, looking for that knight on a big horse whose name I did not know.

But I'd found him; or he'd found me.

I took one of his cigarettes. Truth is, I'm no smoker. It's just not something I ever picked up, although it's a nice way to pick up men. Then he started talking about himself. The words came right out, as if he were offering me a gift, kind of like: "Take this, Tommy. And my body will follow."

So I listened, with the words coming out of his mouth like a small line of angels themselves. I nodded. Our eyes stayed on one another and didn't go anyplace else.

He'd had a screwed-up early marriage; he and Angela (even the name seemed meaningful) had gone to high school together and dated casually for a few years. After four difficult years of wedlock—he would go into no details—she left him for another man. Both familes cursed her, but she was deeply in love.

Niko started to shake, when he said that. It had been a shock to him; he

couldn't hide his feelings of hurt. I put my hand on his shoulder and kept it there. The wind started to whip up. He cupped his hands over his cigarette and looked into my face. "You're nice," he said. "Most people'd never listen to a guy like me. My name's Niko. It's Greek."

"Tommy," I said. I took my hand from his shoulder and put it into his strong warm one. "Tommy Angelo."

"*Angelo*? Angel? My ex-wife's name is Angela."

"Sure," I nodded my head. "Maybe you could use another angel, Niko. Maybe I'd like to be your friend."

He flashed a quick smile under a two-day growth of beard. I could see the dimples on his cheeks, the flashing white of his teeth, the aching, soft sweetness of his lips. They were still boy lips. He turned to me. "Really? I can use a friend now. Cool."

I nodded my head and took another bite of my hot dog, some mustard leaked on the corner of my mouth. I flicked it off with my tongue and for a second I could see his eyes closely watching me. The light in them got deeper. He was taking me in like a camera.

I wondered then if he knew how much I wanted to have my wet tongue in his mouth.

He laughed nervously. "Sometimes I get mustard on me, too."

I nodded my head. "Maybe you need someone to lick it off."

He laughed again. He told me I was crazy and a flirt. "You're a cute kid. But I can tell you're a flirt!"

I shrugged my shoulders, then drank some out of my can of black cherry soda. What would happen next? I was about to say something—*anything*— when he asked me what I was doing that evening. "Nothing," I said flatly.

"Not hangin' out with friends?"

"No."

"Good. Why don'cha come up to the eighth floor, 'bout five. We'll go out and have some drinks."

I called Bert at the loft; he was busy, as usual. He warned me to be careful. "Watch it. That dick of yours can. . . ." He was right; I knew that. I laughed. I hung around Brooklyn Heights, some bookstores on Montague Street, till four-thirty. Then I hurried back to the factory to take the elevator to the eighth floor where Niko had told me he worked. All the way up in that big slow freight elevator, all I could think of was the soft lights of the city reflected in the water. And Niko's eyes, as dark as the East River, and his face, his soft mouth, and trim body.

I wondered how I could hold myself back, once we got on that slow elevator alone together. The smell of him; the sight. My dick already hard, in that soft light. I was not sure I could do it. I'm too lustful; I know. Suddenly I

wanted him, too, to take me in his mouth, like he was kissing me, like my young angelic wet cock was also a tongue, and he was sucking on it, tongue-kissing it . . . and I was reaching a state of Heaven that only I could reach, in the best way I could.

The elevator—a really primitive one—stopped on the sixth floor. Nine men crowded in. They were knocking off, ready for home. Factory elevators seem to go in one direction: one you aren't taking. I was going up; it now headed down. So I went back down with them: literally. I wondered what I must have seemed like to them; my dark, tanned skin but light blondish hair. They looked at me. Latinos, Russians, Turks, Greeks. Blacks. A few Orientals; from Taiwan maybe. Rippling bodies packed into skin-tight jeans and thin T-shirts rolled up to their biceps, showing big arms and chests. Nice faces trying not to show too much interest, but not turned off. Not the faces you saw in office buildings at night, those faces more than half dead.

Sometimes, I admit, when the angelic lust exerted itself, became too much, I followed working men into bars. The kind who still have the wild god in them: it hasn't been completely bred out yet. Beaten; destroyed by the money chase.

I'd follow them into urine-soaked men's rooms, the kind where the tiles have turned gray. They'd take their heavy, piss-hard dicks out at the urinals. They'd beg me, without saying a word, to *suck* it. They would beg with their eyes. *Please.*

Suck this hard cock. Do it for me. Do it and I'll even do you, if nobody's lookin'. I'll get down on my dirty knees here in this john, and you can feed your dick into my face with the two-day shadow and I'll take it and be satisfied like nothing else for a few minutes. I'll do it, if you make me. I'll make myself do it. I'll. . . .

Down one flight, more guys squeezed in. Jokes. Laughs, rubbing. Grabbing. ("Hey, buddy, that's my dick!") Body to body, sweat to sweat, flesh to flesh. Asses packed into jeans at my hands. One man's huge basket packed inside frayed denim brushing against my left hip; another butt bumping my crotch. I stopped breathing. I counted backwards. The air got hot. Steamy. Finally we were back on the first floor. I could breathe again. Everybody got out, without glancing back at me. But I knew; they'd seen me.

Once it was empty again, I took the elevator directly to the eighth floor. I got out; Niko was waiting. I looked around. The floor was jammed with oily machinery, barrels, stacks of wooden sofa parts, and thick bolts of upholstery material. "I wasn't sure you'd show up," he said sheepishly.

I nodded to him.

"Lemme get my jacket." He ran towards a work area, grabbed a nylon bomber jacket, said good-bye to some men, then we got into the elevator. It was empty. My knees felt . . . oddly watery. I looked into his face. A few

93

scars on his brow and cheeks. Maybe from skin problems, maybe fights; maybe just work. It was hard to say. Life marks you up. I knew it.

Outside it was getting cloudy. We drove in his Mustang to a bar nearby. Loud, very dark. Casa Julio. Yellow and blue neon lights flashed in the window like a buoy marker out at sea. There were some quiet hetero couples; some men drinking alone. We settled into an empty corner by ourselves. A middle-aged waitress, probably Caribbean, came up, smiled, brought us some beers, then left us. We started to talk close to each other, the way Greek men do, without self-consciousness. Our skin was touching; I felt good. Our thighs pressed together. He put his hand on my knee, and sometimes I let my hand linger for just a moment on his crotch. That did not seem to bother him.

Other men came by and smiled at him. They shook his hand and shook mine. I was glad that I didn't have to get up, because I was getting hard there in the dark. It was difficult to control it. I kept counting backwards, because I did not want him to see this if I did get up. All I really wanted to do was just unzip his pants and play with him right there.

He smiled at lot. I bought him two more drinks, and he did the same for me. Beers and a schnapps that tasted like licorice. I started to get drunk. I wanted to kiss him on his mouth. "Niko," I said, and then stopped myself, because . . . well, I knew that I couldn't kiss him there. *Rules* forbade it. The rules that hold you apart from other men.

"Yeah?" He was smiling, then he turned to me and said, "You're blond." He compared his dark Greek forearm to mine. I was lighter than he, but my hair is really a strange color. Sometimes it seems almost transparent, light comes through it and in green light it appears greenish, or blue, or whatever. He looked at my eyes. They're the luminous pale blue of certain Siamese cats' eyes at night; so pale that light passes through them, like water. "You have strange eyes," he said. "I like them."

I smiled. "They can see *all* of you, Niko."

"Shit! No kiddin'?"

"Yeah. All." I smiled. "They see you're lonely. You're pissed off about your wife—"

"Fuck! I never cared for her. We got a *yos*, a son. Cute little kid. At least I got to take him. Mama takes care of him. He's so beautiful. He's three."

"You're lonely . . . and horny," I whispered.

He turned from me; I think I really embarrassed him; I hoped I hadn't blown the whole thing. Then he said, "My kid's beautiful. Can your eyes see that?"

"Of course," I said. "He'd have to be beautiful. My eyes can see that. They'd like to see him."

"Sure. That's cool."

"How about now?"

"I don't know. He's asleep."

I laughed. "That's all right." Then I suggested, simply, "Just show him to me."

He nodded his head, then suddenly ran his hand through my silky hair and laughed out loud. "Sure, I'll show him to you," he said as his hand brushed slowly down across my face. I licked it, kind of like a joke, when it reached my mouth. I put my hand on his knee and left it there. He smiled, then casually placed my hand on his crotch and nodded his head. He smiled at me and I knew that the wild god was winking.

I wasn't sure how I'd get up, because now I'd really gotten hard. My dick was thumping, flashing inside me like the neons outside. But nobody noticed in Julio's; it was dark enough. I put my Levi jacket back on. We left the bar.

It was really black outside. Light rain started to come down. I told Niko he was too drunk to drive, so he laughed and pretended to hand me the keys. "I like having a young man drive me," he said. "Makes me feel important, like you're my driver!" He laughed, then said, "But let me drive. I know the way. I'm not too drunk. See. I was just pretending to be. That's all." We got into the car.

Julio's was in an area full of dark empty streets. There were warehouses, winos and vagrants outside. Some of them stood around, rubbing their hands over oil barrel fires. "This can be a bad area," Niko said.

"Can't be too bad," I said, and suddenly in a friendly manner put my free hand on his crotch, like it had just landed there by accident, but this time I started to rub it. He let out a funny kind of "Wow!," then said, "You're *bad* to do that, you know, Tom?"

"Bad?" I looked surprised. "What's bad? We're friends, right? Friends can touch each other . . . right?"

He nodded slowly, then he said, "Sure. And maybe one can suck the other's dick, too?"

"Maybe." I smiled at him. Sure, I thought. But *maybe* wasn't even in the question.

Then I got bolder and undid his zipper and started to reach in. He grabbed my hand. "I'm not sure if I'm into that right here," he warned.

I told him that was okay, and a minute later he was into it. I did everything I wanted to him, got his cock into my mouth, sucked his ass; then, as I remembered, he started the old Mustang. And a bit later, we were in Astoria, where the story began—and then I was back at the table finishing dinner with his parents.

"Your parents are nice," I said after we returned to his room. "I guess they don't know anything about me."

"Just that you're my *filos*," he said. "That's enough." We had the door

closed, and he was now on top of me. "I don't want you to think I'm a queer," he said. "I ain't no *pousti*." Then he unzipped my jeans, pulled out my cock and put it into his mouth for a moment. "That tastes good."

"You don't have to stop." I told him.

"I don't know when to stop. That's my problem."

I told him I understood. He started to kiss me, then he said, "I'm so confused right now. I'm scared."

I told him it was all right. We all got confused sometimes.

"It's just," he said, "this is kinda new for me. I sucked dick before—okay, I guess you know that. I been gettin' blowed for years. I like it. My wife never liked doin' it. I asked her once to do it and she got upset. 'That's not something nice women do,' she said. She could not even talk about it. I guess the truth is she could screw a *malaka*, but she couldn't suck my cock."

"She doesn't know what she's missing," I said.

"Sure. She didn't . . . it's just . . . well, I never thought I'd ever have anything going with a guy that could go on."

I told him again not to worry. The most important thing was that he liked me and I liked him. I looked into his face and for a moment I forgot about the problems I'd had earlier in the day—finding a man dead in a hotel room; escaping I was not sure what, but something. He asked me what I wanted to do with the rest of the evening. I shrugged my head. His room was getting small, and I did not feel like facing his parents again. Their English was about as extensive as my Greek.

"I have an idea," he said suddenly. "I know a club over in Brooklyn. Some of the Spanish guys where I work go there. It's wild, you'll see. I been there before, you know. We'll go there."

Chapter 8

The club was called MaloMalo—it was in a series of gigantic old warehouse rooms in Greenpoint, above Williamsburg, not too far from the bridge. I could not have found it; the streets twisted and turned and held you with their own sense of foreboding. Finally Niko stopped on a dark narrow back street, all garbage cans, cobblestones, feral cats; filled with thuggish-looking guys who never stopped eyeing us—"They keep your car safe," Niko assured me as he locked up and we walked out among the other cars on the narrow pavement. "They're brothers." I nodded my head, but still wondered what he meant. A phalanx of dark young men in big baggy pants, all popping elastic bands of white undershorts at the tops—hot muscular brooding guys, way too serious for me, I thought—nodded at us. "Buyin'?" one whispered to Niko. He smiled. "Whatchu got?"

"Pot, crack, X, K. Some H, for later, if you want."

Niko smiled. "I'll check you later." We walked on. "Never buy from the first guy," Niko whispered to me. "Just a bit of advice I give you."

I nodded. We got to the elephant-sized, black industrial door. There was already a line of thirty or so people, mostly straight couples, dressed fairly down but very party, to get in, with a few scattered gay men waiting with them, in pairs or alone. What looked like the human versions of two Mack trucks stood at the door, smiling briefly, checking people out—including patdowns and flashlights on faces.

One was about ready to pull me aside, when Niko smiled at him and said, "Hey, he's wit' me," and then, as if old Oz himself had spoken, we went in. "They usually charge bucks, but they know me. I been here enough." Niko Stamos broke into a big smile and shrugged. "So I guess I'm a regular."

We walked down a few stairs, past a ticket window where somebody said, "Hey, Niko!" and Niko beamed, and then we turned a dark corner and passed some young guys and a few girls who might have been guys, too, at some point; and then we got into the first room.

MaloMalo exploded in front of us. Huge walls reached back only to dis-

appear into mists of falling color. Spinning shafts of light; ear-splitting music. The beat totally nuts. It stopped, rearranged itself, doubled back to blow up in your face. Again and again. Latino/Caribbo/Arab/African/House. Heavy drifts of perfume; smoke; laughter.

A night storm of screaming voices blew through the place; music rolled over it or pushed it from one side to another. The club was crowded already. Not late, only 11:30 or so. "This ain't nothin'," Niko warned, lighting a Camel. "By one o'clock, it's gonna be jammed. Wait. You'll see the most beautiful people in the world here."

I wasn't sure about "most beautiful." But they were wild, crazy, and high. We found a tiny empty table with tall bar stools in the back. We sat down and Niko stared out at the crowd, as the scene moved on and off the dance floor. Spotlights swirled around the club, sometimes melting down to a soft gray or pink, other times shooting back up right into your eyes. For a moment I felt kind of dizzy, as people kept pushing around the tables, posing, shouting, talking.

Nothing registered. It was like all blank, like trying to pick out one pink feather in a flock of flamingos. Then a gorgeous, flame-haired, cinnamon-skinned girl appeared. She was all legs and swan neck. With cute dark reddish freckles on her bare silky shoulders and back. Her face, kind of pixyish, was painted like a parrot's. Little round peppermint pink lips. Crimson blush. Two thin emerald-green lines around her very dark eyes. "Niko! Niko!" Her long fingers went up into the air. She hurried over towards us on her high heels. "Chu are th' one I wanted t'see!" He beamed at her.

"Tommy," he said, getting up slightly. "This is Paula. Prettiest girl in the world, right?"

I nodded. "How you doing, Paula?" But she could not hear me over the loud bar noises and the Afro-Brazilian beat. She swayed back and forth, then bent Niko's ear to her lips. He looked over at me, then smiled and told me he'd be right back. They were off for the dance floor.

She had on a polyester flower-print dress, gathered so tightly that I wondered how she walked in it. Then I saw that it was cut open in the back, all the way up to . . . anyway, it stopped just at that point where she could sit down without being completely bare-assed. Her purple backless heels didn't skip a beat as she melted next to Niko and the two of them fell into the next dance, a slower samba. The lights came down. I watched, mesmerized: now I was really lost in myself. A very handsome waiter who looked half black and half Asian came up. I ordered a gin-and-tonic.

He came right back with it and I gave him a ten dollar bill and he smiled and left. I lifted the glass to my lips, when a short, light-skinned, kind of fleshy guy, Celtic-Irish—his nose slightly punched in, broad and flat like a pug's—wove his way towards me. He was, maybe, early forty-something, I

figured. He wore a pair of loose dark khaki pants and a tight dark blue polo shirt. It said Perry Ellis. "Mind if I sit?" he asked. I nodded. There was no telling how long Niko was going to be with Paula, and I did not like being alone there—it was too crazy; too easy to get numbed out by all this.

"You new here?" he whispered to me under the noise.

"Yeah," I answered. "My name's Tommy."

"Billy. Billy O'Geech." He started laughing. He had a strange, loud giggly laugh, like a bird or a dog from a cartoon—it spilled right out of him. For a moment he couldn't stop. "My name always breaks people up! Sometimes it even breaks me up, like I can't believe I'm really Billy O'Geech. I'm kinda high. You high, too?"

"No," I whispered. "I'm not really a drug person."

"Good. Stay off that shit. There's a whole lot of bad shit here. Heroin, 'specially. Don't let nobody shoot you up with that. But if you need it, I'll tell you who to buy from. But—anyway—stay away from it. I just drink. I just had about six beers and a couple of gins." He smiled at me. His eyes looked like pinwheels, they were revolving. Or maybe it was only the strobe lights revolving in them. I could tell he was nervous talking to me—a stranger—but he wanted to. Despite all the craziness here, it did not seem like a place where you just went up to somebody and talked. For one thing, it was too loud. And for another—well, the place was too edgy. Some guy might come up and kiss you, or knock two of your teeth out. There was no telling; so I'm sure there were a lot of things that kept people away from each other.

"Do you dance?" I asked him.

"Naw. You? I feel like a fool out there on the dance floor. Those Latin guys can dance the pants off anyone. Just watch 'em. Mostly I wish they'd dance the pants right off me. I'd give 'em my pants any day!"

"Is that what you're after?"

He looked at me shyly. Maybe I was being too forward. "Naw. Not really." He started that funny laugh again. Then he stopped. "But I could dig a guy like you."

"I'm here with somebody else," I said.

"Shit, the good ones are always taken! You with a he or a she?"

"He's out on the floor"—I pointed—"dancing with a girl named Paula."

"Ahhh, he's with Paula! She's hot. The guys all go for her, even some of the prime straight ones. She's still got her dick, but they don't mind it at all."

"A *dick*?"

"Yeah, she's a tranny. Gorgeous body, nice face. She can be a bitch, but I'd like to pop her myself. Imagine sucking on something like that, with those sweet little tits and a nice face?"

I nodded my head. "I guess a lot goes on here," I said.

"Everything goes on here. Come on, I'll show you around."

"I should stay here for Niko, my friend. The one with—"

"Forget it! He's busy." He pointed me over to Niko. He and Paula were working together on the floor like peanut butter and jelly. He had his hands on her small hips, then down her dress. One of her perfect little tits, like a scoop of pink cantaloupe, had popped out. She appeared embarrassed, but Niko quickly had his hand on it. She laughed; he pushed it up with his palm for a moment, then kissed its tiny nipple. He let go, then she put it back in place, all to a hardcore salsa beat that unleashed, all by itself, could have raised the room temperature by fifteen degrees. "Come on," Billy said. "Come to the men's room with me. I'd like your company."

I got up and we walked through the crowd to the men's room. It was jammed with guys and some girls dressed as guys, or was it vice versa? In one corner, a tall, espresso-dark, macho type, his nicely pressed pants only slightly dropped, was getting his big cock sucked by a woman, or someone of that ilk; frankly, I couldn't tell.

I saw the back of her long blonde hair at his crotch as she crouched in her heels and carefully worked on him. He had his eyes closed. He was vaguely smiling. Other guys either watched from the corners of their eyes or ignored this, or were busy snorting drugs, or, in the back, in half-open stalls, were shooting up. They would come out, looking dazed—like the light had left their eyes. Sometimes the life, as well, as they tried not to trip over anyone and then left.

Billy went over to a line of white porcelain urinals to pee. I decided I'd better do likewise while I had a chance. I unzipped, took my cock out and realized that despite trying not to be, I was halfhard; peeing would not be easy. Maybe it was just the atmosphere—so saturated with sex and drugs and this wild beat that you could taste it. I wasn't sure what the taste was like; maybe one of Paula's little nipples. Billy looked over at me, then reached over and started to stroke my cock gently. "I'd sure like to suck that," he whispered.

I felt strangely embarrassed. Maybe I was not high enough, or maybe something about all this unnerved me. It reminded me of a tense kind of war game, one where you could land on the wrong square and get blown up. I knew that I had to watch out for myself. "Uh uh," I told him. "This is all too crazy."

"We'll go someplace else," he said, and stood next to me, casually pissing and smiling. My dick got soft enough to pee, and I let out a quick stream, then rezipped. More guys came. Latins, Koreans, blacks, Chinese—and mixtures of them all. A few handsome white guys who looked very New Jersey, flashing ropes of gold jewelry, shirts unbuttoned close to navels, mingled cautiously. No one was too pushy or difficult; there was a strange—and

strained—funny kind of quiet. I guess you knew what the rules were. And if you didn't like the show, you just didn't look.

Maybe the drugs were all working right. The couple at the end of the room stopped. She got up on her open-toed heels. Very pretty, but her dark face was just too thin for the mop of blonde hair on her head. She had wide bony shoulders and wore a tight gold lamé dress with thin straps. She smiled, giggled nervously, then flipped open a tiny shoulder purse and applied a coat of cherry-red lip gloss on her wide mouth.

She was with an ebony god; very big and confident. His biceps were the size of a car and he wore a simple white dress shirt with the sleeves rolled up to show them off. They walked out and the ebony god looked at me and winked. "I'd sure like to suck that dick of yours," Billy said after we'd left the men's room.

"Maybe we should get back to Niko," I said and we managed to thread our way through the crowd to the same table. Niko was not there.

"I know where he is," Billy said, nodding. "He went to Heaven with her. She must have gotten something for him."

"What are you talking about?"

"Heaven. It's another room. They don't let just anybody in, but I'm sure Niko knows where it is. I've seen him here before, plenty. He must have seen you gone, so he figured you're there already, being such a good-looking kid. Anyone ever tell you how good-looking you are? You look like an angel, something out of a painting."

"Not all angels look like that."

"You do." He paused. "Can I kiss you?"

I shrugged my shoulders. I was not at that moment so turned on to Billy, but what could I do? After all this going on around me, he seemed kind of direct and sweet. "Sure."

He leaned over towards me. He cupped one of my cheeks with his hand and brushed his lips against mine. There was something so shy and tentative about the way he did this; vulnerable, really. He smelled of beer, gin, cigarettes. Still, I liked the hardness of his lips as his mouth opened slightly. With a warm sweetness that got to me, he gently sucked my bottom lip. Suddenly he laughed, then made this noise like a sob. A funny, bubbly kind of sob. "I don't do this a lot," he whispered. "Y'know . . . jus' kiss somebody. I ain't really so drunk. I just saw you. I had to come over; what can I say? I want to show you everything. Will you let me?"

He got up and took me by the hand; his hand was much bigger than I'd thought it would be. It was work-hardened and callused, but he held onto me gently, like we were small boys. I felt moved. We squeezed our way across the dance floor, with hardly room to get a knife blade between dancers. The music had slowed. Lights glowed at half level, ruby red, misty. It was like

walking through a sunset.

Most of the dancers were in couples. Some were in threes, usually with two guys and a girl. The guys were trying to act slightly macho, at least around each other, with the girl in the middle. I wondered what would happen if the girl disappeared. With some that had already happened. The girl was way out by herself in drugville; I saw guys melting together like caramel, their lips finally not afraid of one another in the slow duskiness of the music.

The sight of all this was turning me on. I knew it; I had got my own high just being there. I felt like a balloon, rising up off the floor, trailing Billy gently by the hand. We passed out of the room, into a dark stairwell. Three bouncers stopped us, and Billy said something to them, and they nodded and pointed us down the hall. We got to an elevator, got in, and someone in there took us up.

Now it was all brightness, like being in a moving cube of light. We got off at the top floor, and Billy held my hand as we walked through another door. It was dark and quiet, then as I became more accustomed to the dim light, I realized we were in a series of cubicles and alcoves, each with its own separate action. The first was for shooting up and smoking. The acrid, unmistakable smell of crack hit me. "We ain't going there," Billy said.

I nodded, and we walked past another room without going in it. It was filled with people, but seemed innocent enough. "What's this?" I asked.

"Voodoo. Plain witchcraft. Some of these people go for it."

"Can we go in?" I asked.

He told me we could in a minute. He pulled a joint out from his pants pocket. It was wrapped in tin foil. "How about some of this? It's just weed with a little hashish in it. Sometimes you need that, you know? It'll loosen you up. You seem kind of . . . scared, I don't know. Something."

As a rule, I *prefer* not to do drugs. In my profession as a massage worker (okay, there is some aspect of the *whore* in that), as I've said, you have to be at least slightly in control of yourself. I don't drink on the job . . . but I told him okay. We went over to a big industrial window and lit up. I knew that the night sky was somewhere out there, but I could not see a single star. Someone came by and asked if we wanted a little coke to go with it. I thought at first he meant Coca-Cola, which shows you at that moment how dumb I was. Even angels aren't supposed to be that stupid.

Billy nodded and said sure. He put a tiny white bit of it up his nose, then licked the rest and handed the guy a ten dollar bill. Then he handed me some, and I did the same thing.

I felt as if my head had been lifted off my body and it was now speeding through a dimension I could not name. Billy was on top of me, and he led me quickly into another room—this one bigger and darker. There were couples

page number at bottom left

of all sorts in it. They were smoking, and doing other things. Fucking. Sucking. Skirts up. Bare bodies. All I saw were shadows and silhouettes, but I knew what was going on.

Very quickly Billy found a private corner of our own; and there he took my clothes off.

Chapter 9

A gray, silverish light from a dirty upper-hatch window, like an eye from the night's private world, fell in a puddle about us. It trembled, passing; had a life of its own. What an odd, fabulous, naked creature this raw light made Billy O'Geech become: like he were swimming in it. All thick, muscular thighs, slick belly, soft merry nipples. Big arms. And a cute, funny little dick like a pig's, coming to a slight, fleshy curl at the end, where his foreskin gathered in a satiny twist. We were now both stark naked. No shoes even . . . and maybe it was the marijuana, the coke, the . . . anyway, I felt like I, too, was just swimming through him.

Doing a smooth evening breaststroke into the tunnel of his mouth, as he mouthed my dick and stroked my body and felt so warm and cuddly all over, something men really can't get enough of, and he was a good cocksucker, skilled, attentive . . . his tongue hitting all the live nerves in my tool, the veins under the shaft and the warm ridge of the head; then him kissing, sucking and licking my balls, all the way down to the magic fabled Gold Spot, where the little pleats of the scrotum and anus meet and all those smart, wicked sensations linger to shake hands. The Arabs call it "the doorway to Heaven." And I know that's true . . . because as much as I enjoyed being in Billy O'Geech's sweet heavenly mouth, I realized that I had left him there at MaloMalo . . . with only my body to play with . . and I, in another form, was with Bertrand again. I had passed over the bridge. . . .

. . . And we were passing under the raised grated gate of a distant castle; it was at the end of a bright afternoon, before *aefen* torches were lit, and the waving glint of gold and blue banners yet sparkled from its towers.

I thought my heart would catch in my throat; never had I been in anything that even *resembled* a castle before. How could I, Thomas Jebson, son of a pig farmer? And there was so much . . . to look at! My eyes could not keep from going back and forth, trying to take in everything. Never had I felt

this magic; this excitement . . . and the wondrous importance that I had while holding onto Sir Bertrand as we paraded on his steed Fire all the way into the front courtyard. A small crowd of faces, perhaps twenty-six in number, came out smiling to look at us.

The castle was the keep of Sir Bertrand's friend, Sir Garet du Fontayne, a worthy young knight who only recently had come into his inheritance. Sir Garet was one of Sir Bertrand's two *confrères* that first morning, that seemed so long ago. My lord had told me nothing of our approach to this keep; I had been sleepy, surprised! Surely this had to be a dream, as the drawbridge was lowered and we passed over a moat, then under the raised portcullis itself and into the bailey, the fortress's central yard.

It had been planted with merry flowers, some fruit trees, and boxes of herbs and seemed the fairest of all fair places; though, as I have said, never had I been inside a keep—and knew nothing of what was in store for me.

The fortress had been placed at the boundary of a beautiful park land, a thick holt studded with ancient oaks and great trees. Now riding away from the ugly, fearful land of my birth, I felt such relief, as if, truly, I had been born again. We trotted on a clear promenade through this park, until the castle appeared there slowly, guarding a knoll before us, with nothing behind it but graying mist, which foretold the evening as the land itself dropped off (securing the fortress, from the rear) . . . and my mouth, from surprise, dropped open.

I had not expected to see before us this picture in stone: four guard turrets climbing, spider-like, above thick walls cut with slits for archers. And in its midst, one central tower, rising, I told myself, to a truly mountainous height, where, I supposed, Garet du Fontayne himself must sleep. At sixteen, my breath was taken away; my heart raced. Never had I seen so many faces who were strangers, and who smiled so graciously into my eyes.

Then, soon enough, accompanied by a guard of eight warriors with ceremonial torches and a few other worthies in finery, the noble Sir Garet emerged from within the keep to greet us.

Bertrand and I dismounted, then he bade me remain back with his horse. I watched nervously and held the bridle, while Fire barely contained his desire to prance forward and follow his rider. "Easy, Fire," I whispered into the horse's ear. "Be good now."

Bertrand strode ahead, until he bowed before the young lord of these towers, dressed in ermine and spotless white, who bade him rise and then kissed him on both cheeks as his small court nodded their heads. Sir Garet whispered a few words into Bertrand's ear, and Bertrand smiled, then Sir Garet said, in a more public voice, "Our friend Sir Bertrand of the Land at the End of the Mountain has returned to us in good health. I rode out with

him into the sad lands of our foes, those villains led by Sir Odred de Campe, but a week ago. Shortly after, Sir Bertrand felt a calling," Sir Garet stopped, smiled, then went on, "to venture on his own. I prayed to our Virgin that Sir Bertrand would be secure. And that his venture would be to our credit and God's will. We thank the Lord Jesus that he has returned to us with—"

"*Bon*," said Sir Bertrand, clearing his throat. "He is Thomas Jebson. *Mon*, uh, groom."

"And a pretty and gay lad he is!" proclaimed Sir Garet. "So we are pleased to welcome this Thomas, Sir Bertrand's groom, who will—" Sir Garet gazed about, then said, with a smile, "sleep in the stables where a spot will be made ready for him!"

At this Sir Garet clasped Sir Bertrand to him. Then they turned and marched up the marble stairs into the keep, followed by Sir Garet's small court, as it chattered away, with the torches, the banners, those fine clothes and everything, while I stood outside, miserable. Sorely disappointed. Like a pig with his nuts cut off, looking for a bit of soft muck to hide his snout in.

So, I muttered to myself, I will not get to sleep in a castle after all. And certainly not in the furs and silks which Sir Bertrand had promised me.

I, cast into the stables. With only horses!

(I might as well have remained with the pigs. . . .)

The thought saddened me, but this seemed to be so. Sir Bertrand and Sir Garet du Fontayne disappeared, and I was left in the courtyard, alone. Then an old man named Wilfred shuffled up to me. "Aye!" he called. "This way wi' you. There'll be supper f' ya soon, and good! Barley bread, groats, porridge. Bean soup! You'll like our bean soup—make ya fart till ya see our Lord!"

I walked, downcast, with him, until we were at the big hammered doors to the stables. We entered. At first my eyes were overwhelmed with darkness. Then I was introduced to two other grooms, another Tom, who looked about eight or ten, then Dirk, a handsome young man of about my age—perhaps three years older—with long red hair, even longer than mine; fine, pale, slightly freckled skin; and already the massive shoulders and arms of a good blacksmith. He had a slim waist, and, I could tell, even with his breeches on, huge muscular thighs.

He was bare-chested from scrubbing the horses, and I could not, no matter how much I tried, keep my eyes off him, and he smiled at me, too. The skin of his broad chest was as white and fine as flax. He was all muscle and sweet manliness, as beautifully made as Fire, my Lord Bertrand's horse. As beautifully made as . . . oh, surely, I was glad that there was so little light in the stable. For anyone could have seen my face redden and blush with the misery of my own admiration, even under my tanned churl's skin.

He had even white teeth and a handsome Saxon face, though not as fine

107

as Sir Bertrand's. Soon our smiling eyes could not leave each other and they stayed there, unashamed, with no recourse to embarrassment. Then, quickly enough, to my happiness, Wilfred left and took young Tom with him, and there I was, alone with Dirk.

He asked me where I was from, and I told him that I came from the lands of Baron Odred de Campe. He grimaced. "A bad lot, them," he said, sadly. "We have known for years of their meanness against God's laws. They burn the fields and many good folk with them. They burn the forests, too." Then he lowered his voice and added: "And the forest men."

"Do you know of these foresters?" I asked.

He nodded his head. "Aye, yes. Good men! Some fear and hate them, just as they fear the Ealdcraeft itself. But there are other reasons why: they want to own it all! And give nothing to those who are poor Saxons, and are from here. Sir Garet is of Frankish line, but not Norman. His old people came before the Normans, even afore the Danes. He's a good man, and has little to do with the Norman lot. He is not a powerful knight—as you can see, our forces here are not grand. But a fortnight ago, he went out riding with Sir Bertrand. They wanted to see what had been done; a bit of a look-around. But only Sir Garet returned. We have not yet seen the third, Sir Ansel. Our lord Garet fears for Sir Ansel's life. He is the oldest of the three, and also good. All whiskers and gray, but smart. Tell me, have ye washed yet, young Thomas Jebson?"

I told him no, and he led me over to the horse's troughs, where fresh water had been laid out for them. "We wash in this too," he said. "The horses mind not a bit."

I took off my tunic and dipped my hands and arms up to my elbows in it. Then Dirk sneaked around me, and bent my whole head down into it, and kept it there but for a moment. I bucked and pitched to escape his horse-strong grip, and finally did, gasping and spitting water all about me and directly into his face, while he laughed at me with joy.

I had water in my eyes and screamed what a knave he was, until I realized that I was now caught in his great bare arms and he had pulled me to his chest. "Now let me dry and console you, Thomas Jebson," he said, as he put his mouth to mine and kissed me.

I opened my darkish green eyes and saw that they were now looking directly into his own, which were the purest jet black, despite the snow whiteness of his skin. "You are true good, Thomas Jebson. I kouth why Sir Bertrand wishes you to be his groom!"

I could feel Dirk's cock pressing with all its force against his breeches, and his hand groping that place where my own piece had become excited and was leaping to get out of its confinement. He kissed me more, and then we heard the shuffling sound of old slippered feet returning to us—"Shhhh,"

108

Dirk warned, and took my hand. "There is a loft above the barn. Wilfred cannot get up there. He's too old."

We hurried quietly up to the loft and then watched Wilfred scratch his head, and leave. Dirk whispered into my ear, "Old Wilfred is not a friend of forest lust, as Sir Garet, Sir Bertrand, and we are. Understand?"

I nodded my head and soon felt very happy as we had all our clothes cast off, and I was in Dirk's arms again, with his long red hair falling down into my blond. How well-made Dirk was, his stomach tight and coiled with muscles, his chest beautiful, smooth, muscular. He had no hair upon it as Sir Bertrand had, but was most handsome nonetheless. We soon began to cavort with one another, feeling each other's cock, kissing and sucking one another, until Dirk turned me over and began pressing the thick thrusting head of his tarse to my arsehole. I had never engaged in this play before, and was sure it would be of great pain to me. I remembered the gloomy warnings of the priests—"The Devil's backdoor," they screeched on—and I told him that I surely could not do such a thing. Besides, if anyone possessed this entrance into myself, it would have to be Bertrand himself, my liege lord.

Dirk begged and begged, but I still told him no, then I began to suck his cock as skillfully as I could, which made him happy. He burst forth finally, releasing great spurts of white liquoring cum, and coming himself into a great happy lightness; whereafter, soon enough, he fell asleep with his massive arms about me.

It was then approaching real darkness, and I knew that I had to go someplace. To see Sir Bertrand—no matter what.

I reclothed myself, and carefully climbed down the rickety wooden ladder of the stable's loft. When I got to the bottom, in the darkness a gloved hand reached from behind me and grabbed me by the mouth. "There you are, you roaming ape!" The hand released me enough so that I might turn about and see my lord's dark face before me. "Where have you been? Kouth you not I was seeking you?"

"No, sir," I said. "I kouth that my liege was with others, better than myself."

"*Pas*," he whispered into my ear, then kissed me full on the mouth. "No one is better, Tom. You killed that dog Mars, who would have murdered us both. We are up against terrible things—you and I. You will learn that." Then he said, "You will sleep with me tonight. Sir Garet only had to say that for the others in his court, his relations who do not know him really, nor his heart. He has given me his blessing that we sleep together. I told you I'd bed you with furs and silks. Now is the hour for this!"

Sir Bertrand led me through the darkness in front of the stables to a rear stairway. He unlocked a door. We climbed up the steep circular stairs to a tall back tower. At the top was another door, which Bertrand unlocked to our

chamber inside. With a flint, he lit a spirit lamp, and I looked around at the circular room that was like nothing I could even imagine.

The chamber was . . . so beautiful. My heart still aches to think of it. Bright and rich with colored silks, tapestries, carpets, and a bed all laid with linens, soft white ermine and sable furs, quilted silk covers, and plump pillows. "It for you, *mon confrère*," Bertrand announced, "to share with me."

I smiled. He had not lied. He had told me I would sleep with him in furs and silks, and there they were. "Let me wash you myself," he whispered, and he poured fresh water, scattered with tiny pink flower petals, from a pitcher into a shallow bowl. Then he carefully removed my dirty clothes and laid them aside. I know they smelled of horse, hay—and Dirk—just as I knew I smelled of him. But I hoped that my liege would not notice this, as I stood before him, totally naked, my sixteen-year-old "stick" throbbing just so slightly with excitement, almost jumping, but not quite hard. Not yet.

He was still completely, richly garbed, but he took a soft cloth and dipped it into the fragrant water and slowly began to swirl its warm wetness over my face, the back of my neck and its blond hair, and then, even slower, back and forth over my chest. Each place that the satiny washcloth went, his lips followed as he gently kissed my neck and chest with his slightly chapped mouth; then he went down my tight young stomach, making it tingle with delight. His mouth and tongue stayed on my little nipples, as he excited them greatly, making them flush with a hardness and warmth I had not known before, in such a sweet place.

"Does that please you?" he asked.

I nodded my head.

"Tell me," Sir Bertrand asked seriously. "What other men have you known in this manner, and what in the past have they done to you?"

I told him that I would tell him, but only if he made himself as naked as I was. He did so, and then continued to wash me, this time concentrating on my lower belly, all silky as it was with short, curly blond strands, down to my pubic region. He washed this area until water beaded off the hair tufts, then he sucked the water from them, and slowly kissed the shaft of my cock, just running his tongue and then lips over it, until each vein stood out upon it, flush with heat, thick and almost purple with rushes of boyish excitement.

"In truth, sir, I have known only the men of the forest," I confessed. "Crude knaves. Nothing like you, sir. No one truly . . . as noble as you, my kind *seigneur*."

He stopped and looked up at me seriously. "Do not lie to me, Thomas," he ordered. "Or I shall beat you here on the spot."

I hesitated. I did not want to be beaten by my young, dark-haired lord. But if it were his pleasure to do so to me, then, I decided, so be it. "If that is your pleasure," I professed, "then I am prepared for you to beat me, until I die!"

"I am saddened," he continued with all seriousness, "that you will not tell me truthfully with whom you have lain, as you have lain with such lust with me."

"I cannot, sir," I said to him. For I was afraid that in his possessiveness, if he learned about me and Dirk, he would order me away from his bed and I knew, then, that I would die, if that were the case. But I also knew—even in my own unlearned youth—that it was impossible for me to hold myself solely to him. He had professed, surely, no love for me; only his possessiveness. As a high-born knight, Sir Bertrand would protect me, but not love me. I thought myself to be only his vassal, to do with as he pleased.

"Then it is for me to beat you, Thomas Jebson," he declared seriously. "I shall beat you soundly and since we are here alone, you may cry out as you want, but no one will notice you."

I told him, then, that I was prepared to accept any violence from him. I threw myself down on the bed, so that my tender stomach met its softness, and waited for him to attack me.

" I must first find a device of discipline," he said, and he started to look around the room. He picked up his long leather glove, and began to flog me with it—one stroke, then another, then another on my back—using it as a whip; then he became tired of that, and it hurt me very little. "You are not crying out," he said. "So I will choose another device for your discipline."

With this, he went to a large oaken chest, opened it, and took out a favor, a square of black silk, doubled it, and then used it as a blindfold on my face. "Can you see?" he asked.

I told him no. It was true. The favor left me as blind as a church bell bat. Still, I felt a bit . . . I can only say "merry" to have it on.

"*Bon*," he said, then he bound my hands behind me with a slender rawhide length and told me to get up and accept my punishment. I managed to get off the bed, then stood, but only found myself being tripped, no matter in what direction I walked.

Sometimes I was tripped because there was a wall directly in front of me, other times I was tripped by something under my feet. I had to be careful to keep from falling on my head, or landing flat on my rear! Finally, after several attempts to stand on my own, my young Sir Bertrand took me by the hand and bade me stand alone, by myself, and wait.

"You will be punished soon enough," he warned with a sneer in his voice; then I felt his mouth go briefly to my lips, and I followed its warm, slightly chapped course down my chest, until, there, at that area below the bottom of my stomach, I felt his mouth on my swelling young tarse. It rested there, filling me with longing, hardness, and a warm wet softness at once. He sucked and licked my boyish tool, while at the same time I felt on the muscular round cheeks of my arse the cunning sharp tongue of a whip—a real true

111

whip this time—though, definitely, a small one.

That I would bet with my last coin! It was a small whip, but still I flinched and flinched. Even so, my lord was able to hold me perfectly in his mouth; even as my arse was being whipped handsomely by some hand.

But, how could this be *his* hand, I wondered?

Could Sir Bertrand of the Land at the End the Mountain administer such love to me with his mouth, while at the same time flogging me so expertly from behind with a small whip? My arse, though, I knew was getting warmer—and, most probably, redder—until, finally, I began to find this "punishment" almost pleasurable. Except that I wanted, more than anything, to have my lord Bertrand kiss me. To have him raise himself to my lips, and stay there, quite simply, with his manly, slightly chapped mouth upon mine.

I yearned for this. Hungered. How much, I can only barely tell you. I wanted his lips on mine, even as much as I delighted in the attention he was giving to my excited tool. Soon enough, though, he pulled away from me. I stood now, blindfolded, bound, my cock twitching from excitement as it stood, fully hard and desperate to be relieved of its bounty of warm thick juice.

"So, Thomas Jebson, how does this punishment meet with you?" my lord asked, as the flogging hand continued to lay its rhythmic strokes on me.

"It grieves me. Because I would rather you kiss me, sir, than punish me."

"Very well—" my lord said.

Then his mouth came up to mine, to fill me with his tongue, getting it deep inside my throat until I thought I would faint from sheer happiness, even as I, still, was being flogged. Yet, as he did this, suddenly the flogging halted and I felt something other now also enter me. A slickened, warm thick cock entered my tight, but pained arse, which opened slowly, as this member pushed skillfully into me.

I cried softly, moaning with the sheer warmth of it, as it passed my reddened flogged cheeks, then deeper into the reaches of my gut. Now, surely, I might pass out from another hunger, deeper than that even for food, as I wanted this excellence to hold and enfold me, and not stop.

Instead, I felt many strong arms taking me back onto the bed. This was done even as I was being taken from the rear by this beautiful, and not small, organ working its way down into my breech, with another pair of lips now softly nibbling and kissing the back of my neck.

On the bed, my legs were lifted up. With this tool still working its way into me, and slowly moving up and down to a rhythm of its own, my cock was also being sucked attentively, as yet another mouth made love to my chest and nipples. "Please," I whispered. "Unbind my eyes that I may know who is doing these good acts to me."

"But that means you do not like your punishment," Bertrand whispered,

and then another voice said, "We must punish him no more. I command it."

At that command, my blindfold was removed and I saw that I was being fucked by none other than the young Sir Garet du Fontayne, and that Dirk's mouth had left my cock and was now licking my chest, as my lord Bertrand kissed me over and over again.

I then took my liege Bertrand's organ into my mouth and sucked him until he delivered his juice directly to me. I lapped it like milk, and it was by my taste as good. Still I was not fully satisfied, and would not be until Sir Garet had his way with me, fucking me slowly and then hard and fast, delivering himself to me from the other side, and with that, Dirk sucked me to completion, and I did him yet again, and then we were all, as one, tired on the great bed. So much so that I did not even witness Sir Garet leaving Sir Bertrand's dark chamber only a short time later.

I stayed there that night, with Sir Bertrand on one side and the handsome groom Dirk on the other, his beautiful red hair sometimes falling into my face and his mouth upon my chest, even while Sir Bertrand kissed me and held me from the other side. It was a night of pure happiness, but it was not to last for long.

For early the next morning, before the sun's rays had penetrated the narrow windows of our chamber, Dirk returned to the stable to see Wilfred, who knew nothing of Dirk following the ways of the forest. Once in the stable, he would have to pretend to be asleep—and give a ready excuse why I was not there. ("Oh, Thomas Jebson has been commanded to Sir Bertrand's chamber to help his knight dress, Wilfred. You understand the ways of noble folk— they are quite helpless without the work of us!")

I was allowed to sleep later, at least until cock crow, but then saw, once my eyes were open, that Sir Bertrand was now fully garbed in the most handsome red and black. Two colors that reflected his own state of mind. "Get up!" he ordered. "We must get up! A *catastrophe*! *Très dangereuse*!"

I asked him what he meant, but he only took my face into his hands and whispered to me, "We must take courage. You and I. I will be there always for you, Thomas Jebson. But we must have *courageux* heart. For nothing shall part us, I give you my knightly oath."

"What are you speaking of?" I asked him as I struggled to dress myself quickly in a new outfit that had been waiting for me in the large chest in Sir Bertrand's room. And handsome, it was, too, with green hose. Green hose! What I had wanted always; and a yellow tunic, and a shirt to go over that.

Bertrand looked away from me, his beautiful head down, so that I could see only his glossy, raven black locks, shining in the fresh morning light. "Come. *Regardèz*."

We walked from the chamber down the parapet stairs, and entered through a series of passageways the big hall of the court. There, with Sir

113

Garet seated on a raised polished chair before us, we saw, on a black catafalque, the pale bloodless corpse of an older knight. How handsome, I thought, he must have been in life with his gray whiskers; though now he was stone white, with no color on his face, even about the gash of his mercilessly slashed throat.

"*L'Ansel*," Bertrand announced to me, his voice barely able to suppress the cry in it. "He was . . . 'delivered' to us just before dawn. Two hooded messengers came up to the keep and called out for Sir Garet du Fontayne."

"We suspected an ambush," Sir Garet said. "So I came down from my bedchamber and brought my men out with me. Then we found this awful sight, dropped by the moat, like a load of wood . . . to be burned!"

"*Mon Dieu*," Bertrand said softly, "Imagine our grief!"

"He must be avenged!" Garet cried. He strode down from his chair—I thought it had to be a throne, but learned later that knights do not sit on thrones, only kings—and planted a kiss on Sir Ansel's cold forehead. "He was like a father to us. Uncle, brother, all of that."

"True!" Bertrand shouted. "Surely, none other than Odred de Campe did this. *Monstre*! We had to kill his lackey, Mars, who tried to ambush us. We were unarmed, naked from river washing. Now he has done this to Sir Ansel. I want Odred's head, *mon cher* Garet. I swear!"

"*Non*," Garet said. "As much as I love you dearly, *cher* Bertrand, I cannot let you go alone. I shall find twenty men—the best, the bravest. I shall go to the Baron's keep and demand that he fight with me, one on one, in *combat de honneur*. Then we shall lead him to trial. If he is found guilty, we will hang him—and then burn what is left of him, publicly in our courtyard!"

"*Pas*," Sir Bertrand said sadly.

"Why?" Garet argued. "I want Odred to be brought back here alive. I want all to see that justice is yet alive in England!"

"*Cher* Garet," Bertrand sad sadly, "you are a good man. You have understood me as few have. You know my heart. I fear you will be the one to burn, and faster. You have only a small force here. It is justice in this part. Odred will destroy all of you. He is cunning, and without mercy. When you are gone, there will be no one to fight his allies. But I have another plan."

"*Oui*?" Garet said, listening.

"In an hour, I will set forth from here with Thomas, my groom."

"Thomas? Your—"

"Yes, Garet. *Mon* Thomas. He is from the region of Odred, he knows that area perfectly"—I *do*? I thought—"and I am not afraid of the Baron. The two of us, if we must, are completely prepared to die. Believe me, *vraiment*, that is so."

I was sure that the beautiful dream of last night was turning into a nightmare, as Bertrand went on—"Thomas knows my heart, that I will not die without him. So to prove our affection for each other—"

"Exactly!" Sir Garet du Fontayne exclaimed. "And your own nobility, Sir Bertrand, *mon cher ami!*"

"*Oui*, therefore, with stealth we'll do what must be done. We shall pass into Odred's keep easier than any force of yours. I can be cunning, too. And if we do not return in—"

"Holy *Jesù!*" Sir Garet said, as I listened, unable to say a word, but turning stone white already. "*If* you do not return in a fortnight, I will send a message to my cousins, the Celtic Fontaynes on the Irish coast. They will come if they have to. And then *if* the two of you die, we can then avenge all *three* of you!"

"Your Celt cousins, *bon*," Sir Bertrand said, nodding his head. "*Très bon.* But I believe after we are through, there will be no need for them."

Chapter 10

"Are you frightened?" Bertrand asked me, a short time later. The sun was still low behind us. We had left Sir Garet's small castle with only a rushed meal, breaking the fast of night before mass. We did attend mass together, and on our knees prayed in front of the Virgin and her Son for our deliverance, and I prayed as well, in silence, to myself, to the old gods, for they had kept me alive so far and brought me the good fortune that I had received, as much as Jesus Our Savior had. Of this I was sure.

At least now I was on my own horse, an old nag named Rose, the red-brown color of clay, who despite her age was good enough for someone like me, only a vassal. Ahh, I thought, if Grett and old Jeb could but see me—their only son—dressed finely in green hose and a new tunic and shirt. Even if I must die, at least I had my green hose!

And on a horse! A genuine horse! Despite that her back sank in the middle, her hind legs gave way every now and then; and, sometimes, she just stopped. Then I'd have to give her a good kick to get her going. But what did that matter? No one amongst us churlish pig farmers had ever had a horse of his own. Or, better yet, rode with a real knight . . . who could read letters and spoke so well!

"No," I lied to Sir Bertrand, trying as best I could to smile. "I have no fear at all!"

But as we rode farther on, the mask of courage I wore started to fall away. The sweet countryside of rolling hills and peaks gave way to strips of charred land, the burnt remains of huts and woods, and the gristly bones of dead horses, pigs, and other beasts. These sights became too regular as we rode on towards the castle itself of Baron Odred de Campe, a villain whose face I could not say I had ever seen, but whose very name brought fear forth amongst the villagers I knew.

"Tell me, sir!" I called up ahead so that Bertrand could hear me. "What

does he look like?"

Bertrand smiled back at me. "*Oui, mon jeune* friend?"

"The baron! Odred!"

The knight slowed down, leaned back towards me, and shook his head. "*Grand* belly. Tail. Horns. *Vert*—green—"

"No! Play me not for the dolt. What does he look like?"

Bertrand smiled shyly; dimples settled into his cheeks. "I fear I cannot say. I saw him only once, at a great gathering near London. It was like a *tourney*, but not a real tournament. What you'd call a 'tilt,' or as we might say a '*plaisance*.' Kouth you that?" I told him no; I did not. "Mostly for show. Goodly knights came—in splendid dress with horse, and fought—but not to hurt. It was, you see, near the mass of Christmas, ten years after the coronation of our King William"—he saw my face flinch. "He is still *votre roi*," Bertrand went on. I bowed my head, then looked up. "Many men of gentle blood were there, and ladies. Amongst them was Odred de Campe. There was much gossip about him—his strange tastes, his 'morality'—even many Normans hate such things, but bear with him. I saw little of him. Only at a distance."

"His 'morality'?" I asked.

"*Oui*. Look around you." He surveyed the charred land.

I nodded my head. "Were there other great thanes about, sir, like Sir Garet?"

Bertrand laughed. "You are *gentil*! Sir Garet is but a poor knight, compared to the splendor of royal ones. You should see them. They walk on sables, and always protect each other! Sir Garet has a few nice pieces of fur . . . but, truly, he is but a knight from a good old family. Frankish, here before the Normans. From the death of his elder brother, Ernest, he inherits that small castle. But before, when we first clasped hands, Garet du Fontayne lived on the edge of a good forest. Hunted, sported with *galant* young men, was a *doux jeune homme*. Inside, he still is."

"And how did Sir Ernest die?" I asked, while I tried as best I could to get Rose to keep up with Sir Bertrand.

There was quiet. Bertrand gazed attentively to the right, then to the left. He was taking no chances; then he looked back to me.

"Whilst traveling one day towards dark," he answered, "Ernest went over to help what he saw was a fallen knight. It was an ambush. Another of Baron Odred's allies charged him from behind with a lance. Killed the poor man. That is why Sir Garet and I go out to spy on the Baron and the other Normans of his area. We want to know what he and they are doing. *Comprend*? That is why we were out there in the dark that morning, when I first saw you. We will bring him to justice yet, and hang him!"

My hands began to shake. I steadied myself. Baron Odred de Campe rep-

resented the power that I had feared from birth—the evil, overbearing Norman landlords who bade us pay forever, merely for the right to eat and breathe.

"You are afraid," Bertrand said. "I can see that." He slowed down, and reached over to stroke my face with his gloved hand. "You are much younger than I, in many ways. It is unfair, my friend. But fear not. No matter what, you will never die without me."

I looked at him, while my lips humbly kissed his glove. Had I wanted a simpler life, I told myself, I could have stayed near the forests of Oakum— and as easily be murdered there without the protection of Bertrand. "It makes no difference," I asserted. "I will do what I can, I have no fear! I will take this Baron Odred, and cut him open myself if need be!"

"*Bon*," Bertrand said. "You have a true heart."

"And by truth, sir, I am not much younger than you."

"Yes. And that is why I looked for you, and—" he paused, then said— "Why I love you."

I thought my heart would leap in my throat. "You do, sir?"

"*Oui!*" He looked down, as if he were too shy to say what he had to say, him a knight. Then he looked at me. His blue eyes glistened. "I love you because I must. I have given you my *honneur*. Why else would I invite you to all the most secret places in my heart?"

I nodded my head. He *loved me*, though his love seemed more an obligation than real love. Real love, I thought, was gladly given. It was between equals. Still perhaps this was only the way of knights; and they spoke thus. Surely, I thought, one day he would go off and leave me. He would return to the Land at the End of the Mountain, and there marry a woman of his own rank and forget about me.

Still, he had melted me; he always would.

We broke our ride at noon and ate and drank from a small store of victuals Sir Garet's cook had prepared for us. Bertrand told me what a good cook Sir Garet employed. He was a Frank, very low born, a cussèd sort, who had trekked all over Europa, and knew amazing secret recipes, some for poisons and others for the passions. One, from the stewed heart and testicles of a gallant stag, was sure to inspire lust and good sex in all who ate it. I made quite a face when he said that, and Sir Bertrand smiled. "Of course, Tom, you do not need such a preparation. You are quite loving enough."

He leaned over and kissed me long and very sweet, and I was glad once more that I was with him. I felt as if he and Sir Garet had already planned my death; but, again, this was also only the way of knights. A way that I, a churl, could not fathom.

We remounted—Bertrand in chain mail armor this time, not plate, and me in my fine new hose and togs—and we got back on the trail. I did not ask

any more questions, but accepted that Sir Bertrand knew the way, that we were riding in the right direction, and that I was as happy as I would ever be.

Fear left me as the sun made its slow, ruddy descent into the West. Soon we found ourselves riding deeper into a thick, gladed forest whose name I did not know but whose leafy depths I found more comfortable to myself, since at heart I knew myself to be a forester.

"You have no fear here," Bertrand noticed.

No, I told him eagerly, I did not. Soon we had to dismount and lead our horses. We found a clearing and decided to make camp there for the night. Bertrand stripped off his armor, and wore only his under breeches with a wool vest over them. I took off my new green hose and tunic, and wore only a nightshirt and breeches. We secured the horses, pitched a tent, and then Bertrand invited me to go out looking for dinner. "This place is teeming with game," he said.

Taking a small hunting bow, he proceeded me, working his way easily through the underbrush. We soon spied a covey of quail, running here and there, flying over us, and in the same place several dark squirrels and even a funny little badger, who disappeared into a hole as fast as a wink.

"Shhh," Bertrand warned me, then he carefully started to trek ahead, sinking his shoes into the soft ferny forest floor, making no sound at all. He passed through a close stand of great trees. Then he was gone.

Suddenly, I realized I was alone.

Alone, and in what seemed—in one more wink of the eye—pitch darkness. I looked up. All I could see were the black, tightly joined boughs of high leafy trees, and not one star. Not a wisp of moon. Then I heard noises about. Crackles. Little snaps of wood. A few birds calling.

The noises died, then resumed. I called out as low as I could to Sir Bertrand, but heard nothing. Then, with no warning, I was immersed in a total blackness which I can only compare to that of the grave itself. I struggled, and found myself immediately knocked to the ground.

A sack had been pulled over my head (hence the quick darkness), and soon I was up and being led someplace. Where? "Go quiet!" a voice growled. "Or ye'll be dead as th' good pig at Christmas."

I did as he told me, and was led under low boughs, about hilly places, and then up. I was surrounded by men (for I could hear their voices), but I had no idea who they were or why I was being led. My immediate fear was that some of the Baron's own men had caught up with us, and I'd be clubbed in the head and dead as a bagged rabbit with my next breath. Then, we—or they—stopped. I decided to start begging them for my life. It seemed like the only thing to do.

I sank to my knees, and lowered my head. In a flash, the bag was removed from my head. I was sure that my head would be removed next, but

I looked around.

Light, even in the night forest, was all over me. I was in the middle of a clearing, men all around me. Then I heard, "Tom! It's our boy, young Tom Jebson!"

Jesus, Mary, and the green gods! Yea, there in front of me were the old forest men, though some were not that old. I almost sobbed with joy! And, next to them, hands and feet bound, a gag tied into his mouth, was Sir Bertrand, struggling to stay on his feet, despite the bounds.

"Tom!" I heard. "We're so glad t' see ye!"

The voice came from Richard Smart, hearty, bearded, a most decent sort, from the wooded glens near Oakum. He led the men there; how could I ever forget him? He had brought me secretly into their rites and had been pleased with me. He smiled at me; I smiled back at his big bearded face. Then he embraced me fully and kissed me on the cheek. I wondered what he was doing in this strange forest, and he must have wondered the same thing about me, because he asked me that question outright, with many men in rude forest dress bearing in around us. "I'm on a journey," I answered.

"Good!" Richard gleamed. "Good t' have you wit' us. Now this rascal, we got 'im, too!" He pointed to Bertrand. "The rich nobles rob and kill. We should kill this 'un. Hang him! Slice his gut out! Look at 'im, wi' his fine ways—"

"He is good," I said. "He's with me, or I'm with him. His name is Sir Bertrand of the Land at the End of the Mountain, and he is fine. As fine as any man. He is from Provençe—"

"A Frank," Richard said. "We never liked them Franks!"

"You must take his gag off," I said. "And he will tell you what he is."

"You sure?" Richard asked me, then winked at me. I told him I was sure—as sure as I stood there. Then Bertrand's gag was removed, though he was left in bounds.

"Thank you, sir," Bertrand said kindly. Though still tied, he made a slight bow to Richard Smart. "Please kouth I am not Frank, nor Norman, but Provençal. From the land of the troubadours. We love song and poetry, and are pledged to aid good men like yourself—and your friend Tom, whom I have taken to my heart."

Richard nodded his head, then apologized and bade his men untie Sir Bertrand.

"I ken it now," Richard said. "Methinks sorrow that I treated ye bad. Ye must ha' supper with us." He clasped Sir Bertrand to his big chest—he was easily twice my knight's size, with huge thighs, arms, and calves. He was a mountain of a bearded man, truly. "Then you will sleep safe wi' us, and go fort' in the morning. You are looking for Baron Odred, I'd say."

"How kouth you this?" Bertrand asked.

"We' here," Richard explained, "because the Baron's been robbin' and burnin' more than e'er. We ken he murdered one dear Sir Ansel—a bonny ol' boy of yours, no doubt."

Bertrand nodded his head.

"He a ugly bugger. He tries to burn us out o' our own good forest, so we come here."

"Jeb and Grett?" I asked, suddenly frantic with care. "Ken ye of Odred's serfs—has he been killin' 'em as well?" I was lapsing into the regular talk of the area. I knew that.

Richard shook his head. "Nay. We ken nonce. Besides, yer old Jeb is smart. He kenst how to keep his throat in one piece. Nay, but yer mama Grett, is fair yet. Odred's men astick the eye on her. No lie! I would astick the eye on her m'self, if I kenst not she a good married wench." Richard winked at me.

The other men, about twenty of them, were all about us now, engaged in gathering, cooking, and making do with what we had to eat. There was a dressed haunch of deer, baskets of wild roots and berries that the good men knew to prepare so well that they tasted much like regular parsnips and turnips. Also jugs of sweet mead and ale, the best I ever truly knew. We sat now in that deep clearing in the sweet-smelling wood, and I was very pleased, what with the tasty food (there is nothing like deer meat cooked outside over a wood fire) and the good drink. "If Odred kenst we killed his deer," Richard said, smiling, "he'd hang us all—and burn the holt so the deer would die anyway. Nay, we kill to eat. Not the other way, as Baron Odred de Campe and his mates do!"

"Has he been around here?" Bertrand asked.

"Aye. He stalks about wi' his men. Plain doltish. One day, he'll be cut off from his knaves—a' then we c'n cut his throat like a gay cock."

"What do you do when he's around?" I asked.

"He'll not come int' the wood a' night. No wise gentry will. That's why I ken your friend Sir Bertrand wa' bad. Anyway, when Odred rides through, our lookouts warn us. So we hide and spy on 'em. We listen to e'ery word they talk—a' times from the trees, a' times from the ground, all covered about wi' bush. Tha's how we larned of tha' sad dog, Sir Ansel. 'Twas routh about 'im. Pity. Have another slosh of ale, Sir Bertrand," Richard offered, and poured him forth another huge helping of the foaming brew.

While Bertrand was drinking, another forest man, Zachary, thin like a fox and all quick, and I went back to get our horses and the tent. Zachary found them in the dark as easy as anyone might in pure light—he knew the holts like his own face—and we brought back all. By this time I saw that Sir Bertrand was quite happily drunk from the ale and the mead, and that Richard had most of his clothes off, except a breechcloth, as the fire provided

enough warmth. Bertrand then asked me to pitch the tent, so that he could fall asleep and we could ride off in the early morning. But Richard Smart would not permit it. "Sleep wi' us. We make our beds next to the fire. There we sleep besides each other for warmth and happiness. Look at those stars way up! There's no need for a tent a' night."

Bertrand nodded his head sleepily. He was too tuckered out and drunk to argue, and Richard even helped my lord out of his togs, so that now the young knight was stark naked there by the fire, with Richard smiling at him. "You're a gay bonny man," Richard said, nodding his head and smiling at him. Then he clasped Sir Bertrand to his huge naked chest. Now most everyone else had gone off in twos and threes to their bedrolls, and I only watched as Sir Bertrand hugged Richard, as much to stand up as to hold him.

"And thou!" Bertrand said. "Are by truth a hero and a *gentlehomme*. I swear this! To take such care of me and my *jeune* friend Thomas."

"Aye, sir, you are barely out of boyhood y'self! But I took care of Thomas afore—" he winked at Bertrand. "When Thomas was e'en younger!" Then Richard brought me over to him, and he felt his way into my breeches to stroke my hardening cock. I soon released it from its cloth hammock, took off my nightshirt, and was as naked as they. Soon we were rolled together in Richard's bedroll, clasping to his huge warm furry self, both for warmth and pleasure. His cock was as thick, fat, and indeed, tasty as the rest of him, and I brought him close to release several times with my mouth, as he kissed and hugged Sir Bertrand, who being drunk did not seem to mind mixing his gentle self at all with a wild, hairy forest man.

I wondered how he would have behaved on a more sober evening, since Sir Bertrand was a noble knight, and not one to sully himself, I felt sure, with merely anyone—which was why I felt truly honored to be his groom. Suddenly at one point, while the two of them were stroking one another and whispering manly endearments, Sir Bertrand said to Richard, copying the big man's speech, "Ye are truly a' angel, Richard Smart."

Richard looked over at him in the fire's warm glow. "A' angel, sir?" he said, sighing. "That is most genteel."

"*Vraiment*," Sir Bertrand whispered in a voice so low I could barely hear it. "I am one . . . I lie not. It is . . . I keep it from Thomas . . . my time here is short. I tell you, but . . ." Then I heard almost nothing except— "a secret . . . please, I pray you, keep it."

With these words—which I admit I could barely hear—they kissed more in great manly affection. And I turned and sucked them both, enjoying both their sweet cocks one after the other and sometimes even at the same time, until Richard could last no longer and gave all his juice to me. Then he took Sir Bertrand himself into his mouth, so that Bertrand was relieved, too. At that I handled myself gleefully, and soon fell asleep with the three of us

123

blissfully entwined.

But unfortunately, I could not sleep for long. Something woke me up, out of the deepest soundest sleep, a sleep that still snored with Richard and that kept my lord Bertrand in his great warm arms.

I got up, naked as the day of my birth, and walked for a short while beside our camp in the forest. I thought about the forest men. Why did the "good" nobles hate them so? Why did they try to snare and kill them? I tried to understand all this, about the Church, the priests, and the nobles, but could make no sense of it at all. I tried to understand what I had overheard from Sir Bertrand. At times he surely was like an angel to me, but what did he mean when he said that to Richard Smart?

Then I heard a noise. It was Rose, my horse—she was all shaking bones and nervous fear. Skittish, you'd say. Something had broken out in her; I felt it. I edged over, still naked and now kind of shy about it, to where she was tethered, and petted her browny-red head. She looked up at me and smiled, I swear, in this silly horse way. Except for her bridle, I was as barebacked as she was; but as horses can—since I have been told they bear a sense we men do not—she sensed coming danger.

I walked over to Fire, and saw that he, too, bigger and much more sturdy than Rose, was alarmed. He was tugging heartily at the rope that staked him to a great tree. I petted him, too, whispered into his ear, and calmed him down.

Back with Richard and Sir Bertrand, I awoke them. We all quickly dressed. Zachary was already up. He had heard the neigh of the horses, too, and was lookout that night. Richard gestured to him, as if to ask "Where?" Zachary pointed him into the direction, and then quiet as mice we crept from the camp with Richard in the lead. Pushing through the thick surrounding stands of brush and wood, he pointed us to a trail that emerged, clear, from the forest. We walked along it in the moonlight. He showed us how this trail circled the woods, only, later, to backtrack through it once more.

"Someone must be on th' open part o' this trail," he said. A short way off, a line of tall gray cliffs rose along it, and he took us over to them. I was not used to rock climbing, but managed to make my way up, using my shoulder muscles and the callused grip of my hands. Bertrand had no problems at all. He was a natural climber. Once at the crest, Richard ordered us to get down. We did. There, below us, in the first haze of morning light, were four horsemen; nobles obviously, riding together.

"Who are they?" Bertrand whispered to Richard.

Richard shook his head. We could see only the tops of their heads, until Richard took a pebble and hurled it directly into the black rear flank of the last horse. The steed careered up on its hind legs, and then settled down, but not before I got a look at its rider. His hawkish face was stone cold, pale,

hard-mouthed, with eyes that seemed to be made of ice.

They were of a piercing steelish blue that looked almost transparent; they sent shivers through me. I clung to the top of the cliff with just enough of my brow exposed to look safely at him, but felt as if a razor-sharp wind from the north had suddenly passed over me.

Soon enough, they were gone. They had disappeared around the coming bend, away from our camp.

"Gone," Richard said, popping up. "They won't go int' th' forest. We're safe."

"Who was that?" I asked.

Bertrand smiled. "My young friend kouth not," he said to Richard, and they smiled wisely at one another.

Kouth *what*? I asked both of them, feeling a sense of nausea and dread mounting inside me.

Then Richard answered, "He, my young man, is yer Baron Odred!"

Chapter 11

And so it was . . . that face, icy, intense, startling . . . hung in the air before me. In a flash it froze the close-to thousand years that separated me, Tommy Angelo, from the younger, curious Thomas Jebson, as both of us, shuddering at the same time, separated once more, holding the Baron's demonic features in our two minds.

Suddenly I jackknifed deep inside, ripping open all of my nerves and the secret experiences I'd had of being away and Time travel. My naked skin, on the body I had left with Billy O'Geech, crawled with cold goosebumps, as if an army of frozen ants were doing maneuvers across my chest.

At the same time Thomas Jebson swallowed hard, trying to keep from peeing on himself out of fear. He gazed over at Sir Bertrand for help, as I looked directly at him. Then I realized something: Thomas could not see me at all. For even angels can not be in two places at once.

That moment—that timescape which Thomas Jebson inhabited—had closed. He was my guide, my earlier form, there. I felt sorry that he was so afraid. Should I say something, give him my experienced hands, my warm lips . . . ? Yes, but it is unwise for angels to do so. We do not perform tricks with the centuries.

The Baron's cold face had compacted that near millennium of Time into a short, crystalline bridge of ice leading directly from the distant past. I sprinted back over from it.

Now all I felt, too, was cold.

My eyes opened into dim light. I stared at Billy O'Geech, as he emerged from a background of music and noise so loud that it pierced my eardrums after the roaring quiet of that icy bridge of Time. I could still feel the goosebumps on my shoulders. My neck muscles felt tight.

"Oh, man!" said Billy, who actually looked much cuter naked. "You just did the wildest jerk"—he shook his head—"like all your muscles went BANG! It made me stop suckin' your dick." He reached over to my shoulders and then touched my nipples. They were icy, too, I knew. "You feel

127

cold; you okay?"

I told him I was. He started to massage my neck. That felt good. I was really starting to like Billy.

"I thought you were gonna have some kind of seizure," he said as he carefully rubbed my neck, then my chest. "I know about guys who *pop* before they pop, but, man . . . you sure you're all right?"

I nodded. "Sure," I said. "Maybe it was just the . . . I'm not used to drugs." I had to say something.

He laughed. "That little bit of weed musta really done it to you! You look like you been about a million miles away. I couldn't get you to come for anything!"

"It's true," I confessed. "I was a *long* way off." I looked around at the strange sinister shadows flitting around the large, dimly lit room. Suddenly despite everything, it hurt to come back; I longed for the forest men, for Sir Bertrand . . . for Thomas Jebson himself. Then I realized how dumb that was. I had never known fear the way Thomas had. (Or, I will admit, adventure for that matter—he could walk five miles and be in a different world!)

"I liked what I was doin'," Billy said. "I mean, gettin' to play with you. I don't get t' meet a guy that looks like you often." He laughed nervously. "This place is so wild. It's kind of like going to the old baths in New York, except that there's more going on. You got men, women, drags, trannies, all sorts o' shit!"

I wondered: what was really going on? There were people here, but how many of them were actually connecting—directly—without all those drugs and craziness in the middle? I looked up. People were around us. Not crowds, but their shadows rolling across the walls of the room. These shadows seemed so much less real to me than going back in Time to be with Bertrand; and seeing, for that first time, Odred, an individual filled with evil . . . judgmental, harsh, always covering his own guilt and sordidness.

I was really chilly. I got up and put my clothes back on. Billy looked at me, puzzled.

"You know what your problem is?" he said, nodding and smiling. I asked him what he meant. "You ain't in the moment. That's what you gotta be here. It's like you're someplace else." He put his clothes back on, then pulled another joint out of his pocket, lit it and passed it to me. I tried to draw some smoke from it, but only ended up coughing. I tried it again, and some of the peppery smoke slid down my throat into my lungs.

At that moment, Niko suddenly turned up with Paula. They both looked much worse for wear; Niko had eyes like a crazed zombie. I could barely recognize him. And Paula's dress had come apart; it resembled the tablecloth at a kids' party, after a food fight. The top part was ripped, stitching had come out the back, a shoulder strap had popped.

"MaloMalo!" Niko shouted. "Ain't this the best!" He had a creased, frantic look on his face. He did not look like the beautiful man I knew. Billy looked at him and whispered to me: "Looks like your friend's been suckin' on the ol' crack pipe."

"MaloMalo!" Niko said again, and started kissing both Paula and me at the same time. "This must'a been what ol' Greece was like. Everybody jus' doin' everybody else!"

"Niko honey, chu better behave yaself," Paula said. "I think your friend's not ready for all dis."

"*Shiiiit*! you should see what he does for me!" Niko said, his voice echoing in the room. "Tommy can give the best blow job in the world! He's a' angel with that mouth!"

I became embarrassed; I knew it. Even a lustful angel like myself doesn't like his name just flung around. I turned away and Billy looked at me. "It's okay," he said, trying to keep his voice down. "It's crack talkin'. They get nuts like that. I wish they never had the shit; I hope he's not hooked on it!"

"I heard that!" Niko exploded. "*Na pas sto thiavolo!*" He waved his right hand to us, palm outward, with the fingers spread apart. "You know what this kinda hand means? It means go fuck yaself in Greek. I ain't no junkie. And I ain't a queer, neither. I'm married! I gotta son. He's beautiful. His name's Paul—just like her!"

I shook my head. I was sorry to see Niko like that. He was in more trouble than I'd thought, but what could I do?

He grabbed Paula and began kissing her as hard as he could. He became totally out of it, and pulled Paula's dress up and her panties down. She wore something else under her panties, kind of like a jock or something like that. He pulled that down, too. Her cock, long, skinny, and uncut, popped out.

"Niko, dammit!" Paula screamed. "Chu don' know how t' treat no girl attal!"

Niko looked up. His dark, weary eyes caught mine. He looked trapped.

"It's the goddam truth!" he began crying. "I'm a fuck wit' women. *Skata!*" Then he sank down on his knees and began sucking Paula's soft dick, pushing it at first all the way into his mouth, then suddenly spitting the whole length out and licking her balls. Soon he stopped and said, "This is the most pussy I ever get!"

Billy shook his head, and grabbed me by the hand.

"Let's get outta here," he said, shaking his head. "This is way too nuts for me!" And what could I do, but agree?

We left that part of the floor, and I followed him down a flight of stairs through an empty hallway and into another room. At that door, we were stopped by another group of bouncers—three men all in black, their eyes

guarded by glasses so smoked I wondered how they could see us at all. "Where you goin'?" the lead bouncer asked. He was pale-skinned, short, but built like a fireplug. Billy smiled. "The Queen of Spades asked for us."

"Ahh," he said quietly, nodding. "You know the Queen?"

"Sure," Billy said. "We got a game to play with her."

"In that case," he said smiling, "Sergio, let 'em in."

Sergio, at the door, opened it, and we walked into another room, this one lit up like a gaming casino. There was a crap game going on and some cards; with men and girls and some very butch-looking women either playing or circling. "You play craps?" Billy whispered to me. I shook my head. I did not know one end of the dice from another. But who cared? All I wanted to do was watch.

The intensity of this room seemed even hotter than in the sex floor we had been on—and more violent and combustible. Billy knelt down, took some money from his pocket and laid it in front of him. The men around him smiled, and he was passed the dice. At that point, a tall, angular, very black man—truly Nubian, I thought, in his grandeur—with mascared eyes outlined in deep turquoise blue, approached us.

He was dressed in black with silver embroidery and edgings on his ruffled shirt and on his pants. A long, dark blue velvet cape fell behind him and several gold and silver chains hung from his neck. On them were crosses of every sort. Coptic, African, Swiss, French. Some bore crucifixion figures; others were simple and stark. There were additional icons, as well: a tiny gold foot, a clenched bronze fist, a cat in onyx with gleaming gold eyes, a jade ankh; and, finally, most fabulously, a large, all-seeing Eye of the Egyptian deity Horus, encrusted with lapis, rubies, and diamonds, whose design, I was sure, had inspired the Queen's own eye makeup.

"How you, your majesty?" Billy asked.

"Billy! Nice to have you back amongst us! I see you've returned for services!"

"I do—I mean, did—your majesty. Tommy, this is Roland, the famous Queen of Spades!"

"*La Pique Dame*," the Queen informed me. "Though sometimes known as *Le Rôl*. You may kiss my hand, *jeune garçon*. Let me admire you."

I bowed and kissed his long-fingered hand, and then rose. He looked at me, directly in the eyes; I felt even more naked than I had felt when I'd met Bertrand in the darkness out in the wilderness. I tried not to give myself away, but felt now like I was on a more distinctly foreign territory than any I had ever ventured onto.

Suddenly Roland took my hand and pulled me towards him. He wore a very heavy rose perfume; it seemed to gather me into its rich atmosphere. For a moment I felt isolated with him, in a strange enticing privacy of our own.

His supple hand stroked my face. I had a slight, silvery-blond stubble by then, and his fingers walked knowingly through it. "Pull off your shirt, dear," the Queen insisted. "Let us see what Billy is presenting to us."

I did as he commanded and the others in the room watched as the Dame looked me over. I suddenly felt chilly again; those same goose bumps ran across my smooth chest, my nipples wrinkled and hardened. I could feel his eyes staring right through me, and I knew those eyes were already licking my nipples. My stomach started to wobble a bit. "Ahhh," *Le Rôl* sighed, appreciatively. "Billy, put that hard-earned cash away. We'll use what you have brought us here as collateral. You lose, and young Tommy comes to play with me. How about that?"

I looked over at Billy and he shrugged his shoulders. "I dunno. It's up to Tommy," he said. I nodded my head and agreed to go along with this. Why not? I thought impulsively. I was, frankly, somewhat curious, despite my initial nerves. I still have a kind of shyness in me that I can't shake. Blame it on Tommy Smith, blame it on . . . Thomas Jebson; what can I say? In my profession as a masseur and escort, I'd encountered many different situations but none, perhaps, quite as . . . eccentric. Mostly, I dealt with horny, anxious businessmen; not with Nubian queens. I watched, fascinated, as Billy scooped the dice up and rolled twice, winning thick wads of money on each roll.

"So," the Queen of Spades said, parading around the players with me in tow, "you have brought good luck, Tommy. What is your last name?"

"Angelo," I told him.

"Exactly as I thought," he said and lifted the Horus eye to his lips and kissed it. Points of light from the diamonds glittered like little stars against the dark, plummy skin of his lips. "You have cost me a lot, young man—but that, of course, is the way of gaming. You know that also, I am sure?"

I nodded my head. No one had ever gambled for me, although my life—or past lives—had always been a gamble. An angel's moments here on earth are limited. We are neither omniscient, nor all-powerful. We can only hope that we do the best job here possible. "When," I asked politely, "will this be over?"

"That's your call, Tommy Angelo. Tommy of the Angels. See, we're getting tired of the house losing to Billy. Billy!" Billy looked up at the Queen. "Just one more toss for us, Billy. I'm gonna toss in ol' Horus's Eye for you. It's worth a fortune. You win this, and you won't have to work for the rest of your life. How do those bells sound?"

"'Fraid, no dice," Billy answered. "I know when t' roll 'em and when t' fold 'em!" He got up and put the money in his pocket. "Tommy, I think it's time for us to get outta here. You can sleep over at my house tonight. I won you, this time!" He smiled and made his usual funny hee-haw kind of laugh.

He went over to me and gave me a quick peck on the cheek. "You been real luck. I never do this good here at the Queen's game."

The Queen smiled, then the smile dropped from his narrow face. "Billy, you wanna come back and play, or what?"

"Sure, your Majesty, I wanna come back. Just not tonight."

"You're a bad sport, Billy, and we don't like that here. One more roll, that's all I'm asking from you. You win, you get all the dough and Horus's Eye here. You lose, and it's just Tommy's cute ass. No skin off your little dick, right?"

"I can't just—" Billy began to say. But before he could finish, the short fireplug of a pale-skinned guard from the door was next to him. With one hand, he pushed Billy down to his knees.

"Roland wants you t' roll," the guard ordered, behind his black shades.

"I can't," Billy cried. "I know what happens to the guys she plays with. She gets 'em addicted to crack. She—"

"Shut up!" the Queen ordered. "Like I said, I hate spoilsports—and rumor-mongers. Tommy can take care of himself; and I'd sure like to take care of him, too."

"In that case," I replied. "Why don't you let me roll?"

I knelt down on the dirty warehouse floor and the Queen unsnapped the Eye of Horus from his necklace and placed it in front of me. The light from its brilliants encircled me, casting a starry nimbus around my face. I felt protected suddenly, even kneeling there. I looked up and smiled, as every eye was upon me. I took the dice in my hand. "Whatever you do," Billy whispered into my ear. "Don't let her shoot anything int' you. She'll try t' kill you with their heroin. Don't let 'em."

I watched the little dice roll, with my heart strangely stiller than even I had anticipated. Why were men so foolish to believe that gambling is a higher thrill? I knew where the dice would land; exactly. The question was: which part of my own fate would I land in? I had entered the Substance of God before. There the heart merges with the rushing stillness of Infinity: and the heart knows . . . that the Great Plan will always "trump" anything produced by two black cubes.

Two single white eyes showed up.

Then the Queen rolled and, as I had expected, turned up with a seven. "So, this is safe tonight," Roland announced, and snapped Horus's glittering Eye back into place on its gold chain. "Come, my petite," he said. "It's gonna be you and me now, Tommy. And all the happiness money can buy."

I got up stoically and, to keep my part of the bargain, began to walk out with the Queen. But Billy stopped me and asked permission to speak with me for a moment. The Queen nodded, then parted from us.

"I'll wait for you," Billy promised. "I'll wait outside, if I have to wait till

tomorrow. I'll be there—and if you don't come out, I'll. . . . Well, I'll do somethin'. I can't go to th' cops. That's out of the question. But I'll do somethin'. I know some bad characters myself."

I thanked him and then walked out with *Le Rôl*. The Queen had a look of excitement, desire, and something else—which I thought I could detect as pity—on his face. His own eyes seemed certainly as old as old Horus's.

He took my hand and kissed it softly. The guards nodded to us, and we walked through the hallway and then down a short flight of stairs in the back. "This is the inner sanctum," Roland said. "For special guests like you, Tommy. Most people'll come to this club forever, and not get to come in here."

We were now in a small dark room, not much bigger than the bedroom back at my loft. It was locked and quiet, with a big double bed in the rear. I wondered suddenly what Bert was doing; and how had I got myself into this mess. "Can I offer you something to drink?" Roland asked, wearily taking off his cape.

I told him I'd like a glass of water, and he complied with a glass of fresh ice water from a small refrigerator by the bed. In its freezer, I noticed several small gleaming vials and bottles. I drank the glass completely down, and he said, pointing to one of the little vials, "This is the best amyl in the world. We get it from a Swiss maker. It's used abroad for rich folks with heart problems. Want some?"

Why not, I thought, and nodded, my curiosity still driving me. He withdrew one of the dark little bottles from the freezer and slowly unscrewed its black cap. It had an intricate, forceful smell; quickly overwhelming, like violets steeped in something that I could describe only as being like . . . yes, the scent of Death itself. Or a deathly transcendence. Or, even, descent. He passed the bottle under my nose and gently held one of my stiffening nostrils while I inhaled.

For a sniff or two, little happened. Then I noticed that the small dim uninteresting-looking room itself had started to rise, to take on a glowing pale rinse of lavender light . . . then of darker amethyst. Then, finally, a saturated, deepening red.

Like blood.

Like a September sunset penetrating the viny, mossy knees of a forest.

The fumes went all the way through me. My heartbeat accelerated. But I also felt as if I had become very much *more* aware—as I had been at times before—of the sheathing silence between each beat. The void when Time itself clicks; stops . . . and becomes still.

We both stripped, though I cannot remember how we got from clothed to totally naked. All I was aware of was his mouth on mine, and then on my

133

chest as he licked, kissed, and sucked my hardened, urgently wanting nipples. His lips went further down to my always-tanned, silken stomach, to that place where the muscles on it give way to pale fern growths of pubic hair. His mouth was a combination of hardness, softness, sweetness, and bitterness.

How, I wondered, could any one thing be so much, on any particular man?

As the amyl sped its dizzying way through me, I found myself becoming oddly obliterated: like I was no longer there. But where was I? I had not gone back, that was certain, into another angelic self. And yet, neither was I there with Roland, who was slowly stroking the now quivering smooth, full length of my shaft, and warming my testicles.

"This is where we begin," Roland announced. "Now that I have the seat of your soul in my hands, this is it."

Was it? I could not argue with him, even as he began to suck my male organ so expertly that I became with every movement of his mouth all cock, raging fire, blood surging . . . pounding . . . pounding . . . pounding.

I was blasting out, like a once-kinked, twisted garden hose, with the water turned on full blast. But, even as inside I became *unkinked*. . . I felt, strangely enough, stopped . . . I was so far out of it. So far cut off; from anything, except the physical.

I reached, impulsively, for his thighs, for his long cock. It was huge, evening-colored, its length and head covered with lovely, petal-soft, light-and-dark mottled skin. All silken movement; beckoning me with its one closed eye, which, suddenly, like something out of a very strange, coal-forested Eden, crept out, to reveal itself.

He pulled himself away from me. "You'll get that, Tommy, in a moment," he promised.

He then got out a thin leather belt and buckled it to my upper arm, as a tourniquet. I asked him, trying hard to come back into consciousness, what he was doing. "Making things more comfortable for you. I told you I'd give you all the heaven money can buy."

"Money can't buy heaven!" I heard myself shout from an hypnotic distance. "Stop this!"

"Listen, Tommy," he said, seductively. "I know who you are. What you are. And what you saw today."

"How?"

"I'm not only the Queen who controls the game, I'm a witch." He took a small hypodermic from the same refrigerator; it was filled and ready. He stuck it into my arm, then injected me with the chemical in it. "I know . . . know . . . what you saw . . . saw . . . at the Raleigh House," he said softly. I
kept hearing the words reverb; then everything just stopped.

Dead.

But I was not dead.

Everything around me seemed to stop for a . . . lifetime, while I only watched like a patient trapped on a surgical table, watching his soul being cut out from his body. He bent me over and the sweet, seductive snake that emerged from the obsidian-black, glittering hairs of his crotch (appearing, it seemed, like the ancient arm of a bronze Egyptian god—but now cold—its swelling, cobra head and part of its startling length wrapped in pink, translucent latex, with an emollient of slick lotion over it) entered my rear as the Queen began to fuck me. Slowly. Long. And more . . . more . . . wondrously . . . than I'd ever been fucked before.

"You like this?" Roland asked. "I know you can't answer, but you must think of me as the god Itself. For I know all your thoughts, my angel. I can gather up each thought and kiss it. I can hear them as if the skin that lies between the two of us has disappeared—"

I lay there, unanswering. But I felt so wildly . . . strangely . . . heavenly, just being there with him. Him, fucking me so long and nice and sweet, while holding me as I had not been held in . . . but what's Time now?

What? I wondered.

Then I realized, out there, where my mind was still connected to something other than just my body, that *somewhere* all men truly yearn for this: they do. To be embraced by the head of Evil itself, eating its own modest twin Goodness, or perhaps . . . by Evil pushing through itself, to finally find redemption as, and through, this secret, rarely recognizable twin . . . that shy *face* of Goodness that emerges from the *Substance*, we call God.

Now, I was sitting on him, and he was holding me and leaning me slightly over, to guzzle and lick down my cock in front of him, until I said to him: "Roland, Queen, if you are, as you say, 'God,' then, listen, I . . . will leave you with myself. I'll trust you. You can have my body."

And Roland smiled and said, confidently, "It's the truth, Tommy. Trust me. Tonight, we're *both* God."

"That is the *truth*," Bertrand said to me. I was now on the other side. I was Thomas Jebson. I felt as if my head had been beaten open; and as the pain stopped, the younger man had come out. "That is Odred." I smiled blankly, trying to take in the Baron's cold face, trying not to shiver.

Then, looking into Richard Smart's kind simple face, my lord relinquished any promise to bring back the Baron to Sir Garet alive. He could not so bitterly disappoint the forest men. "We must kill him! Only *mort* will do."

We rose from our stomachs on the top of the cliff. "Aye, he's about killing," Richard agreed, nodding seriously. "But how?"

In the gathering light, we threaded our way back through the dense trees, 135

towards the hidden camp. Bertrand was lost in thought, then he said: "I see only one way to go. We need to get into the Baron's keep. He is no fool. It is well armed. So I see a disguise. We must do that, and follow the way to his keep."

Richard Smart nodded. "Yes, sir, a disguise. Like mummers—you pretend to be other than what you are."

"Then," my young lord said, seriously. "One way or another, we kill him. Are you up to this, Thomas?"

I nodded. My life was on the line.

"And I mean t' go wi' you," Richard Smart insisted.

"*Pas*," Bertrand replied. "'Tis enough that the two of us die."

"And not me?" Richard asked. "Ye think I'm but a brigand and a dolt— and not *smart* enough t' die wi' ye?" He looked hurt.

"*Non mon cher*," Bertrand said and kissed Richard's mouth. "*Pas*. Not a word is true. You're no brigand. No knave or dolt, but a true friend and . . . yes, *gentil*. So," he smiled, "if you please, come with us."

We returned to the camp. There Bertrand left all of his fine chain mail armor and I left my new clothes. We donned ourselves in old togs, ripped, dirty, tattered, given us by the forest men. Now we looked similar to Richard Smart and his friends. We stripped Bertrand's horse of his rich saddle and banners, then Richard and I clopped off together very slowly on my old nag, Rose, while Sir Bertrand, in his new churlish guise, cantered on ahead confidently, on Fire.

Day had barely broken, but soon we were on the trail of Odred and his men. Shortly we'd be within the walls of Odred's keep: his great dreary, fortified castle. There our lives would be in his hands. Or, with God's help, his own life—and throat—would soon be in ours.

Chapter 12

Unlike Sir Garet's beauteous keep, Odred's fortress was situated on a slight rise in the midst of a low dry plain. The plain, when wet, was all sticky mud and flood washouts. Now, dry, it was fields of gullies, brambles, bleached animal bones, and tree stumps. Though I'd been born hardly more than a half-day's ride from here, never had I the courage to approach it. The stories I'd heard were too frightening.

Old Jeb had warned me that the only creatures who ever returned from Odred's keep were vultures.

"Bald vultures and black ravens," he declared; and for me as a lad with no horse to ride, it made not a dolt's sense to attempt a journey to Odred's walls. Besides, he sent his own villains, like Mars, enough times to inspire fear in us—so why bother? But there had been some curiosity inside me; some interest in looking this evil *seigneur* in the face. I admit that.

The countryside looked like a thousand killings had taken place there. Even Richard, a man of the forest, grimaced and held on to his stomach behind me. "Worse tha' I imagined," he whispered to me. "Ain't fit for no Christian!"

Sometimes he gave me funny affectionate little kisses on the sides of my neck, like the tickling of a rose bud. "Mind i' I tickle ye?" he asked. I told him no, but the truth was, it made my cock tingle and grow hard, and that kept some fear from me, I'd say.

Bertrand circled back toward us. "They defoliated this land in order to observe for miles and miles," he told us.

"*Defoliated?*" Richard asked.

"*Pardon.* Cut down the trees," Bertrand explained.

Richard nodded his head. "Ye gentlemen speak a finer tongue than I, just a lewd man. What comes out m' gut, I speak."

"I despair!" Bertrand suddenly said. "if they discover me on this horse, I fear kouth they I am *vraiment* a *gentil* knight."

"He means," I tried to explain to Richard, "if Odred's men see him—"

"Yeah, I ken it," Richard roared. "I ain't that dumb! I'll take yer good horse, Sir Bertrand. Keep yer mouth shut and make ol' Richard Smart be that. We'll say we find this animal off to hissself. I took 'im, and . . . we're wood cutters, lookin' for honest labor. How's that clink, m' friend?"

Sir Bertrand smiled sheepishly. He swallowed hard. His eyes lowered, then he looked directly at Richard. "*Comprend*," he admitted, then added: "Ye wants m' steed?" Richard nodded seriously. "Good, Suh Smart. T'is thine. Thou art a gay fellow, and I sha' keep my gullet snapped tight as a ter-rtle!"

I applauded. "How did you do that?" I asked.

Bertrand shrugged his shoulders. "In Provençe, we are all actors. *Oui!*"

Richard then dismounted from my old bony mare, and Bertrand jumped from his dark stallion, and they swapped places. Bertrand got on the back of poor old Rose, who was happy, surely, not to have big Richard Smart there. The knight clasped his fine dark hands around my waist. "That feels good," I told him.

"Naturally," he said. Then he pushed away my blond hair and kissed the lean back of my neck, and we proceeded to trot on. The gray towers of the keep, which seemed at first, in that flat distance, like a mere stump before us, became larger and larger. Soon we were at Odred's very gates. There we stopped, as we spied a wide, deep *fosse*, or ditch, dug between us and the walls.

Closer, we saw that the ditch was armed with a forest of razor-sharp spikes turned point-up at us: worse, I was sure, than any moat, filled with unbelievable sea monsters.

(Of course, I had never actually seen the sea. But I was convinced that such monsters existed, from the stories of the shaven priests about the Book of Jonah, which seemed, even coming from such dolts, fairly believable.)

"Who comes there?!" a voice rang out from the tall battlements. "Tell or die!"

"Three woodcutters, yer lordship," Richard answered. "Simple men doin' honest work. Hungry. Lost f' days. May I ask what worthy's castle we hie ourselves to?"

"The castle of the gentle Baron Odred de Campe," the voice snarled. "I am Turlow, captain of his guard. Your callings?"

"I *highte* by the name of Mule," Richard Smart replied. "And this here be young Tim, and behind him 'is friend, Simple Peter *highte* he. Dumber than a rooster wi' his nuts off. But we let him ride wi' us, t' use his back. He got a strong one for haulin' wood, water, any sort o' stuff like that. Could ye use three more backs and six willin' hands, here in Jesus's own good land?"

A drawbridge was lowered with the creaking and grinding of a set of

rusty chains. Then a fierce portcullis gate, all spikes and bone-crushing iron balls, was raised, slightly, to let us in. We had to crouch down on our horses to pass under it. Once we were in the courtyard, scores of men, more than I had ever seen, fully armed, their swords and crossbows ready, came out to meet us.

Turlow, a tall stork of a man, all bony neck and broomstick limbs even in his leather-and-chain armor, with a simple shirt over that, approached. His graying hair was shorn down almost to his scalp. "Ye are strangers!" he spat out. "Get down from yer horses!"

We did as we were told. "That looks like a fine mount for a woodcutter," Turlow observed of Fire. "Where'd you get him?"

"Riderless, he wuz," Richard explained, "but a li'le time back. Me fears his rider wuz murdered, the horse let to starve. So I just a-took 'im for m'self, yer lordship."

"Now he's mine," Turlow said. "If that's all right with you, sir. If not—"

"Yes, sir," Richard said, bowing his head. "We ken it. Three men alone—one too simple e'en t' fetch a pail o' water for hisself and keep from dyin' o' thirst. Simple Peter's like that, right?"

I nodded my head, and looked warily at Bertrand, who took on the dead-pan, empty gaze of an idiot. He was truly gifted at this.

"Your name?" Turlow demanded of Sir Bertrand, who did not answer him at first, until Turlow pointed his sword at him. Then Bertrand swallowed hard and, without a glint of his native accent, spoke: "Yer lordship, 'tis true. I be bu' Simple Peter. Stepped on when he but a wee babe. Knocked the Lord's sense right out o' m' head!"

Turlow smiled and nodded. "And where you be from, Simple Peter?"

Bertrand looked away from him, swallowed again, then said: "Nowhere much—as the crow flies, suh. But it be far!" He then made a broad gesture to indicate over hill, under vale, and all about.

(I thought I would faint. . . .)

But Turlow only put his sword away, and then smiled. "So cutters, welcome. All of ye go to the stable. There you'll be fed. On the morrow we have wood to chop and haul, water to draw from our wells, some cleaning. Our privy holes could use a muckin' out. The gentle Baron de Campe himself will come and inspect your work." Turlow nodded. "If good, you'll be paid. If not, it's the Forget-It-All—the *carcern*—for you. We have a jail six feet deep. The sun never shines in it. How clinks that in yer ears?"

"Super!" Simple Peter suddenly cried, with a grin all idiot to anyone who did not know him as I did.

I smiled then, while Richard gazed around at all the armed men and hoped that we would not be searched; for we three kept daggers next to our skins, in our boots and belts, and we were determined to use them before we

left there.

We were led to the stable, more a dirty sty than a place where you'd keep good horses. I noticed that they had few good mounts, mostly old slope-backed mares—like Rose, not a sign of respectability if you ask me. Of course no one did; and neither did they ask me about the grub they threw us. That, too, was only pig slops if I ever saw it—and I did see it. In fact, Jeb himself would not have fed good pigs such a mess.

In the dim, foul-smelling rear of the stable—Odred and his men verily kouth not a thing about mucking out—we found a bit of old straw and lay down to try for a sleep. We could not unclothe, since we were armed and wanted to stay that way. Besides, who (except some real Simple Peter) would want a wad of such straw and muck poking next to his skin? It became dark—very dark—very quick. Baron Odred's keep, it seemed, had hardly a candle or lamp in it.

I managed to shut my eyes for a while, though without sleep; then, a bit later in the night, Bertrand turned to us and said quietly, "*Vraiment*, I have a plan." I pushed closer to see him. My eyes had to become used to the darkness.

"What kind o' plan?" Richard asked.

"Aye?" I asked. "Should we surprise them in their sleep, and like lightning cut their throats?"

"*Pas*," said Bertrand humbly. "That we cannot do. We are outnumbered. What I want is more . . . subtle."

"*Sottle*?" Richard asked. "Is that like 'something'?"

"*Oui*," Bertrand agreed, nodding his head in the dark. "*Something*. I think you, Tom, being a . . . *galant* young man, *charmant*," he pushed his fingers sweetly through my long hair, then went on, "will go up to the Baron's quarters *privé*. I sense it must be in one of these turrets."

I looked at Bertrand: my admiration for him sank. Was this rash young knight out of his mind; had he *become* Simple Peter? I had no idea what turret even to start in, much rather . . . Bertrand continued: "*Oui*, now this is what you do. *Insinuate* yourself to him. Tell him you have news of Sir Garet—news of interest to Odred. Then . . ." Bertrand hesitated; his hand ran through his long dark locks, then stroked his chin, which was becoming darkly bearded. He resumed: "Say you must speak with him—here in this stable. And bring that *monstre* Turlow with you."

"Sir?" I asked. "What do you mean, *insinuate*?"

But before the knight could answer, Richard Smart shook his head. "Sir, I like it not. Perhaps it'd be better as the boy says: just run out by surprise—cut their throats!"

"*Pas!*" Bertrand answered. "That is *folie*. No, we'll use this *garçon* to

bring the two back here . . . alone. I have some understanding here. Then we will slice them both, *oui*—if I'm not Simple Peter!"

"I don't ken about no slicing," Richard said; so Bertrand made the gesture of a knife across his throat to drill the point through. But, Richard still had another—"And how," he asked the knight, "will we git our hides out o' here? They got to make *down* that drawbridge, and then *up* that gate."

Even in the dark stable, I could see Bertrand's sly smile. "*Pardon, Seigneur Richard. Vraiment*, you are a man of thought."

"So, sir?" Richard asked.

"Well, suh, *if* I c'n b' Simple Peter in the light, I can also be Baron Odred . . . in the dark. After Thomas brings them back and we kill them, we'll take their garments. I'll direct his villains to let us out. I foresee no problems here."

Richard nodded. "I am glad ya don't, sir."

The bearish forester smiled faintly, then put his big fingers together. Even in the dark, I could see that he was clenching his eyes closed.

Any confidence I had before was shattered. Obviously, to anyone except my liege Bertrand, Richard Smart understood this plan, but had paltry faith in it. I could detect the air moving softly as Richard mouthed a silent prayer. Surely, he was seeing his own grave dug a short way down the road; if he were lucky enough to get a grave.

Bertrand, all smile and ready energy, sprang up from the straw. "Now, *cher* Tom?" he asked. "Are you up, a *la hauteur*, for doing this?"

I must have looked, to anyone with eyes . . . shaken. The plan, though it possessed simplicity, carried very little water. It leaked; it dribbled. I was, in truth, scared out of my own piss. What did Bertrand want . . . nothing other than my own death? I knew that this plan was to please Sir Garet, but it was madness to think that the three of us could stand up to, perhaps, a hundred armed men.

Even a knife in their sleep might have worked better. (But, alas, who was I, a serf, to say?)

And, there was one other fact: I, only a few short weeks away from a pig farm, had never *talked* to any baron, much less Odred. The thought of conversing with him filled me with jitters. Making *him* interested in me was something I could not even imagine. How would I do it?

But I got up and remembering my promise to follow Sir Bertrand through wind, snow, barefoot (etc.), drew myself up completely to my full height and agreed, "If that is your wish, my liege, I will risk"—I had to push the rest of the words out—"death for you."

Bertrand pulled me enthusiastically into his embrace, then called Richard Smart into his arms as well. "I swear," the young knight whispered, "by all that is Holy and our Lord Jesus Christ Our Savior, that I shall never forsake

the two of you. I shall do everything to save you both from slaughter. And if that means that my own noble blood will be shed—"

"Aye, sir," Richard interrupted. "We get th' bones, th' skin, and the mush o' what ye sayin'!"

I smiled, then Sir Bertrand kissed both of us; and I walked from the stable, looking back at them every few steps in the dark, hoping that I would not fall into a rut hole.

I was on my own. I carefully crossed the deserted stone courtyard between the stable and the main hall of Odred's castle. There was little moon to be seen—only a few silverish rays at times, between moody shifts of clouds; hardly any stars to speak of. A portent of rain, certainly, but good for us. If we were to need a hasty exit, darkness and a squall of rain might help. All was quiet around me. It was so silent that I could have heard a rat gnawing his own tail thirty paces away.

Bertrand had told me to go to Odred's turret, but where was this? Perhaps *he* had known, but I was in the dark here, truthfully . . . very much so. I crept as close to the mossy, stony walls as I could. Then, all at once, a powerful but bone-sharp arm grabbed me from behind, knocking the breath right out of me.

It was Turlow.

"Young Tim! The dear childe I seek. Come hither. Baron Odred seeks bright company of you!"

"*Mine?*" I asked, barely able to squeeze the word out. "Why *my* company, sir?"

"By Mary, why not, childe? I prithee, why are ye aventuring out on this night? When a storm thickens like ale out here? You knaves were told to stay in the stable . . . or else. I had thoughts to find you—" Turlow paused, broke into a sly smile, raked his bony fingers through my blond hair, then winked, allowing me quickly to piece together what his game might be: it seemed the captain was probably . . . close to fall-down *drunk*. "And," Turlow continued, burping beerish spit into my face, "drag ye back to m' bedchamber and fick y' silly, sweet lad!"

I nodded my head and smiled innocently. "By Mary, that bothers me not, sir. Verily I kouth how good a man can be, when the good hops sweeten his affections."

"Young knave, yer language is gettin' as pretty as ye. All blond locks and dulcet. Let us be off to Baron Odred's gathering. He is awaitin' for ye in the little hall, next to his own chamber in the far turret."

Now it became apparent that this were indeed so: Turlow had been sloshing at the hops, but at least he was pointing me into the direction I wanted— what luck—and I wasn't even dead yet!

So I followed, with Turlow hardly able to stand any more upright than a dancing bear. We went around several passages, up stairs, and then into a narrow turret, all of heavy black rock. As we passed up into the turret, I began to wonder how I could make do on Sir Bertrand's rash plan.

How could I, only a lad, convince Odred and Turlow—alone, just the two of them without a whole army—to follow me into that stable? What could I offer them? What excuse?

But a different situation, than even Bertrand could have counted on, seemed to be waiting as we climbed up the stairs. For the steps, all of blackest stone, were incredibly littered with men. Many drunk, and dribbling from their mouths. Some fast asleep, as if deep in some witch's dream. Others gazing about stupidly into the stormy air, whereby I must have appeared with Turlow as some kind of strange, blond, youthful spirit, or ghost.

Finally, after stepping over outstretched bodies and dodging a few knaves stumbling about themselves, we stopped. There, an oaken door was hung so low that one would have to stoop to enter. Turlow knocked. A deep voice within called: "Enter, Turlow. Have you the young scout?"

Scout. Oh, no! The very word made me shudder. Did Odred suspect a plan? Was the Baron waiting for me, with the gift of my own death—a gift that, it seemed, Bertrand himself had planned? Turlow entered, and I followed, as I said, bending down to do so. Inside it was wickedly warm, for there were but a few narrow bowman windows to produce air and from these only the meagerest light came in. It settled in fluttering patches as the moody clouds of that approaching storm herded through the night sky.

Most dark it was, and at first I could make out almost nothing. Then I saw that there were eight powerful, muscular men in the Baron's close chamber. Eight all over each other, like anxious eels trapped under the milky ice of a wintry pond. Weaving in and out; some close, it seemed, to fall-down crazy. And all in a state that was as shocking to me as my young churlish mind could take in.

For they were all, these warriors of the haughty Baron Odred, absolutely . . . stark naked. Hanging about, as bare as the day they were born.

True.

They were without one chain-ring of armor, or a stitch of any material. My mouth dropped. Then suddenly an arm was placed around my neck and a knee thrust behind me, forcing me to kneel in front of a pair of muscular calves, whose owner I yet could not identify.

"He's all yours, Baron!" Turlow said, laughing. "He is but a serf, who sleeps in your stable. Do with him as you will. Then we'll see what kind of work we can put him to ourselves. . . ."

"The *cher petite* scout," a deep voice said, as a heavy hand ran through my hair. "Pleasing, he is, Turlow. Fairer than the run of his type about here."

"Yer lordship," Turlow said, "I believe he *is* one of your own serfs, born here on your lands. Mars once described a local lad who resembled this."

"And he did not bring him back for us? He merited his death for that. Right, Turlow?"

"He was a good man for what he was," Turlow said, his voice taking on a sudden catch in it. I looked up. As the dim light from without shifted, I saw that the captain of the Baron's guard had carefully placed in his mouth what seemed to be a touch of gritty white powder. He swallowed, then pushed a pinch of this powder into his left nostril. He inhaled slowly, then smiled.

"Aw, the merry substance of our Lord," I heard the Baron say. "What think you of it, Turlow?"

"Most dear," Turlow answered dreamily. "This flower inspires the simple tongue to poetry." I wondered what he meant, but could not say a word. Then Turlow said to me, "Now, Childe Tim, open your mouth and let sweet words follow . . . without words!"

"Well said," the Baron commended. "Turlow, you have skills beyond meanness. As for young Tim, we are pleased with him truly, and wish his attentions upon our gentle bodies! How does that make him feel, we ask?"

Stupefied, was my only answer, but I said nothing as Turlow pushed my face into the Baron's sweaty crotch, where his thick cock, I am afraid to say, was already at full attention.

Turlow pulled back the Baron's foreskin and fed his tarse to me, forcing me to suck that thing with all my might. I could not stop, and knew that if I did, then Turlow might indeed strangle me or thrust me through with his dagger, since he was the only one in the room fully clothed. And, even secretly armed as I was, I knew that I would be no match for these big men. My greatest fear, though, was that at some moment they might ask me to disrobe as well. Then instantly one dagger would come rolling from my boot, as another came falling from my belt.

So I had to comply, as disgusting as this act of rape was, while Odred pressed me to him with his big hands in my hair. As I continued sucking the Baron's thick but not very long prong, I knew that soon enough he would either come to his completion or perhaps force me to unclothe; and so give away both myself and my two worthy companions.

With this in mind, I hoped that I could simply suck him, until his hot juice blasted down my throat. And, at that point, if he were as "impaired," both from drink and that strange white powder, as Turlow, then he might fall asleep, simple and plain. With this result—and luck on our side—perhaps I could return to the stable, and there tell Bertrand and Richard that, without delay, we might take on these fools.

This was asking for much luck, but without any alternative I continued to suck him, using my mouth as skillfully as I could, feeling his cock thicken

144

and harden even more, no small feat for one so advanced into his own vices. Then just as the Baron's knobby cock started to vibrate thunderously and announce its immediate release, he pulled it from my mouth.

"Well done, childe," he said. "My lust has been quenched for a time, but will repair later. Here, Turlow, take some sport yourself. Let this boy's sweet mouth be the maiden's cunt for you!"

Turlow then dropped down his linen breech piece and let his tarse fly loose from his groin. It was as thin as he was, but with a fleshy head on it that reminded me of some old wrinkled fruit attached to a loose squash vine. Fortunately, by Mary's grace, the vine remained but that. Loose and jiggly. It would not stiffen at all. I now kneeled down in front of it, and as much as I tried to get Turlow's slim attachment to react to my attentions, nothing happened.

"Ish-no use," Turlow slurred. "Theesh flowers from the East got t' me. Makin' me but a soft dreamer!"

"Thou art stupid as a tipsy cat in a brewery!" Odred howled. "A fat fool inside a skinny body. I should fick you bowlegged, knave!"

"Sh-ir!" Turlow drooled. "You may fruck this young man! I'll shrimp 'im myself—and git 'im to you naked as a flucked chicken—and shrice as tender!"

Turlow then attempted to grab me, but easily I rolled from his reach, even though I was still down on the floor, having not risen up from my position there, where I had been forced to do service to the Baron.

At this point, the other naked men started to gather about me. One pulled me to my feet and I then saw them, like a blur circling me, for in the darkness that danced through the turret, I could make out not the features of a single person. Only shadows. This was also true for the Baron, for although I had given my closest attentions to his stumpish cock, I had not been able really to look at his face at close range.

My memory of him was still seeing him at a distance—from that ledge, with those icy steel-blue eyes; and I imagined those very eyes peering down at me in that dark turret room, like two pieces of pale blue stained glass, hoar-frosted on a wintry church window. They were that cold. I wondered what kind of devil—or monster—could have such eyes. I would wonder that even if I lived for a thousand years . . . long enough to know that angels could have such eyes, too.

Angels who lived amongst men, for their own lust.

But at that moment such ideas were not in my head. I only knew then that, soon enough, I would have to be sport for all there. *If* I survived that long. And once they discovered I was armed under boot and belt, it would be all over for me. My hope that the Baron might simply be brought to his completion, then sleep, was broken soundly. Even with my two daggers, I was no

match for these men, huge warriors who resembled the oiled wrestlers I had seen in the tents at country fairs. Brawny. All muscle; all strength. They could unman most men, or even a bear.

Numerous hands started to stroke my face, rifle my long hair, and grope my ass and the strings of my codpiece. I tried, as best I could, to follow them, my eyes darting about. Then, as some of the darkness in the room shifted with another glance from the cloud-soaked moon outside, and a soft, silvery light floated in; one man, bearded, very dark, his hair not so short, and he certainly not unhandsome, leaned his face into mine and kissed me fully on the mouth. He laughed, then his tongue went into my ear.

I did not return his kiss, and he said, "You are not pleasing me, young Tim. Are you shy around us?"

"Neatsfoot!" the Baron roared. "You are always game for a young one, aren't you?"

"'Tis a weakness," Neatsfoot said. "I would like to unclothe him myself—and diddle with him and stick my ready boner right up him!"

"Then you shall," Odred ordered. "For you are handsome enough to please anyone, myself included!"

Neatsfoot smiled, and then said, "In that case, Baron, allow me to have this young knave alone in my chamber. After sport with him, I swear to return him to you. In good use and in good shape! And, by that time, after you have tasted enough of Our Lady's dreaming flowers, thou shalt be truly ready for him!"

"Never!" Odred said. "I am the lord here. I will exercise our right to have game with him—and when I wish, take him into my chamber!"

"You are our *gentil* lord," Neatsfoot replied humbly. "But, truly, sir, we have but a little churl here. Coarse, bastardly, filthy from the stable. Most surely pocked. He will do for sport in the dark, but he is not up to the rank of your chamber, he is—"

"By your troth, Neatsfoot?" The Baron looked concerned; in the gray light, I could see a scowl wrinkle his forehead. "Not up to my standards, you say?"

Neatsfoot nodded his dark head.

"I kouth your meaning," the Baron said. He nodded, then waved me off with one hand. A moment later, after grabbing his shoes, shirt, and hose and hastily putting them back on, Neatsfoot bowed to the Baron and took me by the hand.

Without another word, we began to leave the Baron's turret room. The nine men left there, including the Baron and Turlow, were now so far along in their cups that our absence would make little difference. They were all close to passing out, groping in drunken, rowdy abandon. Several spewed obscene ditties back and forth ("I'll plug yer Sister, that bloody whore!" "I'll

fick your butthole like cow pussy!" "Try m' dick for yer first course, then good, hot cream t' follow!") while falling all over the floor. One, I saw, barely standing, was peeing on himself; another, down flat on his back, was shooting his golden, beer-laden piss straight up into the dark air, where yet another muscular warrior rocked about and leaned over to catch it on his tongue.

I took one last look at the Baron. One of his icy blue eyes winked at me, then his head sunk. As if on cue, the clouds outside again lowered the light, and Neatsfoot shut the door. We quietly rounded the bends of the circular staircase laden with groggy, half-awake bowmen, some passed out over others; one man asleep in his own vomit, face down.

Chapter 13

"have done you a service," Neatsfoot whispered to me, as we hurried away from the turret's stairs, then across the dark, empty courtyard under the threat of a storm to his own chambers. This was not far, it seemed, from the stable. "I could not let the Baron completely take his way with you. You are good. I can tell. My heart went out to you."

"If your heart has gone out," I asked, "will you not allow me to return to the stable and my friends?"

"Those louts and simpletons? No, my young friend, that I cannot do. I did not take you away from the Baron simply to throw you back with them. I want to show my love to you in my chamber, for . . . I believe we have not met by accident. It is by some design; even if its form is not plain to us."

In my simplicity, I knew not what he meant, but followed him. I hoped that my longer absence would not be so noticed by Sir Bertrand and Richard that they might venture out without regard, and then meet, the two of them in this wicked place, some terrible death. Neatsfoot's chamber was small, but cozy. With a flint, he lit a spirit lamp. I looked around. The walls were adorned with curious holy miniatures. Distant saints, I guessed. I had never seen such things—some had words in a script that seemed strange even to me, an illiterate serf.

Books, richly bound in leather, lay on his bed table. I dove over to them and picked one up. Never before had I held a real book in my hands. They trembled as I leafed through the beautiful vellum pages, glittering with gilding. "You can read!" I said.

"Of course; in many languages. And you?"

"No, sir," I confessed. "I am ignorant. A churl, as you said." I put my head down.

He softly stroked my hair. "Do not be ashamed. You have fine stuff in you, I know."

"How?" I asked.

"I lied to the Baron—you are warm, dear, handsome, and unpocked. You

come from good parents, I see." I nodded silently and only looked into his dark face. "And you are truthful, I kouth it. Not like I." He smiled, distantly. "I am not what I seem, Tim. To some I present myself as a Norman; but in truth, my people come from the East."

"The place of Jesus?" I asked.

"No." He smiled. "Greece. The place of all great knowledge. My real name is Gregory; it means 'watchful' in Greek. That, I must be here. But I have another name, my second name. It is Nikolas. It comes from Nike, the goddess of Victory. It is my secret name, the name a slave can not tell. Do you understand that?"

I nodded my head, trying to understand. There were things we could not say to the Norman conquerors, too. About the forest men; our own yearnings . . . .

"But here," he continued, "they call me Neatsfoot, because I am dark, and, yes, guileful. Smooth. Like oil. That, also, I must be here." He smiled again, this time more genuinely. "Now, permit me to write your name. I will write it both in Greek and in Latin."

"If you would!" I said, feeling my soul go out at this very thought, even against all my wishes. My own name in script! What I had longed for. My eyes followed him as he took a clean sheet of vellum from a small quire, dunked a goose quill into sooty black ink, and then looked at me.

"By what are you appelled?" he asked. "Your Christian name? In full and in truth, you must tell me, if I am going to write it."

"It is . . ." I hesitated; my eyes glanced down. "Tim."

"'Tis not," he said, smiling. "In the East, we quickly see the lie on any face; I see one now on yours. Tim is not your name. Tell me your 'secret' name."

He is guileful, I thought. Was this only a clever trap? Perhaps he was a spy for the Baron. He told me he was oily, smooth. I looked straight at him, then collapsed directly to my knees. I started to roll about on the floor, as if I were under some kind of evil spell.

"My friend! Did you take of that dried flower? Is this a fit? What, my young friend?" Neatsfoot's face showed concern.

I managed to roll away from him, thrusting my hands towards my feet, just long enough to pull a dagger straight out from my boot. I jumped up and lunged at his throat, the point directly at him. It waited, only a thumb away from his handsome bronze skin.

He shook his dark-browed head softly. His nose seemed slightly large, but still noble. "Fool," he whispered. "Why would I hurt you? I wanted to save you from Baron Odred, whom I despise. I was brought here as a captive servant on King William's fleet. I had to serve the Normans. I escaped; but
only to serve that monster Odred."

"You are no friend of mine!" I spat at him.

"I saw and loved you. What are you doing?"

"If I tell you my name, you will know who I am—and who my parents are. You will be able to deceive me, and harm them."

"No," he said, his voice at a whisper. "I am saddened that you are so afraid—but so many are. Listen, his men are only a few paces from my door. One move out of here, and—if you don't believe me—let me show you."

He edged away from my blade. Then he turned around, showing his back to me, so I could stab him easily and he knew it. I realized, then, it was true; or else he'd never take such a risk, even with only an armed boy like myself. I followed him to his door, and he began to pull it towards himself, only to whip around at me and grab my wrist that held the dagger.

He was stronger and bigger than I, and twisted my wrist until the blade clanged to the floor. Then he pulled me into his arms and kissed me until my breath melted into his. "I told you I was guileful," he whispered. "But now it is only to be caught in your web. What is your name? Your real name? I will write it, I swear, on my heart." His eyes were filled with tears.

"Thomas Jebson," I said. "But, please, do not ask it for your heart, for I have given its use to another."

"Then allow me but to share it," he whispered, with his lips on my neck, my face, then my open mouth. He pulled my shirt over my head and saw the other dagger in my belt. He unhitched the girdle and my secret dagger fell with a clang to the floor. Its sound pierced me to the core inside. How else . . . could I feel? At sixteen, no one had ever told me so quickly that he loved me—truly, on my own level; and made me feel that way.

No one.

I knew that Richard and Sir Bertrand waited, but . . . could not the two wait a moment longer, for my own death? Sir Garet and Sir Bertrand had already planned it, yet . . . at this moment I was still alive. And somehow, I sensed that Neatsfoot was like me inside: concealing everything; poor, but rich with God. Without another word, we both stripped and fell onto his bed.

We rolled ourselves together in one mass of yearning flesh. Muscles, mouths, cocks, bellies, arse, legs, balls, and thighs. I took his throbbing tarse into my mouth and he took mine into his. For the moment I felt completely transformed, and forgot everything except the wondrous, unexpected beauty of my lover Neatsfoot—Gregory Nikolas—in his bed.

"Man, you look like you just come back from so far away!" the Queen said to me, as he kissed me, his cock still firm and full, all the way up my ass. The bridge had been lowered, as much as I wanted to stay in Gregory's bed. But Time . . . Time is vengeful, too.

"I did," I confessed.

"I know."

"How much do you know?"

"I know you have some power," he said. "And it ain't just heroin that's gonna do it."

"Is that what you shot into me?" I asked.

"It's the best shit money can buy. I told you I'd take you to heaven."

"That is not heaven, " I said. "I know Heaven, and no drug can take you there."

He smiled and pulled his cock out from me. He rolled the condom off his snake, then kissed me. "Then will you take me? I want you to take me to heaven, with your mouth leading the way on my cock."

I knew then what I would do. It seemed the only thing, as I went down on him, taking as much of his big dark dick into my mouth as I could, playing it like a beautiful flute as he groaned and cried real tears from such intense pleasure. "You are so good," he said. "So very, very good."

I licked, slathered, and kissed his cock, swallowing the fat, jewel-like head, and soon we were rolled into mutual sucking, a wild, restless sixty-nine position as the innate energy between us circulated fully, endlessly, with both of us traveling towards a mutual climax, taking every vista of pleasure along the way. Vistas of sense, vistas of Time . . . as I knew then that I had left the Queen, and at that moment Roland was only sucking himself, as he sucked my inert, spiritless body.

And I—I had raced back over that bridge of Time to be with my secret lover Gregory Nikolas, passionately kissing and sucking him in his small chamber in Odred's evil keep—lost, suddenly, at being sixteen and having love, what I wanted so much, flung at me this way; flung . . . and picked up by Thomas Jebson.

Until, in the midst of this, I looked away from Gregory's handsomeness to see Roland, the Queen of Spades—a witch—watching, reduced at that moment to infancy, to being a small child wandering back, through genera-tions . . . into his own deepest sexuality.

That place where I had brought Niko before.

So (the question came), were Roland and I (I, Tommy Angelo, who had sped back to that chamber where Thomas Jebson and Gregory Nikolas made love) back in *Eden*? Were we now, as Thomas and Nikolas sucked one another . . . only two innocents, child-like, both reduced to that guiltless state of Sex itself? Had we returned finally to that place where the body and Spirit separated, only to be rejoined in an unleashed, hot spiritualism for which most men yearn, which at the same time, terrifies them?

(It seemed . . . we had.)

On my own angelic wings (of the Spirit) I had taken *Le Rôl* back and untangled his long roots in the human story, so that now the two of us were

touching one another as if we were only two cherubs. But every tiny touch between us was intensely pleasingly erotic and . . . real. Every touch between us, both in Neatsfoot's chamber and there, back in Roland's own.

This went on and on, I have no idea how long. Time at these moments twists around itself into more complex figures than our "logic" can conceive. But finally our innocence was impossible to continue, and was smashed by the approach of. . . .

Orgasm.

It exploded through me, through Gregory, and through Roland at the same time. I watched my secret lover Nikolas's striking Eastern features disappear. That idyllic time with Neatsfoot, with his strong hairy body, his dark eyes and handsomely bearded face, ended. I saw Roland run off, naked, becoming bigger and bigger, no longer a cherubic enfant; and I had to grab the bridge in front of me, and did so—the bridge that was the Queen's lithe black body, his cock now soft and resting.

Suddenly he jerked away from me and jumped up. I heard knocking at the door of the Queen's chamber, at first from a great, reverbing distance and then right into my ear. Eden was over. We had come back. Roland returned to the bed and started shaking me. I looked up at him, woozily.

"Baby! Honey, you better get up! They're raiding the place!" Roland snapped. "Cops all over here! This is bad shit!"

He threw me my clothes, then dashed into a simple black polyester suit—with a white shirt, black tie, and a small crucifix around his neck—changing his appearance completely so that he looked like a simple Christian minister. I dressed as fast as I could. "There's a secret passageway from my room," he informed me. "It goes back into another building. I had it put in for just these circumstances."

"Why are they raiding us?" I asked.

"Dunno. But I think it's got something to do with the death."

"Death?"

"Yeah, I heard about a minute ago while you were pretty much out of it, that a nice Greek boy O.D'd here. Some chick Paula sold him some bad shit, so he checked out. Shame."

"I'm not going anywhere," I told him and hurled myself out the door as fast as I could.

I ran from the Queen's secret chamber, down a corridor, and into a large room that I had not seen before. Like the Queen had told me, there were cops all over the place and a group of men in suits. They all parted like waves from me as I passed through them. My eyes circled around, then I looked down on the floor.

There was a body covered with a sheet. "You know this man?" a white

detective in a rumpled business suit with reddish hair and a sun-freckled face asked me. He flashed me his I.D.—it said "Morris"—and carried a small notebook.

I knelt down, and two police officers uncovered the face. It was Niko. I started crying. "'Fraid he's been dead for about twenty minutes," Det. Morris said quietly. "We got an anonymous tip that something was happening here. The Mayor's been watching this place for a while. It's time it was cleaned up." He shook his head sympathetically. "Too bad. Young man; drugs; bad company. It's sad. Y' know, you look a little too wholesome for a cesspool like this. What're you doing here?"

I did not say a word, then Morris knelt down with me. He put his arm on my shoulder. "I can see you're hit hard by this," he said.

"I'm—his next of kin here," I lied. "He's Niko Stamos, my cousin. He's got a son named Paul."

"We're going t' have to take him to the morgue. Autopsy. You can get him later."

Light, a first, shy, silvery hint of morning itself, started to float softly in from the high windows that pierced a ring around the room. Obviously the room had been a big factory floor, like the one Niko worked in. The two of us got up. I looked down at Niko. The light had placed a halo around his tranquil Greek face; but who else, I wondered, could see this? Or see how long I had known that face, and where almost a thousand years ago it had really come from?

I asked the cops if they'd leave me alone with him for just a minute. "Impossible," Morris answered. "I can't leave you alone with the evidence at a crime scene. You're off your rocker!"

I looked down at the sheeted body, then heard another voice say, "He's gotta do it!"

I looked up. It was Roland, escorted by two other cops, coming over to us. "I'm the Reverend Roland Du Prè," the Queen said, handing Det. Morris his card. "I heard there's been something awful here amongst my children! This child is grief stricken. He wants a time alone, I can vouch for him. I can—"

"What-th'-hell?" Morris asked, turning the card over in his hand. "How'd you get in here, Reverend? No one knows about this yet, except the—anyway—"

"If you don't give this grievin' angel his moment alone," the Queen warned, "the whole community will hear about it! Family blood is a lot thicker than water out here in Brooklyn. I don't know about you white folks, but we people of color know about blood!"

Morris exhaled, nodded his red head, then resigned himself. He and the other cops walked about eight feet away from me. "You got your chance

now," Roland whispered. "Better move yourself a little bit of heaven, baby. But whatever, when the Big Man comes for me, don't say I never gave you nothin' in this life."

Although the men in suits were not that far from me, I managed to block them from my view. I knelt there next to Niko's still face. I looked up. The Queen continued to stare down at me, slightly unbelieving; then he shrugged his shoulders at me and turned away to give me the privacy that I needed. At this, I lay myself down, directly on Niko's sheeted body, my face on his uncovered head.

I lay there with my arms about him in the echoing, vast stillness of this new morning as its eternal light wafted over both of us. I heard nothing, yet everything. A thousand years. A thousand . . . What could I give Nikolas except what I already had: my own simple spirit . . . the angel . . . alone.

Then, as I asked for nothing, as I was impossibly humble, the sheer, awesome simple power of that spirit, which was not really mine, but which came from a Substance so much higher, moved into my friend's inert form. I knew it. A life was coming back. *Yes*. The morning, the timeless morning, fell around us. A moment later the cops hurried over to me.

I felt Niko's breath gathering back in his chest.

"Impossible!" Morris shouted. "The damn guy's alive!"

They were now all looking at me and shaking their heads. "Never seen anything like this in my whole life," I heard over and over again, as the Rev. Roland Du Prè smiled. "Only fools and devils don't believe in God's capacity for miracles," he announced. Then he confidently walked over to the suited men and began talking with them in a low voice that I could not hear.

"Just the same, we'd better take him," Det. Morris said. "I'll get the ambulance for him. The EMS guys are here anyway. Hey, guys!" he called to the ambulance men. "You ever seen something like this?"

Niko Stamos looked up at me. I was now standing. "Tommy. Where you been?"

"Just here," I said. "All along." I bent down towards him. "You had a bad time, Niko. They're going to take you to the hospital for a rest."

He protested. He needed to get back to his house. His parents. His son. I felt suddenly terrible for him, but what else could I do? It was true that I had known he was in trouble—yes, the moment I saw him, outside the factory— and I had come to save him. The connection with him . . . that great connection. But could I save myself? Morris came over and asked me for my address. I gave him the address of the loft, and took his card. I turned and saw Billy O'Geech. He'd been waiting for me, and managed to get back into the club.

"You okay?" he asked. I told him I was. "There's someone outside who's

155

waiting for you. He says he knows you're here."

I smiled. I was sure he did. After a few words, like "Don't leave town," the cops let me go. I was about ready to leave the big room, when one of the men in suits casually walked over to me with his hand on the Queen of Spade's arm. He was tall, impressive; immaculately dressed in a simple gray, light wool suit.

"Tommy, honey," Roland said, "let me introduce a friend of—"

"That was some trick you did," the tall man said, smiling. "The Queen and I are not exactly the best of friends, but we respect each other. Right, Queen?"

"I respect you like I respect heroin and a rattlesnake," Roland said smiling. "You leave me alone and I'll—"

"Sure, Roland. I'll 'leave you alone.' Get over it—I'm going to buy this place out. That's why the cops were all over here this morning. I brought them in. If that man had died, you could kiss it . . . anyway, I almost got to nail you people—and when I do, I'll be able to control Brooklyn, too."

I looked into his carefully groomed face. He had dark hair, a tan, and features that looked like they had been molded from plastic: too perfect, too sculpted. He was obviously older than he looked.

"Who are you?" I asked.

"You don't know?" Roland asked. "Child, this is—"

"No," the gray suit said. "Let me introduce myself. Tommy, I'm . . . gee, you really don't know?" He smiled, then added: "I'm Alan Hubris."

"I gotta get outta here," Roland said, smiling into my face. The Queen gave me a quick peck on the check, then started towards the door, a good way off since the room was so big. He stopped after a few steps and turned. "Hubris, you can try to threaten all you want, that's what white men like you are good for. But leave that child alone. Okay? He's an angel, if you ask me."

I did not say a word, but only watched the Rev. Du Prè disappear out of my life, out the door, to be swallowed up by this strange morning in Brooklyn.

"Tommy Angelo," the tall man said. I turned to him. "You do look like an angel, at least in the part of Heaven I want to go to. But on a more practical basis, let's just say, I know who you are, and what you've done. And—one more thing—I'll get you, Tommy. I swear. One way or another. You screwed up what could have been a very good operation for me, and I don't like that."

He smiled for a second. Then the smile evaporated from his lips. His face, under the tan, was as cold as ice. And so were his eyes. Like steel. Like death. They had a corruption in them that looked like a swarm of maggots frozen in ice. I hated him, because I knew I had seen that face before. And as

156

much as I wanted to spit into it, there was no end to that face, smooth, icy, distinct as it was. I had seen that face. Surely.

On the Baron Odred.

"What a character!" Billy said, laughing. We were now out of the club. Real morning had come to Brooklyn—and there on the street, as I suspected, waited Bert Knight. He smiled at me. "You're getting yourself into the worst messes, honey," he said, and gave me a quick kiss on my lips. "You think we can find any kind of cab around here to get us back home?"

Chapter 14

We left Billy O'Geech outside the club. I promised I'd call him, which I knew I would. Then Bert and I found a Pakistani cab driver looking for a morning fare into the city, and we settled down into the back seat. Bert pulled me over to him. "You had me worried," he said in a low voice, close to my ear. "No one called or came by about the killing at the Raleigh House, but I was sure that something awful had happened to you."

"How did you know that?" I asked. "And how did you know where I was? I didn't even try to contact you."

"An old friend from our past told me," Bert said, smirking.

"Who?"

"Neatsfoot. The dark, beautiful, guileful Neatsfoot."

"Are you still jealous—that happened almost a thousand years ago?"

"I am. But I know Neatsfoot basically has your interests in his heart. And in other places. He still loves you, what can I say? And he knew you were in trouble. While I was sleeping, or trying to sleep, at least, he came back and told me."

"I was in trouble," I said. "Getting buttfucked by every kink in Time. Drugs. The Queen of Spades—what a character he is. And—are you ready?—the Baron Odred."

"That monster's back again? We seem to run into him about every lifetime or so."

"He's now Alan Hubris," I informed him. "I met him at MaloMalo, that club. He's the spitting image—total complete incarnation—of the Baron."

"That's the problem," Bert observed, looking out the window at the shiny metallic Manhattan skyline as we went over the bridge onto FDR Drive. "We never got to kill him good. Did we?"

"We've got to do it this time," I promised. "One way or another."

"You don't mean . . . ?"

"Yes," I said. "We'll remove his aura. We'll take it away from him and

159

then we'll—" But it was silly to talk about it. Until we were ready to do it. And I was tired. I needed to rest—I needed the rest of angels. For at least a whole day.

I was so happy to be back in my bed with Bert next to me. He turned towards me and put his lips on my forehead. "Wow," he said. "You feel as cold as stone. Are you that cold?"

I told him no. Just exhausted. It had been a long night. I wondered how Niko was—they must have taken him to a hospital in Brooklyn, but which one? I decided that when I got up, I'd call his parents. They'd have to know. I was just glad he was alive. "How'd you revive him?" Bert asked me.

"I didn't really do it," I said humbly. "It was the morning light. The approaching Spirit . . . remember, you showed me first how to do that?"

He nodded. "I couldn't do it for you back then. I would have had to leave you."

"I know. But I could do it for Niko; we won't be linked forever."

"I love you, Tommy," Bert said. "Always."

I kissed him. "Being an angel has its plus side," I said, trying to smile. "Even one as dumb as I am knows that!"

"You're not dumb, Tommy," Bert reminded me. "But you do take chances, you horny little bastard." He sighed. "How'd you ever get yourself mixed up with that crowd in Brooklyn, especially when we have so much to do here in Manhattan? This Alan Hubris mess is getting slimier and thicker. Cops are routinely raiding clubs, closing down bars, rounding up innocent guys in cruising areas—all because Hubris and his rich friends in City Hall want to control gay life in New York."

"It's the same old story," I said. "Isn't it?"

"I guess so," Bert agreed. "When what people call 'vice' and what passes as 'respectability' start to jump into bed with one another, you should expect all sorts of interesting positions, right?"

"Sounds good to me," I said, smiling, while Bert got down and took my dick in his mouth and began to lick the shaft and head of it, like a lion casually licking his paws. I liked the way he did that, just sweet, soft, and affectionate. There's so little affection in the world now: I knew it. The more we try to bring sex out of the closet, the more the other things—warmth, affection, love—seem to take a running leap back in. Why? I have no idea. I was hard now, and we were sixty-nining, because I wanted to take Bert, too. I had his thick, warm balls in my mouth and could feel them rotating slowly, while I stroked his shaft and got him to that old "jolly" point where his cock vibrated, ready to cream. Suddenly, without any warning, he gently pushed my face away from his crotch and I released him as he raised himself slightly up

on his elbows. "I saw it!" he said.

"What? What did you see?"

"*You*. The time the Baron escaped from us. And that Neatsfoot guy—handsome bastard he was, I admit it—he almost got us killed then."

"We owed our lives once to him," I said. "At least, that life."

Bert pulled me to him and started kissing me, the way only he could. His tongue slid across my face, caressed my lips, and then filled my mouth. I felt his words just blow into me—his words, as he said, "Tell me, Thomas. What really happened?"

"I can not, Sir," I answered. "Thou wilt verily be angry and wrathful with me."

"*Pas*, Thomas Jebson, my vassal churl. My childe to love. Tell me what happened. You kouth it all. Tell me!"

With those words, my loving knight dove again down to my cock and sucked me . . . until the thrill of his mouth (slightly-chapped, surrounded by dark stubble) on me brought us both back to the world . . . of Thomas Jebson, my own father, truly, at least fifty times removed. But connected on that light-filled path back, found over the Bridge, known simply as . . . eternity.

A loud iron bell clanged again and again through the darkness. "What is that?" I asked Gregory Nikolas, nestled still in the warm embrace of his arms. I looked out into his bedchamber, at the single spirit lamp's glow, while the bell chimed on.

He pulled his dark head from me and sprang up, naked and powerful, his handsome tarse still thick and stiffened from the excitement of our lovemaking. "Damn!" he shouted. "Odred is mad! Kouth you this: he lives on the shameless thrill of poppies. That white powder, he gets it from the East—it is nothing among his liege men. They bring it back to him, whilst pretending they are battling there on the soldiers' quest for Christ."

The bells clanged more. "What are the bells?" I asked.

"He is mad, drunk—bewitched! It is his old habit: when the white potion goes to his head, he demands a black midnight mass. He and Turlow and most of his crew—evil, bewitched! Now all must attend. He does that betimes: his vices stir him to a vile, stygian frenzy."

"And what means that?" I asked.

"Dark. Evil. Things I cannot speak of, my love. I hate him, my friend. You must know that. I want to cut his heart out, I swear!"

"Then swear unto me!" I said and got up from his pallet and dove into his naked reach, filling myself with the warmth of his shoulders, chest and thighs. "We also want to kill him."

"You three? How could you three—only woodcutters, and one an idiot, a Simple Peter, kill this powerful baron?"

"Come," I directed him. "And you shall see."

"Nay, we cannot go out," Neatsfoot warned. "They kouth me. As I warned you, the Baron's men tread only a few paces from my chamber. If the Baron should see you again with me, he will grab you from my reach and throw you into his dungeon. There he keeps poor boys for his own depraved pleasures; they are only a mouth and an arse to him, that is all. I wish I had my hands on his neck. I would—"

My eyes closed for a moment. "A disguise?" I asked. "Do we have any disguise?"

Nikolas smiled. "Yes. . . ." He went into his chest, a large one next to his pallet, and pulled out two hooded robes, exactly like those monks wear. "I have these. I confess I use them from time to time, when I want to go about secretly. The Baron's bowmen, though not the wisest, still respect the brothers of the Lord; especially since so many of the brothers, at heart, are like the Baron's men!"

"Yes," I said, and nodded my head. A new plan was coming into my head, and Neatsfoot—Gregory Nikolas, now my own lover, it is true; I was taken with him, to my own young torment—nodded, also. It was as if both of us understood what fate had presented us with. He kissed me, nakedly, without shame, one last time.

We got into the robes, and pulling the hoods over our faces, withdrew carefully from his chamber. Two of the Baron's men saw us, but quickly turned their faces from us. Then we followed the short path to the stable. There we met Richard Smart, who had been worrying, and my lord Sir Bertrand. They were both surprised to see our heads emerge from the robes of monks. I introduced Neatsfoot to them. The knight smiled at Gregory—he was curious, and also impatient to know what had taken me so long.

I could tell him nothing of my time alone with the handsome Greek. Bertrand wanted to possess me, and yet could not offer me the love that my deepest feelings wanted. I was sixteen and the vassal of my liege knight; but the lover of another.

"What means these bells?" Bertrand demanded to know. I told him we would explain the bells; but first he was to know that only through good Fortune had I met Neatsfoot, a learned Greek, who had waxed to be our friend and who would help us with Baron Odred.

"But why would you want to help us?" Bertrand asked, looking directly into Neatsfoot's unhooded face.

"For God's goodness," Neatsfoot answered. Bertrand's blue eyes narrowed. He gave him a hard, unbelieving look, which even I could see. Then Neatsfoot added: "And, I confess, out of my affection for Thomas here. A good and simple lad, I kouth."

"Ahhh," Bertrand whispered. "Your affection. *Très bon.* I kouth that, too. And what plan have thee for this?"

We could still hear the midnight chimes and learned that, soon, almost every warrior in the Baron's keep, except for a small number standing guard, would be in the chapel. Not to be there would incur the Baron's rage.

Neatsfoot explained it thus: "We shall all wear the brothers' robes, I kouth a true lard of them. Then we shall walk into the chapel beside the main hall of the keep, and, at a certain point in the Baron's service"—then he told us the rest of the plan.

Neatsfoot withdrew from us to retrieve the robes, while Bertrand, Richard Smart, and I looked at each other.

"Be he trustworthy?" Richard Smart asked. "He don't seem like a forest type to me. If ye get my point, he's a bit rare and foreign." He looked at Sir Bertrand, and caught himself. "'Beg yer pardon, sir, but his manners are a bit . . .'"

"*Pas*, Richard. He is only taken," Bertrand explained, "with love—and some lust—for *charmant* young Thomas here. It is evident. I believe him. But at some point we may have to—"

"You will do him no harm!" I commanded Sir Bertrand, something I had never done before. My words rang out in the stable's darkness. His eyes met mine, unbelieving. He looked stung, as if I had slapped him. I could not believe his reaction. I hung my head in shame. "Forgive me, sir," I said. "But he hath been good to me, I swear. And hath saved me from a hard fate—the Baron and his men, all drunk. They take into themselves this stuff made from. . . ." I hesitated. How could I say it? I knew nothing of this powder.

"Poppies?" Bertrand asked. "Is that it? Soft? Golden-white?" I nodded. "*Mon Dieu*, that is what I heard. So all the gossip about Odred is true; that is why I sent you looking for him, Thomas. I knew he likes boys and can be manipulated—"

"What does that mean, sir?" Richard asked.

"It means he can be *handled*. He likes to fuck boys."

"So?" Richard asked. "Ye think we can get him just 'cause o' that?"

"*Pas*," Bertrand said. "Not because; but he is *doubly* cursed. First with the vice of greed, and secondly, with this powder from the East made from poppies. It quickly makes the brain go soft."

And other parts, too, I thought, but did not say so. "Neatsfoot understands this," I said. "That is why I think his plan will work."

Neatsfoot returned then with the two robes. From the high windows gouged into the walls of the stable, we could see the yellow lights of torches bobbing outside, on their way to the chapel. Bertrand and Richard pulled the dark robes over them, and then the four of us, with no torches to guide us, trod on in the heavy, menacing air to the chapel. We walked up a steep flight of stone stairs lined with clumsy, groggy-looking warriors, who bowed to us as simple brothers of Jesus on our way to a midnight service. 163

The chapel was large and imposing, lit only by a few thick beeswax candles, which shed silence and mystery on the place. It was, in truth, so dim that I could barely see a single face and could distinguish only the powerful bodies of Odred's men who stood now in this benchless space. And many of these men, I realized, were also almost naked, wearing little about them—a strange appearance for chapel—but Baron Odred de Campe's keep was indeed a strange place; that was certain.

Still, even in such faint light, I could see how handsomely appointed this chamber was. Up on the altar table were many fine chalices of silver, and there were, as well, windows of leaded colored glass and many amazing tapestries covering the stone walls. It appeared that the Baron, when he was not a villain, had a . . . darkly religious bent to him. Yes, *darkly* seemed to be the right word.

All the swordsmen and bowmen bowed their heads, as we walked in. The Baron himself, at the front of the chamber, up on the raised altar, called out, "Aye! Brothers! Welcome. Come! I have called us together at this midnight service to dedicate ourselves. Dedicate, friends! Dedicate and direct ourselves to that proper place, just below Heaven. Is that not so, Master Turlow?"

"I deem ye right, Lord Baron," Turlow agreed and bowed his thin body, clad only in hose and a leather vest, towards the Baron. Turlow then rose and his eyes surveyed the chamber. I saw that his beady eyes glittered even in the darkness, with a surfeit of ale, the dust of poppies (I gathered), and his own lust, which, I am sure, had not yet been quenched.

I wondered, then, what dark service would take place within these walls. First because the Baron himself wore only a pair of hose and was naked from his waist up. On his bare, hairless chest he wore only a thick golden chain. From this hung the small golden skull of a bull—or some other horned creature, perhaps even a man.

Then I noticed not a single Cross or motif of the Lord's Presence was to be seen in this place. But only strange images that reminded me of a presence I could not name, except to speak of it as Evil. The pictures I saw woven into the tapestries were those of torture and meanness, of men cut with daggers or burned at the stake or lashed at the rack, while hideous horned creatures with the tails and wings of dragons flapped over them. Nowhere were to be seen images of kindness, goodness, or warmth in these pictures, and I wondered who could have made these things—and where did they come from?

"This appears like a bad dream," I whispered in fear to my young lord Bertrand.

"*Oui*, Thomas," he whispered back. "It is a dream to me, also. But fear not. I am always with you." He reached for my hand and squeezed it.

"Come forward, Brothers!" Odred ordered us. "We shall celebrate a special mass tonight. A midnight Mass of dedication and sweet surrender, to the Lord of the Night, to the Demon of Battle, the Angel of Power. And to Him, at Midnight Watch, we shall release our eternal souls."

The assembled warriors pushed us forward. With hooded heads bowed, nervously we approached the raised altar of the chapel, until the four of us stood beside the swaying figure of Odred himself, his bare chest sweating in the close air.

Odred squinted and smiled at us; but I could tell that in his condition (and in such faint light), he could not ascertain a single hooded face. He smiled, nodded, and then pulled a large silver cup, set with crystals and shining with points of colored gems, from the table. "Master Turlow!" Odred bellowed, "'Tis time to begin!"

At that, from the altar table, Turlow lifted a headpiece and placed it on his bony skull. It was a crown, one could say, of polished pewter, trimmed on either side with the full pointed horns of a great stag. Then, brandishing a sword into the air above his head, he shouted, "To the Demon! To the Demon Lord himself!"

Now, all the liege men present bowed, lowering themselves verily to the floorboards. Turlow commanded them to stay, and he walked amongst them, waving his sharp sword over their lowered heads, inquiring, "Who amongst us does not believe in the Demon? Lord of the Night? Who?"

"None, Sir," they all answered. Then Turlow walked back up to the altar platform, and the men rose again. "Now," Turlow asked, with Odred looking on, "Which of you will give us golden drink to fill this chalice that we might toast the Demon tonight and ask his blessing at our Midnight Watch service?"

The chapel reverberated with the reply of "I! I! I!" as the men rose up in lusty voice and spirit, but Turlow only shook his head, merrily. Then Odred looked at us monks beside him.

"No, no," the Baron said, shaking his head. "We shall allow one of the Brothers here to fill the chalice this night. Thus we may drink merrily to the Demon from it!"

I looked at Bertrand and he at me, and in truth we kouth nothing of what Odred spake, until he pointed at Richard Smart, and then motioned with a nod of his head for Richard to pull himself up to the table and stand there on it. And with another gesture, he told Richard to pull down his hood, and show his face.

To this, Richard answered: "Nay, Sir. Our Holy Order don't let us show our guises but to the Lord Himself! To do otherwise is true Vanity, a bad sin. But, as a good Brother, I will obey thy bidding—and thy command, Baron, will be mine."

Then, without another word, Richard hoisted himself onto the table and up to his feet, and looked around the room. I could only imagine what the sight from that height must have been: the half-clad men, the Baron stripped to the waist, Turlow; then ourselves, still deep in the robes of monks. And, as I might have expected, Richard did seem a little unsteady on his feet. I saw that, too.

But he did well and stood up there, dignified as he could be, until the Baron commanded, "Now, Brother with the mysterious face, I tell you: lift up thy robe and take out thy naked tarse. Then fill this chalice to the brim with thy golden piss nectar. So we may toast the Demon with it, and slake the Lord of the Night with this salty brew, direct from thy member!"

"Sir?" Richard Smart protested, more than a little nervous, "I—I swear, I have no piss in me!"

"Aww," the Baron commiserated, shaking his head, "'Tis sad." Then he added, as a command: "Well, Brother! If thou be dry, then lift thy robe all the way up, up above thy face! That way, all may see thy naked empty vessel— and with it, thy sweet face."

"Yes, sir!" Richard said. But instead, he slowly lifted his robe and undid his breechcloth under it. Then he let hang down his fat cock, squatting so that it was right at the Baron's face. And there, he let forth a stream of golden urine directly into the Baron's eyes, burning them immediately.

The men let out a loud "Boo!" and rushed towards the table. I feared they would grab Richard and kill him right off, until I realized that Odred was screaming as much with drunken surprised glee as with pain.

"Nay, nay!" the Baron shouted. "Leave him be! By the Demon himself! Ye are a rash brother of the Night, I kouth it!" And he opened his mouth to be filled directly from Richard Smart's cock, gurgling the golden liquid down, sucking the fat head of Richard's cock with his lips and then lapping more of the liquid down, while the men watched intently, dumbfounded, and even (possibly), quite amazed.

Finally, Richard was empty—his bladder depleted—-with his piss all over the Baron's face, in his mouth, and dribbling down the Baron's heaving, drunken chest. "'Tis gone," Richard confessed somewhat guiltily. "I be as dry as a bone. Still, yer lordship, I know a better brew from another stream—outside the gates of yer own keep. 'Tis like mead itself, from the cocks of young night demons and the tarses of witchmen. I'll take ye there— ye and yer headman Turlow and all yer liege men here, if thou agree."

Neatsfoot—Gregory Nikolas—looked at me and nodded his head under his hood.

"And where is this magical place?" the Baron asked.

"No bother, but a *fea* little gallop away," Neatsfoot answered in a voice I had not heard before. Truly deep and with more of a true, flat Saxon accent

than I had thus heard from him. Surely this would fool the Baron, who was familiar only with Neatsfoot's more refined voice; he appeared taken by this, and very interested. "We wants to lead you there, yer Lordship. That we do!"

"And what is there, Brother?" the Baron asked curiously.

"Yea," Sir Bertrand explained, trying to sound as much like Neatsfoot as he could. "'Tis the Spring of the Night. We brothers kouth it goode, as we go and play about there ourselves."

"You do?" The Baron asked. "And what does this famous Spring do?"

Immediately Bertrand answered: "It keeps us ever *jeu*-uh, young, Sir."

"Young?" The Baron's eyes opened wide. "How wondrous!"

"'Tis true!" Neatsfoot put in. "There yer virgins make themselves whole again, and the old leap about like *fea* lambs. For ye see, we are each a thousand years old! 'Tis why we wilt not show our features even to ye goodly men. For it would fear ye mighty to see us, as we are all alive still after a thousand years; and the face of a thousand years is passing strange and a good sight *not* to see, no matter!"

"'Tis true," the Baron nodded, beaming. "A sight *not* to see, surely—I kouth it. But a miracle, nonetheless, true!"

"Aye," Neatsfoot agreed. "'Tis! So quick, take what men ye trust, and we shalt lead you there. And then ye shalt beget long youth, goode looks, and the sweet bodies and souls of nimble knaves!"

"Aye!" the Baron shouted. "For me a nimble knave would be most good! We shalt give thee four fine horses, including the handsome steed Turlow took from that wood cutter and his two simple friends today."

"Sir!" Turlow complained. "That mount is mine!"

"Nay, Turlow. He belongs to youth. Give it to the Brothers here who spake to us of such miracles." Then the Baron looked sweetly at Turlow, as if we were all too simple to know that shortly after this trip out, when the Baron was sure the dead bodies of the four monks would lie below that spring, Turlow would retrieve his horse again.

We were now all horsed, and Bertrand was back on his own fine steed, Fire. We were riding out slightly ahead of the Baron and his men, who followed us, as we managed to gather a bit more distance between us and them. The sky above was densely overcast with a heavenly face thick with churning black clouds. The moon seemed lost in exile now, and distant thunder reached our ears with the approaching storm on its way. Bertrand rode up to me, and suddenly put his robed hand to my face. I kissed his hand.

"Young Thomas, are you good?" my lord asked.

"Yes, sir," I answered, but he looked anxiously at me.

"*Mon cher,*" he said sweetly, "It is not *façile* for me to say this. My faith is yours: I pledge myself to protect you. I am rash. I kouth it. I took us into

this, and now I shall bring us out. I kouth my . . . 'strong head' torments you. Forgive my desire for us to die together; I pray you, leave any killing to me." I nodded my head sadly in assent, as the Baron's men gathered speed towards us. I looked behind and there they were, so we had to redouble our pace to stay ahead.

The hills, the woods—everything—began to spin about me.

Was it merely from my own rank fears, or the thick air, or the heavy wool robe whose damp hood still clung to my face? I am not sure; but a real funk sweat dripped down my neck onto my chest, and then lower, bathing my belly and even down to my aching testicles with my own salty water. I felt, in Jesus's truth I must say, feverish, but I could not stop. And we all galloped on, the four of us, leading the Baron's men deeper into those tangled woodlands that Richard Smart knew so well.

We doubled around and around, going through overgrown fens and grasslands, leaping through thickets, and finally settling into a vast cathedral of trees so dense that we had managed to separate the Baron and Turlow from most of their liege men. Odred was left with only four bowmen, when Bertrand, Neatsfoot, and I got off our horses and walked up to them.

"Terrible dark here," The Baron complained.

Neatsfoot told him that we could only find the Spring of the Night in the dark, and we invited them to get off their horses, and follow us. They did this, and we led them into a deep grove, where indeed a beautiful, clear spring flowed, capturing in its rippling depths the smile of a full moon that appeared briefly out of its exile to brush its way through the grasping clouds.

"Aye, a good sign," the Baron said. "Full moon. Deep darkness. Thunder. Do ye think the Demon will show himself to us?"

"Yes, goode Sir," Gregory answered in his flattest, deep Saxon voice. "He wilt do. Truly."

With that, Neatsfoot bade the Baron to disrobe completely, to reveal his true nakedness to wash himself in the spring, and for Turlow and his men to do likewise. They did as we asked them, and, totally naked, they wandered into its waters, while the moon disappeared and a thunderous darkness fell on us. In this manner, we, too, quickly disrobed, but were not totally naked. For we kept our daggers with us, as we waded into the shifting, whipping blackness after the Baron and Turlow and his men, with the full intent to murder them all.

Chapter 15

"**D**amn!" Bert shouted. "The Bridge appeared. We were in the water, when it appeared and pushed us back."

"Yes, I know," I said. "I guess Thomas couldn't take the violence up ahead." I knew I was sweating, just thinking about it.

"I wanted to suck your cock some more, just to keep us there. Or was I still sucking it? We can't be here and there at the same time, so—"

"We are here and we *aren't* here," I said. "Anyway, for the most part as angels, we can only watch it. Right . . . isn't that the Rule?"

"'Fraid so," Bert said, yawning, then quoted the Rule, a primary rule of the angels: "'What you save, you cannot keep. What you make, you must release to wonder.'" I nodded. It was true: once we made something, it was *over*. It was only wonder for us . . . to wander. "But"—Bert shook his head in disappointment—"Things were getting interesting. There we were, wading in after Odred and Turlow!"

"I'm hungry!" I said. I jumped out of bed and went into the kitchen and made us some coffee and some breakfast cereal. I knew why I had come back; I knew why the Bridge had suddenly appeared—and it was not simply the cold water of the Spring that did it, that pushed me forward into the new third Millennium—it was something other.

I wolfed down the cereal, and popped two English muffins in the toaster, and went through those as well. I took a shower, while Bert went back to his work on *InQuire*. He had to get the "damn thing out soon," he told me—the advertisers were waiting; but he wanted a juicy story and it seemed that the police storming into MaloMalo would be it. When I got out of the shower, I went into Bert's office area and he grilled me about everything. Of course I knew only as much about it as he did—except that I knew Alan Hubris was at the center of it. It was true, Hubris was trying to control all the gay venues in New York, and he was using his own political connections to do it.

"It's a typical story," Bert said. "Some queen gets his fingers in the power honey pot of power, and grabs as much of it as he can for himself.

Then he can set himself up above the rest of us poor queers."

"Even the angelic ones?" I asked.

"Yep, even us. I just wish there was a way we could find out what's going on—"

"What good would that do?" I asked.

"We could get Hubris—or—"

"The Baron Odred?" I asked.

"No one would believe he's that, if we . . ."

"Killed him?" I asked.

"Shhh," Bert said, then added: "But of course we'll kill him. Or try to. The Baron's always scared, I know that. But sometimes fear can keep you alive, as much as courage can kill you."

I nodded my head. Well said, I thought. Bert had a way with words, and with me. I realized then I was tired. Much more exhausted than I had thought, and also pretty feverish. I realized I was feverish as soon as I returned from the cold Spring of the Night. I put my hand to my head, and Bert followed it with his. "Wow, kid. I think you should go back to bed. I'll do some more work on the magazine, and get you up if anything interesting happens."

I told him to get me up anyway. Besides, after a certain amount of time in bed, I liked company there. He winked at me, and I went back to our sleeping area and was hardly in bed more than a few minutes when I was overcome with sleep. It hit me like the old ton of bricks. Suddenly I felt . . . blacked out, without any dreams or anything. Just vague memories of a thousand years, wandering around. Wars. Sex. Bert. Bertrand. All of it dancing around me, until I became . . . cold.

I could feel it penetrating through me, even with the down covers on. I was wet, cold and wet—and this was not pee or perspiration. I started shrinking into myself, trying to hold on to my knees, my thighs, my stomach, my cock, every last bit of me for warmth; then I realized I was no longer alone. The *Bridge*, icy, silvery, flooded with pale light, appeared, drawing me into that stormy darkness.

I did not want to go, I did not want to see what was both up ahead, and almost a thousand years behind me. But I had no choice. It was the only way I could stop, even for a moment, the spiraling madness of ice and heat within me.

I left the loft . . . and the three of us were entering the spring.

The water felt so cold on my young feverish body, as my bare feet sank into the silty grasses and soft mud beneath. Gregory and Bertrand were next to me, while we heard the Baron call out, "Where are they, Brothers! Where are these witchmen and the Demon you told us about?"

"Out, Sir!" Neatsfoot called forth in the dark. "Ye must go out a long good way and let the water come all the way up to yer necks! And ye wilst feel it!"

"Thou art mad!" the Baron called. "This is madness! Where are the witchmen, the Demon, the youth thou promised?"

"Here!" a voice called from the other side of the spring. "Here we are, yer lordship. We all be here!"

And truly they were, for Richard Smart had been able to ride around and get his own foresters to wade in now, into the spring, and they had surrounded the Baron, Turlow, and the four men, and were about to kill them, as we gathered in closer. But at that very moment, the sky opened up into a torrent, pouring down sheets and sheets of rain, so that I became separated from both my young lord Bertrand and my lover Gregory Nikolas, as well as Richard Smart. The morning, like a faint red bloom, came up in the East; and in the water around me and the water below me, I saw, too, eddying currents of fresh, red blood spilling about.

Blood! . . . *Blood*! . . . So much blood! I cried out to myself, shivering through every bone and muscle in me. I knew I was raging with fever; and there were now currents of swirling blood all around me, up to my knees. With that tormenting rain up above me, too. I bent over in pain but made myself get back up. I had to keep both hands on my head, just to keep from heaving my dry guts out into the water.

I became too frightened; too awash in fear itself. But I knew I had to go in deeper, even if from where I stood there were no telling what waited on either side.

Richard's forest men might be on one bank and all the Baron's men on the other. But I had to go in, and I did—wading, trying to hold myself up— for I could not swim at all. Then suddenly, I felt something partially submerged pass by me, brushing my naked stomach with some unknown waving articles. *Fingers*. Hands . . . cold, pushed on by the spring's raging current swollen by the storm. Then a whole body—naked, face down—pushed itself up out of the water.

It brushed my own belly as I shivered in the spring, with gushes of rainwater almost blinding me, streaming down my face. This form, a young man's, was so beautiful that it stopped me quite still for a moment. Who could it be? One of the Baron's brigands? Or was it, perhaps, one of the young good foresters, now dead in the water, face down?

His back, dark and muscular, brushed up against me. His dead cold hands, spun around by the current, were quickly at my thighs. Then, in this game of the dead, they frisked me, playfully, even between my bare legs as I stood without moving, panting in the water. I felt frozen, but knew I had to hurry on to catch up with Bertrand and Neatsfoot, I could not tarry a bit;

but I had to see whose face was hidden below the churning surface.

I grabbed the back of the brawny neck, and, going with the current, pulled this dead weight up towards me, as my blond hair for a moment slipped below the surface. I steadied myself back up. The rain was now sheeting between me and those blind eyes, eerily open, like a ghost's. I had to brush the water from my own face, as I realized then whose empty gaze was staring at me.

It was my own Nikolas. Neatsfoot.

Dead. Stabbed. Strangled, too, for even I could see his neck broken. I pulled him to me and began both to cry and throw up dryly in the rising water. I had not imagined anything like this . . . that I had fallen so much for him; it was impossible. I belonged to Sir Bertrand. My lord, my knight. And now I felt as if a piece of me had been ripped out and Neatsfoot, my own secret lover, handsome—dead—had taken it.

I could not let Gregory Nikolas's body go; even as I attempted with all my strength to wade in farther, I held one of his dead hands in my own. Then up ahead, I saw Bertrand, alive, with his arms and shoulders down in the water. I had to make a decision: I had to let go of Gregory, and I pushed on towards Bertrand, though my eyes could not stay away from Neatsfoot's corpse as it drifted away from me and into the dense rain and a rapid swirl of current to go . . . who knew where?

Bertrand looked up and smiled at me, his black locks dripping rain, the water almost up to his neck as he crouched in it.

"*Mon Dieu!*" he shouted. "I have him! The Baron! He's down here, Thomas. We're free of him—he and his men will do us no more harm!"

"Good! Good!" I answered. Then the joy ran out of my voice. "They killed Neatsfoot."

"Neatsfoot? How—he was here but a moment ago? Sweet *Jesù*! Deemst you this was but a plot to ambush us? Odred is truly a devil! He was on to us, perhaps?"

I could not answer, but only looked back, at the gloomy place where I had last seen Neatsfoot's body.

"The Baron's men are devils!" Bertrand shouted. "I tell you—devils! They kouth what they were doing, but we have him! *Bon*! At least I killed him myself. I must be humble in glory; he is but a corpse now. I'll hang his body up and let it rot in the trees! That is fitting for a devil!"

At that moment, Richard Smart and four of the other forest men waded up to us. "Go!" Richard shouted. "They are at the other side! They wilt circle us in the water!"

"*They*?" Bertrand asked. "Who? I have the Baron down here! I killed him, I got him by the neck! Who?"

Richard put his rough hands to Bertrand's face and then tried to hug him

in the water, putting his big, naked bearish body close to Bertrand's trim dark one. "Please," Richard said. "Lift him. Lift up our prize. See the face!"

Bertrand nodded, and then, with big swells of rain still lashing down on us, he lifted the body up from the cold water. I held my breath as the spring's sullen dark surface slid away from it. I wanted so much to see the Baron's face, but there, in Bertrand's hands, was the broken neck of none other than his captain, Turlow.

"*How*?" Bertrand asked. "How could this be? I deemed I had the Baron in my very hands from the back. He's an eel, he tried to slip away. But I got him under the water. I would cut him open like trout, but first I had to get to my dagger and thought—why not just strangle him and be done with it?"

"So ye had yer hands on him all th' while?" Richard asked.

"*Oui*! I did!" Bertrand screamed, springing up out of the turbulence with anger and frustration, his strong naked chest slick with the tangled, reedy black hairs of Provence. "This is *catastrophe*," he cried, his voice sinking as he slid, like a water god, back down into the rushing white current. This was my young lord's natural element; I knew it.

"It was dark. Hellish," Richard explained. "Evil. The Baron reigns in the dark. He is evil, we ken it. He must have thrown Turlow into your reach and then escaped. His men are all around us now from the meadow side—they slew some of our forest men; thus runs all this blood! We must go to the deep forest end, yonder. If we try to go back, they'll have us."

"What'll we do with Turlow and Neatsfoot?" I asked.

"Nothing," Richard answered as we hurried to clear the water, me hanging on as best I could to them when it was over my neck. Water all around me. Rain water still lashing down and the spring rising up quickly. "Nothing. They are theirs. Let 'em have 'em—fear not, boy. The Demon Beast *has* been here, and he's kept his pact with the Baron!"

I felt stupid. Empty-headed. Gregory and I had believed we were so smart. But perhaps, in truth, my liege had been correct, and Bertrand's plan—to lure the Baron and Turlow alone back to the stable—might even have worked better than this. There was no telling, but at least we had our lives.

This had been only a plot; a device—an ambush against us. The wily Baron had only winked an eye at it all the time. But Gregory . . . what could I do with him? To leave Nikolas's body to the Baron's fiends? That was too horrible. Then I saw it drifting miraculously back towards me.

Naked, his beautiful dark buttocks up slightly out of the water, indeed, like a water sprite—an *eld* god of the springs as the forest men worshipped (and, even dead, as much a natural part of this water as my liege Bertrand)— I had to bring him to me.

"Thomas, where deemst you go?" Bertrand demanded.

"I must bring him!" I called.

"They wilt kill us!" Richard shouted. "They are on to us!"

Bertrand looked at me. He could see everything on my face, my feelings were as naked as I was. "Go on!" Bertrand called to Richard, and the knight swam beautifully over towards me. I could not swim, but could only hold carefully on to his legs as we both approached Neatsfoot's body. Then Bertrand, with all of his strength and skill, pulled us both—me and Neatsfoot—over towards the other side of the roaring spring. Its sound thundered over us.

I got out. Rain still lashed about me. Bertrand followed, hoisting Neatfoot's body easily over his shoulder, though he panted and was tired, I could see that.

I was coughing, heaving cold spring water out of my young chest, and about to faint—I had come to the complete end of my strength. Boys of my age do that, even if we look grown. I shook. "A sick-un," the foresters said to me with pity. They threw a simple shirt over me. It clung to me. I felt like a cold stick. "We'll take ye back. Give ye nettle tea. It'll do ye fine, lad."

"We need a horse for this," Bertrand said, pointing to the corpse. "I must have one."

"Leave it," Richard told him. "That will slow us down. Let the ravens have it, if they want!"

"Nay," Bertrand said, looking at me. "I cannot, for the boy."

Then Bertrand's own horse, Fire, who had escaped and would not be led by any Norman, was brought to us. Bertrand gently hoisted Neatsfoot's body across his back, face down, and then he led it, naked as he was, away from the spring, with the rain now easing up and the morning beginning to reclothe its bright, warm self in the midst of darkness.

"Where's the Baron?" Bertrand asked as we walked back, barefoot, towards the other horses that the forest men now kept.

"They're gone," Richard announced. "But never for long. Medeems that the Baron will follow ye for the rest of yer days. And only when ye kill him good, will ye be done with him!"

I wanted to sleep. I was tired the way young men become—completely, without reserve—and all I could think of was sleep. I felt as if I were only skin and fever, with no muscle or will in me. We came to a good clearing, protected all around. There Bertrand bade me stop. He found a bit of cleared ground and soft leaves for me, and ordered me to lie down. The foresters covered me with a blanket. I was very feverish. Bertrand knelt at my side; he took my cold hand and kissed it. "Will I die?" I asked him.

"No, Thomas, you will not die. But you must rest."

I started crying. I felt like a dolt—a fool—too stupid and foolish. Perhaps it was my fever, my exhaustion. "You will bury Neatsfoot?" I requested.

"*Pas*," Bertrand said.

"My good lord, I beg. Please do not leave him for the ravens. It is not Christian. It is . . ."

Bertrand put his hand to my forehead. I could feel its coolness next to my burning skin. Then he put his lips there, and, as I remember, they felt slightly chapped but very good. I closed my eyes. Suddenly I felt better than I had felt in many days.

"You will stay here," Bertrand said softly, "and I will bring Neatsfoot to you."

Bertrand then brought his horse over, and bade the other forest men to leave him alone with Neatsfoot's body and me. The others, including Richard Smart, left. Then Bertrand, the Knight from the Land at the End of the Mountain, lifted Gregory's bare body from his horse, and pulled it away from me, so that I could see the two of them only at a distance. There, on a slight knoll, the sun began to rise and shed its rosy bloom on the earth and on Neatsfoot's paling, naked length. It gilded him, turning his cold, dead-white self into pure gold.

At this point, even worn and feverish as I was, I got up, and shyly went over towards my dead lover and my lord. Then, with the blanket wrapped around me, I sat on the ground and watched, silently, as Bertrand lay on top of Neatsfoot's corpse, so that his own, still naked body completely covered the man.

He lay there silently. I found myself drifting off into the most pleasant, peaceful sleep. It was something I cannot describe, except to say that, truthfully, I had my eyes open, yet felt as if I were . . . sleeping. Dreaming blissfully, yet all around me was still . . . and . . . and as real as life itself. The forest. Bertrand. And under him, Neatsfoot . . . Gregory Nikolas, whose body soon began to glow on its very own, as if the morning sun that had seeped into it had brought him back to life; or was it only my liege lord's presence lying over him?

I have no idea, but only know that soon Bertrand rose from atop Gregory; and Neatsfoot himself followed, slowly.

Neatsfoot looked at Bertrand and brought his mouth to my young knight's lips and then kissed him.

"*Mon cher* Neatsfoot," Bertrand said quietly, "Thou must quickly leave." The young knight shook his head. I could see tears in his handsome face. "I will bring thee garments, but thou must part. It is something you cannot understand, but . . . I cannot have thee here with Thomas and me. My love . . . please see, for both of you will not allow it. I thank thee for thy part in our escape from Odred. I believe thou art good—but we cannot take thee with us. *Tu comprend*?"

Gregory Nikolas closed his eyes and nodded his head. He whispered

something to Bertrand, and Bertrand assented. The knight then walked away, and Neatsfoot came over to me.

"I must go," he said. I nodded my head. "I am smitten with you, Thomas, completely taken. I believe it is only for this that Sir Bertrand orders me away. I kouth it. One day I would rashly kill him for you, though I owe my life to him and will always. I am in painful anguish; I shalt have to hide that pain forever. I love you, but you must obey him always."

I nodded my head. It was true, I had to obey my liege. But for the first time, I hated Sir Bertrand. I was only a youth, and my feelings mirrored the storm that had just passed. A tide of anger washed over me, then broke on its own rocks—reality itself. The one to hate was Baron Odred. He had brought Nikolas to me, and now, in his way, had taken him from me—twice. "I shalt miss you," I said, trying to blink back tears.

"Thank you."

"I love you, Nikolas, victorious one."

He shrugged. "My only victory is that I live—the gift of Sir Bertrand. Your love, Thomas, must always be first for him. He will protect you; there is no question in that. And no matter how often you try to find me, you will return to him. I kouth it."

Then Gregory knelt and kissed me, and took my hands in his. We both got on our knees and prayed, both for Bertrand's deliverance and for our Lord Jesus's help. A moment later, Bertrand returned with Richard Smart.

"He alive!" Richard shouted. "'Tis a miracle. Blessèd be the Holy Father, the Mother, the Son, the Green saints, the Blessèd Be, and all that do good deeds!"

Richard Smart handed Neatsfoot some clothing, some rations to eat, and gave him a worthy dappled saddled horse and a sword. Neatsfoot clothed himself, mounted, and then raised his sword.

"To the death of the Baron!" Gregory shouted. "To Baron Odred's death!"

Bertrand smiled and raised his hand, and I got up and watched Neatsfoot—my own Gregory Nikolas—trot away from us. He turned his head back once towards us, smiled, and called for the Baron's death once more.

"Yea!" Richard Smart called, "to the death of the ol' Baron!"

"We have to kill him good!" I cried out, only to be held by Bert, who was dressed and sitting on the bed next to me.

It was dark now. I must have slept through the entire day. "I know we have to kill him," Bert said to me.

I asked him how, how did he know—and who was he talking about?

"This Hubris character. The Baron. You went back, but you left a little part of you anyway. That part began talking in your sleep. You told me the

rest of the story; I wish I could have been there myself, but I guess I was. I just forgot about that part about saving Neatsfoot—I mean, why he had to go away. He couldn't stay with us on that earthly plane, right? It's not what angels do."

"No," I said. "It's not . . . as much as he'd like to."

Bert smiled knowingly. "I see," he said. Then he added, "Oh, there's someone here who wants to see you. Do you feel up to it? Are you still feverish?"

He put his hand to my head. It was cool now. The fever was gone. I felt fine now, completely rested, but wondered who could be there. I got out of bed and put my terry cloth robe on, wandered out into the loft, and saw the dark back of a man. He was wearing a leather jacket and tight jeans. His hair was glistening black, even in the dim light of the loft. He turned to me, and I saw that it was Niko.

"I owe my life to you," he said. "I had to find you, so I did. I just hope that no one followed me."

"Why is that?" I asked.

"The cops took me to a hospital. I was okay, really. That heroin—I'm never gonna do that again! I swear. I ain't no addict—it was just that Paula girl, she's too much." His eyes went over to Bert. "I guess this is your friend here?"

"Sure." Bert chuckled. "I'm his friend. Bert. You must be Niko. So what else happened in the hospital?"

"You gotta match?" Niko asked. Bert went to the kitchen to get some matches—neither of us really smoked. Niko pulled a cigarette from his jacket pocket. He held it, playing with it in his fingers. He was nervous. I could tell that. He had never seen Bert. Or had he?

His eyes darted around the loft like a trapped animal. I knew this was not easy for him, being in my space—with Bert and me.

Back in the hospital, he said, the cops had questioned him about the drugs—he'd expected that to happen. He'd told them nothing—had no idea what went on. What drugs? It was just an asthma problem—a lie, but what else could he say? He'd had an asthma attack and almost died, but his friend Tommy (me!) knew what to do. "It was nerves," Niko explained. "I told 'em that I get these kind of nervous attacks, like I'm dead. Cops are funny. Sometimes they jus' wanna believe you, so they do."

"And they believed that?" Bert asked calmly, when he came back in. "Are you sure they weren't just using you as bait, to get to Tommy, or me?"

"I dunno," Niko said. "Sometimes the liar gets lied to himself. I know that."

I looked at him, as he looked at Bert. Was he talking about his wife, or some event that had happened a long time ago . . . ?

"Sounds fishy," Bert said, "But, frankly, I don't like it that you were in the middle of that kind of stuff. You're a good person, we got you—"

"What do *you* care?" Niko said. "You got Tommy here, I got—"

"It's all right," Bert answered, then struck a match and brought Niko's face closer to him. He gently cupped Niko's dark furry cheek with one hand, then lit his cigarette with the other. He kept his hand softly on Niko's cheek, until it was time to blow out the match. I watched, and realized that Niko'd had his eyes on Bert's face the whole time.

"Now, what happened after the cops left?"

"I dunno," Niko said. "I just know that this man in a gray suit came in after the cops. Wanted to know all about Tommy. How to get to him, who his friend is—how would he even know he had a friend?"

"Good question," Bert answered. "Maybe the guy's really evil; he has a way of finding out these things. He was just using you, that's all, Niko."

Niko's body started to tremble. "Evil!" he screamed. "You got that right, that's what he was. Fuckin' evil! The asshole said that if I didn't tell him, he'd have me arrested. He'd stick me so far in jail—'I got big friends,' he said—I wouldn't get out till I was a hundred years old. He'd get me for drugs; dealin'. He'd have my son Paul taken away from me. Paul's all I got. I got so scared I thought I was gonna shit all over the place."

"What did you do then, Niko?" Bert asked, placing his hand on Niko's shoulder to steady him. Suddenly Niko fell into him, and Bert held him for a moment, then released him.

"I told him . . . I said I'd tell him everything. But then . . . I pretended like I was having another attack. Coughin' bad. So bad it hurt my throat, lemme tell you. Then I rang for the nurse, and a bunch o' people piled in and they got rid of this jerk. They told him to come back tonight, when I was better. They said they'd call the police if he stayed. So he looked at me and just stared."

"Must have unnerved you," Bert said. "The guy in the suit's a real shit, isn't he?"

Niko nodded. "When they all cleared out, I escaped. I jumped into my clothes, made sure nobody was around, then got out. I was scared the whole time. I couldn't go back to my parents in Astoria. It was too dangerous for them. So I came here. I got your address from Detective Morris."

"You did the right thing," Bert purred at him, putting his hand softly on Niko's shoulder. "You have real heart, I can tell that. With some men, it's frozen in ice; but not yours."

Niko smiled and looked into Bert's eyes. "Thanks. You're like Tommy, a real *filos*, a friend. It's just . . . sometimes I don't know where my heart is. I'm not really gay, you know."

"Sure," Bert said. "You mean you're not like us, right?"

"I didn't mean it that way. I just meant—this 'gay' stuff, it escapes me. All the gays I know, they're just fluff. They care more about their muscles and hairdos than about other people. I don't see myself like that."

Bert nodded. "So how *do* you see yourself?"

Niko exhaled loudly, and then took a deep drag on the cigarette. He shook his head, and then started . . . I can only describe it as weeping. Tears came out of his eyes. "I dunno. I jus' dunno."

"Maybe that's the way most people are," Bert said, and gently led Niko over to a couch. It was piled with manuscripts, books, and photos, but he managed to scoop them up and clear them off so that he and Niko could sit down. I stood for a moment, then sat on a nearby chair. Bert held Niko, and drew him closer to him, while the handsome Greek continued crying.

I could not tell what was going on. Was it simply exhaustion? Or had some intense realization moved Niko, who tried to appear so working-class tough, to tears?

"That's all right," Bert said. "Cry if you need to. If you want to talk about it, it's okay. But if not, I'm here for you. I'm the friend you want, though you don't know me."

"But I do, Bert," Niko confessed. "That's what so funny. I feel like I've always known you. You dunno how strange this is. It's like I'm falling into something I can't stop. Ever get that feelin'? You know, like you're drowin'?"

"It's all right," Bert said. "Really." And he drew Niko over to him and kissed him softly, his graying bearded face on Niko's darker cheeks.

Niko shook his head. "I wish you wouldn't do that."

"Why?" Bert asked, as I looked on, dumbfounded. Maybe I was still too lost in that other time, that moment when Bertrand, naked, had lain on top of the pale corpse of Gregory Nikolas, but I could not help but be mesmerized by Bert, great ancient angel that he is.

"'Cause," Niko explained, a shy smile breaking on his face, "You're giving me the funniest hard-on."

"How funny?" asked Bert.

"It's like the kind of hard-on I had when I was a kid. I couldn't control it. I just let go of myself and it happened."

"Good," Bert said, kissing him now fully on his mouth. "Just let go. Will you?" And Niko did exactly that. I could see it; his whole face and body relaxed, as if he were on the most amazing drug, though in fact it was only Bert's voice. His presence. His soft, warm, tender, powerful presence, that seemed to flow like some kind of celestial honey through the dark loft, as he led Niko to our bedroom, and then quietly pulled off the Greek's clothes, until he was stripped totally bare.

Of course, as you can imagine, I had to join them, and as soon as Niko   179

had his pants down, my mouth was at his cock. I licked and sucked him, while Bert kissed and caressed his body, starting with his face, then reaching down to his nipples, poking sharply out of the sweet, black forest of hair that swirled on his chest, then further down to his trim stomach, until Bert's mouth reached mine, engaged with Niko's dick.

There he kissed me and licked and sucked Niko's cock at once, and I became, really, just limp with happiness. It filled me all over. I had not had such happiness . . . in almost a thousand years, I thought . . . because then I realized that Niko's cock was formed exactly like Gregory Nikolas's . . . the secret lover I still loved, despite myself.

But I did not have to say anything of the sort, because I knew that Bert was aware of it, too. And that in his own, powerful way, this no longer bothered him. In the meandering travels of my life, filled with lust, tenderness, anger, and joy, I had not picked Niko for no reason. I knew that this handsome Greek man's spirit was somewhere linked closely with that of Neatsfoot's.

There is life after death . . . even if we can only see it as more life.

Bert stopped what he was doing, and then went back to Niko's face, kissing him again, as Niko embraced him and returned his kiss with total surrender. "Do you wanna fuck me," he asked Bert. "I don't let guys fuck me. I always try to play the man, you know. But I want you to."

Bert nodded his head, and searched beside our bed for some lubricant and a rubber. He was already completely hard, and his beautiful swollen cock was ready for a dab of lubricant, then the rubber. I got back up and helped him get it on, and Niko sucked me while I did this, sticking his head in my lap, and holding onto my waist. Then I drew away from him, and Bert pulled him up and then slid under Niko's butt, so that he could enter him as gently and yet completely in control as possible.

Niko let out a slow, soft sigh. "You're good," he said. "You know jus' what t' do."

"Yeah, I do, Niko," he whispered.

Then I leaned over Bert so that he could suck me while he fucked Niko, and at a certain point Niko sucked me as well, until it seemed as if all of our energies were going into a complete circle of pleasure and giving and taking, too, until Bert's commanding, complete strokes, that he shaped and controlled so that sex to him was more like a work of art that just . . . sex; anyway, they signaled that he would soon come. His eyes closed, and I could feel a real prayerfulness coming out of him, with light and heat circling the bed, as the three of us edged closer to orgasm and its own descent into the magical, fantastic world of night . . . a night leading, yet, to another morning.

"He shalt return," my young lord Bertrand said to me, as our eyes fol-

lowed Neatsfoot's dappled horse until its form was replaced by only a ray of the emerging day.

"And will you kill him, if he does?" I asked.

"Nay. I cannot slay him, as I have saved him. That is our rule."

"Pray, tell me. Who are you, Sir Bertrand?" I asked.

"I am the Knight—"

"Verily I kouth that," I said. "The Knight from the Land at the End of the Mountain. But . . . who are you, or"—I hesitated then said, "What are you, my lord? What form do you take that permits you to do such things, such magic?"

"It is no magic, Thomas. But I cannot tell thee now. Kouth only that I am drawn to thee, Thomas Jebson, son of a pig farmer, though a good one, I believe. In your birthing, there must be nobility! *Mon Dieu*, I kouth that verily. I am drawn to you, as you to me, and will have no one in your stead. You may love another, but will always be mine. And even death shall not separate us, I bid thee that. I promise on my oath as a knight and as a—" His lips closed and then found their way to my mouth.

"As a what?" I asked, after this handsome, dark-haired young knight had stopped kissing me, rashly but tenderly.

His eyes closed, then reopened. They seemed filled with light, and gold, and all manner of majesty. "As an angel," he whispered to me. "It is the truth; I forbid you not to kouth it.

I shook my head. "I kouth not what that means, sir," I said.

"*Mon* Tom, you shall learn."

At that moment, Richard Smart came back upon us. His head was down, as if he were as crestfallen as a gelded rooster. "I see that Neatsfoot is gone from our pleasant company. Nay, nice lad he be."

"He is gone," my lord Bertrand said. "But *e vive*. He lives. Now we must go off again to find the Baron and kill him. Wilt thou accompany us, Mister Smart?"

"Nay," Richard said. "'Tis pure stink, but I must say nay. We lost men in that battle with the Baron's deceit. I must stay wi' m' men in this here forest. But verily as I be, if ever you come back, you will have a home and friends close t' yer bosom."

Now, all I, Tommy Angelo, can recall was seeing the youth Thomas Jebson and Sir Bertrand—the Knight of the Land at the End of the Mountain—in full armor, ride off; and that was when that visit, brought on by the magical spell of orgasm, came to an end . . . the Bridge fell. But instead of coming back cold, I felt warm.

I got up from our bed, naked, while Bert and Niko Stamos slept in each other's arms, and tiptoed into the kitchen to find something to drink. I realized

it was ten o' clock and time for the local news. I turned on the small TV in the kitchen to Channel Five and turned down the volume. Constance Tschu, the always unflappable anchor woman, was on. She went through the usual news—all the local miseries—and then came to this. My ears pricked right up.

"If you've been following news of the recent murder of Charles M. Knoedel, a Los Angeles resident, in the very posh Raleigh House on Central Park South, we just got an interesting tip that may be of interest to you.

"The investigators have been looking for an attractive blond male 'massage therapist' who made a call on Knoedel just before he was strangled. They found Mr. Knoedel's date book, clearly stating that he had scheduled a 'Massage from Tommy' only an hour before his demise. So far no 'Tommy' has been located, though witnesses among the staff did say they saw an attractive young man enter the man's suite shortly before Charles Knoedel's death.

"It turns out, though, that Mr. Knoedel had been brought to New York to work for the Mayor's powerful new friend in the gay community, Alan Hubris. Hubris has been buying up gay bars and bathhouses by the drove lately—all with the Mayor's public blessing. Hubris declares that he upgrades these establishments, cleans them up of drugs and on-site sexual activities, and makes sure that the Mayor's campaign coffers are well stocked from funds whose origins the Mayor never questions.

"The Mayor, who has stated that he has every faith in his friend, feels Mr. Hubris is an asset in his dealings with this controversial community."

Switch to clip of the Mayor and Alan Hubris linking arms and smiling. Voice of the Mayor: "Alan Hubris has done more for his community than anyone else in New York. He has given gay men a real model to aspire to. He has cleaned up their clubs and bars of illegal drugs, sexual activities, and that underworld element that used to prey on these people. He is a—" Voice of Hubris: "Thank you, Mr. Mayor. I want to show people exactly how *good* 'gay' can be in today's competitive world."

Suddenly, Bert and Niko appeared, both still naked and a little fuzzy from sleep.

Niko's eyes opened wide. "That's the guy! The one in the suit who threatened me."

"Sure," Bert said. "We know. We know who he is. He and the Mayor have been closing down clubs to rebuy them again—cheap."

The screen switched back to Constance Tschu. "Now, after last night's raid on MaloMalo, a club in Brooklyn that was not specifically gay but had a large gay following, word has gotten out that Mr. Hubris was behind this police activity—he knew about it—and he might have encouraged the event to make it easier to buy the club.

"We wanted to interview Mr. Hubris about this, but his office refused all

calls from us. But since he and the Mayor are so close, we have some questions for him. Did the raid on MaloMalo have any link with the death of Charles Knoedel? Did Knoedel know something he should not have? And if raids on clubs like MaloMalo make them easier targets for Alan Hubris, what will be the next target in his campaign to buy up gay businesses all over New York?"

Video clip: outside of club on the wealthy Upper East Side of New York, followed by interior footage of a large, gorgeously decorated nightclub space, filled with flowers, carpets, murals of naked men, and stylish banquette tables.

"Mr. Hubris's latest venture has been Xanadu, a club on the fabulous East Side that he bought six weeks ago. We have learned from our own investigations that Xanadu is now the main office for Mr. Hubris's enterprises. And though Mr. Hubris has made a public show of cleaning up this club—which once featured naked go-go boys and a back room area for more private activities—word has it that for certain special customers, the sky's still the limit there. So despite the Mayor's attempts to clean up the gay world all over New York, his friend, the dapper and always nicely suited Mr. Hubris, runs a very *raunchy* club." Constance paused for a second, as the three of us looked at each other. Then she continued: "We just want to know if this is true, Mr. Hubris—and if it is not, why won't you talk? Now, after this brief message, we have 'What's New on Wall Street' and our Sports Rundown."

"We've got to get down there," I said. "Somewhere in that office, there must be everything to convict him. Chuck Knoedel knew that. That's why they killed him."

"But if they catch you," Niko said, "they'll try to pin it all on you."

I could tell Bert was thinking. He looked at me and smiled. "Suppose we make Tommy into even more a blond than he is? Then he could get into Xanadu and see if they'd hire him as—"

"I think," I said, "the new word for them is 'host.' Right? I could be a host there. I'm such a whore anyway."

Bert smiled. "Tommy, you're not a whore. I know whores and you are not one."

"Naw," Niko chimed in. "He ain't a whore. But I think maybe the blond bit's no good. He should be *dark*. Kinda like me. And then maybe I could be blond!"

"You're not going to be a blond!" I said. "But the brunet idea's appealing. My hair can really be anything—and most of the time so can I. There's an all-night drugstore, I think, about three blocks away from here. We'll go in, get a little Clairol, then I'll go by Xanadu this evening about midnight and we'll see how far we can go."

Chapter 16

I t was slightly after midnight before I got over to Xanadu in the East Sixties: so far east that you were literally pissing under the Fifty-Ninth Street Bridge into Queens. The block in front of the club was lined with limousines, Cadillacs, expensive sports cars, BMWs, and even some yellow cabs with their drivers waiting.

My hair was now jet black, with deep blue highlights in it. That alone gave me a funny feeling, like I was no longer myself. For some extra pizazz, I wore a small, fake dark mustache; and I'd even blackened my pubic hair and the slight trail of soft hair on my stomach. Did I feel strange, or what?

Every time I passed a window or a mirror, this other mustached face looked back. Sometimes it surprised even me: who *was* this guy looking back at me—but at least I knew. We needed to get to the bottom of this, but who knew where the bottom was, or even, *who* the bottom was? Was Alan Hubris at the bottom . . . of Chuck Knoedel's death, and at what was now starting to look like an attempt to silence Niko?

Or was something even deeper there, at that bottom?

Seeing Hubris—surely the Baron Odred incarnate—with New York's sullen but talkative mayor was pretty shocking. But why be shocked anymore? The longer I lived (in no matter what "form," I came), the more I saw that things had a way of reverting back to much older situations—and what seemed to be only the "result of chance," usually wasn't.

"How do you feel?" Bert asked me half a block from the club, with the streetlights bouncing over us. "Fine," I said. I was okay with this. But inside, I was more frightened than I let on. There was still this stormy kid inside me, Thomas Jebson by name, who never went away. I knew it.

"Good," he said. "You know how to reach us?" I nodded. I'd signal him telepathically—through Neatsfoot, if I could get him. And, if Neatsfoot were not available, Bert was carrying his cell phone. At this Millennium, you had to have a back up even for telepathy. Every angel knew that . . . then, a moment later, I was at the big locked door of the club. "*Private*," in small let-

ters, was engraved on it. I rang a buzzer. A camera looked down at me. "Yeah?" a voice inquired.

"Mr. Hubris," I said slowly. "Uh . . . told me you're looking for new hosts?"

The door opened, and a bald-headed man with skin pale as a peeled cocktail onion appeared. He was in his early forties, with strange "V"-shaped black eyebrows and a short, hawkish nose that had probably been surgically "improved." He wore a charcoal-striped, burgundy-shaded suit that looked too cheap for this neighborhood. Maybe he should have just worn the box, because he was as wide as he was tall. All shoulders, neck, and chest, even in the suit. "I'm Steve," he said, with a kind of funny, crooked half smile. "I manage da club. We just reopened. Maybe you heard."

I followed him through a narrow entranceway, graced with a lavish, though slightly wilted, arrangement of "Moo-shu Dynasty," expense-account-restaurant-style purple spider orchids on a spotlit Roman pedestal. Then we headed down a short flight of stairs that popped a quick twist *up* to another floor. Steve gave a nod to another doorman, this time younger and thinner, but equally built (in another eye-kissing suit, this time: cobalt blue), who let us in to another room.

The cocktail lounge.

Very loud. Very dark. Very *abuzz*. All just buzzy with *abuzz*. Mostly older, wealthy-looking men; and some expensive "W"-type ladies who might (or might not) have been born female. So? . . . it happens. The ladies were *dressed*, some in fetching little hats with veils. Also, I observed quite a shoe effort; equally disarming little gizmos. None could take you more than six blocks; but, hey, who walks? As I looked around, the *La Cage Aux Folles* disco medley was coming to its climax.

"That's Mr. Hubris." Steve pointed me to him, seated at the bar with a tall, stork-shouldered blond who had mascara trouble and a chin like a moose. I walked over. This was nothing, I said to myself. In my business I met strangers all the time; some of them stranger than these people. Grown men who wee-weed in king-sized diapers. A fat guy from Atlanta who told me while I was massaging him that he liked to munch dog food out of the can; then Alan Hubris, in a double-breasted, tastefully attractive dark jacket, looked at me and asked, "Who've we got here, Gilda?"

"I don't know, but he's quite a dish," the blond said, looking me over with a smile. "Our little publicity is starting to get you big talent, Alan."

"Thank you, my dear," Hubris said, modestly lowering his eyes. "I want this club to *ooze* class. I want it to be, you know—the sort of place our kind of people can hang out at and be proud of!"

"You've done great things for your community, I salute you," Gilda said. "I'd better get back." She giggled. "There's some pressing press business to

do. Do I get an escort?"

"Of course, Gilda," Hubris said. "You don't want to stay for the show?"

"I'd love to, Alan," Gilda said and planted a light kiss on his cheek, "but you know how it is. Meetings, meetings, meetings."

Hubris waved his fingers and Steve rushed over. Gilda got up and Steve's burgundy suit escorted her out of the room. Hubris beamed as he watched them disappear, then he looked at me. "Sorry," he said politely. "What can we do for you? Have you ever been here before?"

"No," I said, shaking my head. "But I heard from a friend of mine at my gym that you're looking for hosts. Go-go boys, jobs like that."

"Perhaps. You're sure you've never . . . " I just looked at him blankly, then he said, "We do have a show later on that we do for some of our preferred customers." He smiled. "What kind of stuff do you dance in?"

"Mostly nothing."

"That's just what the job calls for. I'll take you downstairs, show you the dressing room, and let you meet some of the other guys. We run a good ship here. Tips are fabulous. Select clientele. All very high class."

He got up and we wove our way through the dense, overwhelmingly male crowd. Hubris smiled, winked, and shook hands, while a few of the men, quite drunk, grabbed me, groped me, and tried to hold on to me. Hubris laughed and said I'd be available later. They were mostly older men with money, but who discriminates? There were also some younger men with money, too.

"You're quite a draw already," he said when we left the cocktail area. "The show's up here." We climbed another flight of stairs to what must have once been a restaurant area—it was wide open, but was now set up with seats, tiny cocktail tables, a bar and a runway. Waiters in uniforms milled about and smiled at Hubris, who ignored them. "You seem to draw men to you. What's your name?"

"Tommy," I answered. "Tommy . . . Smith."

He looked at me with those steel-cold blue eyes. "You remind me of someone. I swear I can't say just who, but I feel it."

"Happens," I said. "I remind a lot of people of people. Maybe it's because I'm still young."

"How young?"

"Twenty-two."

"Come on. How old are you really?"

I hesitated. "Twenty-four."

"That's good. You're probably twenty-six, but who cares? What's important is that you know how to make people happy. That's what we do here." He smiled to himself, then broke into a cold giggle. "Gilda liked you."

"Who's she?"

He started to laugh again. What a cold laugh, I thought. It really sent shivers up me, like icicles breaking. "The Mayor."

"The what?"

"The Mayor. He likes to come over here like that. It's kind of a goof for him. You see, he really likes gay people. Especially those with money."

I nodded my head, then we walked up another flight of stairs, went around a couple of corners, and were soon met by a dark green closed door. The door had an electronic combination lock. Hubris leaned over to punch in the numbers. This was too easy: I didn't even have to work hard at seeing the numbers. Could it have been a trap, or just Hubris's own . . . well, hubris?

The numbers. One-Zero-Seven-Seven. Idiocy, I thought. Who could not remember that?

Hubris gave the handle a quick flip, and there I was: in his office. How did this happen so fast? But things were happening fast anyway. We were in what must have been his outer office—too presentable to be the inner one. No ledgers, bills, and rubber stamps flying around, like in Bert's office in the loft. I looked around and saw a door. I immediately walked over to it and tried it: it was unlocked, with the light still on.

Pay dirt. Books all over the place. Ledgers. A computer on. "Hey!" Alan said. "Where you going?" He grabbed my arm, led me back into the outer office, and I said, "Sorry. I just thought you wanted to go in there."

"Why would I want to do that?" he asked. "It's a mess in there. Why don't you take your clothes off?"

"Sure," I answered. I began to strip for him and he watched me, enjoying himself, I could tell. Some men have a thing about just making you do what they want you to do. I was sure Hubris was one. I pulled my loafers off and flipped them aside, then slowly started to unpeel the snug black Lacoste polo shirt I wore. His eyes were riveted on me as the shirt slowly skimmed over my tight stomach, revealing just enough of the silky skin underneath. His hands went up to feel the soft dark fuzz there—now I was glad that I'd colored that part, too. He nodded. I let him touch me, then drew away a bit, to continue the full peel.

If you're going to strip for a man, you have to do it so that he feels like you're doing it naturally. Like you, say, could be in a "Y" locker room; and taking your clothes off is no big deal. I wanted him to feel that way, so I stopped every couple of seconds and smiled. Then, once I had the shirt off, and I flexed my chest, like I was just happy to be bare-chested, and watched him from the corner of my eye. I grinned, then began to unbuckle my pants. They were dark gray cotton chinos and I wriggled out of them easily, so I was now down to my white Calvin briefs. I walked slowly up to him, and he put his hands on my thighs and ran then down my naked legs, then reached in and groped me inside my underwear, so that my cock, almost hard already,

188

edged up and the head managed to peek out of the waistband.

"Just stay like that," Hubris said. He sat on the edge of his desk and then pulled me over to him and began licking my chest, and then softly sucked one of my hard little nipples. I moaned. "You like that?" he whispered.

I told him I did. "Want the briefs off?" I asked.

"No. Not yet."

Hubris looked at me, licked his lips, then unbuckled the pants of his suit; he was still in the jacket though it was now open. He let the dark pants drop, halfway down to the floor. Then he pushed my head down into his crotch, while he fished his very pinkish-looking meat out from a pair of sky-blue boxer underwear. I figured this must have been part of every audition for Mr. Hubris, although I'm not sure if the regular customers got this kind of royal treatment, unless they were really paying for it.

I always think it's funny sucking a man's cock who's wearing an imported suit. There's that chemical dry cleaning smell up your nose, along with the crotch scent as well; it's even funnier trying to do it with a fake mustache. I'd stuck that on securely with surgical glue, but I had to be careful it didn't snap off. For a big enough man, Hubris did not have an impressive dick, though it was adequate and somewhat, finally, responsive. He was cut and, I have to admit, I enjoyed the plummy softness of the head in my mouth. I'm a sucker for such things—or just a sucker anyway.

I think he did not want to take this very far . . . it was just a casting call, right? I stopped after a few strokes, and got up. I casually checked the mustache with my hand, and he smiled, like he was going to say, "Come back next week," then his cell phone rang.

"Shit!" he said, pulling his pants back up. He popped open the receiver. "Okay," he said quickly on the phone, then snapped it shut. "Some nosy asshole reporter's downstairs. He heard the Mayor comes here—wants to know if that's true. Of course it's not true, *right*?

I looked at him blankly.

"Listen, if you want to stay alive and healthy here, don't repeat anything you hear or see. Understand?" I told him I did. He finished zipping himself back up. "The show's a little after one tonight. I'd like you in it. I'll take you to the dressing room, you can meet the other boys. How does that sound?" I smiled. It sounded good to me. "Something tells me you've got something special, Tommy. It's one of those feelings I've had before; it's really unique."

The dressing room was right next to Hubris's office. I noticed a mirror in it that he could probably see through, if he wanted to spy on the artists at work. There were four other boys in the show, and they gave me a kind of blank look when he walked in with me. "Introduce yourselves afterwards.

This is Tommy Smith. He's the new talent for tonight. Tell him how we run things, how he'll get paid, stuff like that. Good luck, and have a great show!"

Then he left, and the other guys approached me. They were already in costume—our first appearance was in tuxedos that popped apart from Velcro openings. Two, Randy and Rip, were big Midwestern-type blonds. I was glad my hair was black that evening, if only not to look like them. Something told me they had something going between them, and it was not particularly healthy to try to figure it out. They kind of smiled at me, coolly, then turned away.

Carlos, a handsome Latino, was bare-chested, and he should have stayed that way all his life. He looked like he'd been chiseled out of the most beautiful tropical wood I had ever seen. He nodded at me, slipped on the false tux shirt and jacket, and I felt disappointed.

The last man was big, beautiful, and darkly black. He was built like a linebacker, with a strikingly handsome face, the kind you'd see on a statue of a Roman emperor. He was in his tux already, but barefoot, and he shook my hand and smiled at me. His eyes lit up, then I realized why. He was Ernie, the gorgeous man I had played with in the steam room of the gym only a few days earlier. But, as they say, what a difference a few days can make.

"You better get out of those clothes and get into this," he said, handing me a hanger with a complete outfit on it. "The thing's adjustable—the question is, are you?"

I told him I was.

He stared at me for a moment. "Were you ever a blond? Funny, but you look familiar." I did not say another word, but just smiled; then he told me how we got paid. We collected our own tips, but our real salary came from the private "dance" lessons that we gave upstairs. These were put on the bills of customers, so we'd carry a small pad with us. Since customers paid a lot of money for the "lessons," sometimes as much as six or seven hundred dollars for one, everything was billed to a credit card. Some of these were corporate accounts, so the whole thing had to look very legit. What was important was that Hubris always knew exactly who was giving the lessons.

"It's simple," Ernie said. "You make as much money here as can you hustle to make. Call it 'American enterprise' at its best. You bring in your own salary. I worked on Wall Street for some flaky junk bond guys before I got this job—and let me tell you, Wall Street sucks compared to this!"

"It must be hard to keep all this straight," I said while I got out of my clothes and into the tux.

"Naw. They probably keep a couple of sets of books. One's just for us. It's not all that different from a lot of Wall Street—there they have the 'fiction' books and the real stuff, too. They can move stocks up and down whenever they feel it. Anyway, it sure keeps the tax guys guessing."

"Oh," I said, nodding my head. A light suddenly went on: that was what Chuck Knoedel was doing: fixing up the "fiction" books, while trying to keep the "straight" books straight. "What happens if you don't bring in the lessons?"

"You won't be here very long," he said, then added: "Oh, and another thing. Don't ever cut in on anybody else's lessons. That's asking for it. Lucy and Ethyl over there"—he looked over at the two blonds—"would just as soon kill you, if you did."

Chapter 17

I was trying to stay as calm as possible, though my palms were getting pretty moist as we lined up on the tiny stage. My big intro to show business, and I was about ready to pee in my rip-off tux. I checked to make sure my mustache was okay. I figured it was. Then I felt this funny kick in the back of my shins. I turned around and spotted (even in the dark) blond Randy and Rip smirking. "Good luck, girl," Randy hissed between his teeth. "Just remember: Seniority counts here. We get first pick of the johns, uh, I mean customers."

"Watch out," Ernie, next to me, whispered. "Ty Rex and Godzilla are getting ready." I nodded my head, gave Ernie a quick kiss, then heard Steve's dry monotonal voice pierce the darkness, as the curtain went up, with: "Ladies and gen'lement. Dis evening for yaw pleasure, we present again . . . de Xanadu boys."

We were out on the runway; those little blue lights all around us, music exploding—everything sounding like Sir Andrew Lloyd Weber stuffed with cocaine—a moment later, the Velcro snaps were popped. Then I was dancing between Carlos and Ernie, in nothing but a sequined jock strap, with Randy and Rip already out front, doing a double show of Jayne Mansfield pecs. Almost everything about them, including their faces, was identical. Were they taking the same steroids?

The two blonds were great hustlers. They were in half the laps out there, feeling the well-suited men up while managing to stay just ahead of the sea of hands around them, except for a flying assortment of twenty-dollar bills stuffed into their jocks. For a second, I had that same lost feeling I'd had at MaloMalo—too much, too quickly. What had Bert been thinking, trying to get me into this place?

"You better get your cute tail out there," Ernie warned, flicking the back of my jock and snapping me right back into the action. "This ain't no time to be doin' Alice in Wonderland."

Then he jumped out in front, while the two blonds continued playing the action like a roulette wheel—knowing just how to get the sparks going—whose chest to stroke, tie to loosen, neck to nibble. And face to push (gently) into their bouncy crotches, which soon looked like two big overstuffed deli sandwiches, with lots of meat dropping out on each side, surrounded by wads of fresh green lettuce.

I was surprised at Ernie; suddenly he was all over the place. The reserved, smart exterior he showed before, snapped apart. And there he was—friendly, smiling, hustling the whole joint. Getting all kinds of hands into *his* jock, which was also starting to get stuffed with big bills. Carlos, on the other hand, was *macho*. He kind of let men come to him. He had a smoldering intensity and it drew attention to him. He was not a party boy like Siegfried and Roy (my new names for them), but he knew how to get what he wanted.

Now it was my turn. I had to go out there and produce the goods. Ernie had told me that dance lesson requests would be given to me at the end of the act—either Steve would hand them to me, or sometimes customers themselves. I got out into the audience, strutting my stuff, while the music blasted away around me. It was pretty tacky music—it seemed to stay somewhere with Jerry Herman—but it did what it was supposed to do.

We could not dance totally nude up front and out there with the audience, it was "against the law." But we could reach down and either grab our jollies or let something poke out for a few seconds, especially if the right customer showed any interest. I was out dancing among the tables and suddenly, there at a table, alone, was Bert, dressed in the only dark suit he owned, with his ultra-cool, wraparound Vuarnet shades on.

He smiled distantly, nodded to me, and I played up to him. "How are things going?" he whispered.

"Fine. The office is upstairs, just above this room. Dark green door. Combo lock: One-Zero-Seven-Seven. Can you remember?" He nodded. "Go to the inner office. Files all over the place. Real mess, but we can get what we want." Suddenly Ernie's eyes locked with mine. He gave me a quick "move on" look, and I had to add quickly for Bert: "Whatever, we'll do knock twice. Okay?"

He smiled and nodded to me, then leaned over and kissed me right on the mouth. "One-Zero-Seven-Seven," he said, his voice so low and deadpan that for a second I thought: He's reverted back to Bertrand *totally*. Then he added: "I may just kill Hubris and get it over with."

I nodded. What could I say?

"Niko and Billy are downstairs," Bert added, suddenly grabbing my face and kissing me again.

194

"I'd better go," I whispered, and smiled as broadly as I could. Hubris was

only two tables away from me and, like a barracuda, was moving in closer.

Bert grabbed my waist with one hand and my butt with another. He made it look like he was just drunk. "Billy," he whispered, "knows the layout here. We'll be upstairs in room *eight*. That was his idea. He told me he has an 'in' back from Brooklyn, with Steve the manager." He grinned. "Funny. All these characters know each other."

A second later, I turned. Alan Hubris was behind me. He had his hand on my forearm, and managed to get Bert's hands off me.

"'Scuse me, sir," Hubris said politely to Bert, "he'll be back"; then he led me away. "You're great, Tommy. You already have some requests for lessons. You may be busy all night. Hey, let me introduce you to a special friend and customer."

I nodded my head, then followed Hubris's double-breasted jacket off to a table at the far side of the club. There a short, chubby, vanilla-custardy kind of balding man in baggy charcoal gray waited. He was in his late fifties, and wore a "power yellow" tie from the 1980s. I recognized him instantly, but hoped that he couldn't return the favor: he had never seen me with black hair and a mustache, and as close to naked as this—and, it was fairly dark. (And, for good measure, he wasn't holding the amount of alcohol in him too well: I could see that.) "Gil," Hubris said. "My new boy, Tommy. I told you he's hot. Look at him!"

Gil Levenberg looked up at me and smiled. He was all smirk, and near-sighted, too. "You're cute!" he said. "I could jus'-eat-you-up, kid!"

I thanked him and smiled, but not too close. Why take chances? No: he did not recognize me. I knew it. So there, ladies and gentlemen, was Gil Levenberg, our ever-scheming landlord, the creep always trying to put us out on the street. Hubris took me aside. "Gil Levenberg's a gentleman and a player," he told me. "He's interested in some of our projects, so treat him right. I better get a good report from him on you."

"Sure, Alan," I promised. "I'll treat Gil right."

"I want him to be your first customer. He's easy. Just jerk him off a bit. You may have to suck him, that's all. But don't take any tip from him. Tell him the tip's on the house."

"Is he a friend of the Mayor, too?" I asked, as I saw Rip and Randy, like overbuffed chipmunks, rushing back to the stage for our second number.

"Yep. Mayor loves him. He's one of those landlords that keep our Mayor happy. They're turning the city around. Hey, you better get back on the stage—you know what to do next, right?"

We were soon back on the small stage, where the lights were squeezed down to a dense, purple semi-darkness: time for total, blue-balls, hands-off nudity. Simulated sex with the Xanadu Demi-Gods, as we were called. Ernie had his cock out—nicely out—and I went down on it, or had to appear to do

195

that. No actual physical contact was allowed, since the club had to stay within the Mayor's safety guidelines. The idea was just to get the audience hot enough that a lot of them signed up for "dance lessons" afterwards. "How you doing?" Ernie asked me while holding on to my shoulders.

"Strange way to make a living," I said.

"Could be worse. I could come out of here with four or five hundred bucks tonight."

"Or dead," I whispered.

"What d'you mean—hey, what *do* you mean?" Even in the dark, while he was pretending to be doing something other than just talking to me (suddenly his eyes shot over to Randy and Rip, to make sure they weren't listening), I could see that his mood had changed. "Who are you?" he asked. "I *know* I know you from someplace. Are you a cop?"

"No," I whispered, and brought my mouth up to his ear. "But what's going on here is even worse than the cops. These guys here play for keeps—"

"Of course they do. It's the money, dummy . . . it's serious here. You think the guys on Wall Street are any nicer?"

"I'm not talking about Wall Street, Ernie. I just don't want anything bad to happen to you. I want you to be on my side."

The music was starting to change. It was now "Last Chance for Love." Our cue. "Listen," Ernie pleaded. "If you know something, tell me."

"They'll kill you," I whispered. The lights started to go back up; Randy and Rip stopped play-fucking each other; Carlos tucked his big Latin sausage back into white bicycle pants (new quick costume change), and then Ernie and I, in small, tight white tennis shorts, were back out in the audience for one last go-through with the crowd. By then they were slobbering all over us.

Bert winked to me. I had to ignore him for a moment. The money hustle resumed, this time with an extra dollop of feel-ups to rope in customers. Several older men were all over me, stuffing tens and twenties into my shorts pockets. Hubris was no dummy; you can shove a lot more bills into shorts than jockstraps—and one fairly mastodon-ish customer with a huge, very red nose in a Christmasy, silver-colored tux and Stetson hat, kept trying to tongue-kiss me while asking, "How's m' best pardner?" I had to do a half-gainer flip away from him to keep my mustache on.

He started to press his mouth on my nipples, and I lurched away from him. I knew you did not give away freebies like that, but shoved his sweaty hand down into my shorts and let him wander in there for a moment. "Your best friend's doing fine," I answered as his fat fingers grabbed my hard-on.

Then I fished his hand out and took Tex with me back to Bert's table, where I bent over, unsnapped my shorts, and let my new pardner get a quick crotch-lick for himself. Before he came back up for air, I whispered to Bert, "I don't want anything bad to happen to Ernie, the black guy. I think he's on

our side."

"Okay," Bert said. "Can we trust him?" I nodded and he took out a twenty, and made a show of putting it behind my ear. I hitched my shorts back up, and sent Tex happy back to his part of the Alamo, as Hubris walked over. "You're new here," he said to Bert. "Don't think I've ever seen you before."

Bert smiled. "I just came into town from San Francisco. I produce computer networks. Things like that. I like your club. It's classy. My name's Knight, you must be Mr. Hubris."

Hubris smiled knowingly. "Are you interested in Tommy? I think his dance schedule's still open. We offer private lessons, you know, upstairs."

"Sounds good," Bert said. Hubris told him he'd need a credit card, and Bert pulled out his Amex card. Hubris took it from him, then came back with a slip for him to sign.

"Tommy's got one appointment before you, if you don't mind. If you do, we can get you Ernie, who 'aims' to please, let me tell you, or Carlos, our Latin stallion."

"I can wait for Tommy," Bert said. "I'll be in room eight."

Hubris looked puzzled. "*Eight*? How'd you know what room to be in, if you've never been here before?"

"A friend of mine back in San Francisco likes it. It's the leather room, right?"

Hubris nodded. "Okay, but it's booked now for the cute blond boys. They have a regular who wants it."

"I want it all night," Bert said. "I'll pay you a grand for it."

"Sorry, " Hubris said. "But since that room's been pre-booked and you want . . . a lot of service there," he hesitated, then said: "It goes for fifteen hundred. Flat. Is that all right, sir?"

Bert shrugged his shoulders. "Fifteen hundred? Sure, no problem. Let's just say my company's gonna be throwing a client party in that room. Okay?"

"Yes, sir," Hubris said. "I understand what you mean completely." He withdrew the charge slip. "I'll get a fresh new slip, we'll put in that figure, and you can sign it." Hubris hurried off, and I watched him speaking with Steve.

"Wow, fifteen hundred bucks," I said to Bert.

"Greed has no limits," Bert said. "He closes down every bathhouse, every bar he can—he and the Mayor—then they open this place."

"He and Gil Levenberg are friends," I said. "In fact, my first appointment is with him."

Bert chuckled. "Let me know what room you'll be in," Bert said. "I think we'll give Mr. Levenberg a surprise."

Hubris returned with the totaled slip. "This does not include tip," he 197

announced to Bert, who signed it without even looking at it. He handed it back to Hubris and put the yellow customer copy into his jacket pocket. "We hope we'll see more of you, Mr. Knight."

"Oh, you will." Bert nodded his head again, and briefly took his dark glasses off, then replaced them. "Perhaps we can have a talk, Mr. Hubris, before my party with Tommy begins. In your office, just us. I hear you're looking for investors."

Hubris smiled. "That may be possible. But like you see, tonight's really busy. Can you come back, say, tomorrow night?"

Bert shook his head. "Sorry. Time's now. You're either interested in my money or you're not."

"Do you know where my office is?"

Bert said no, and I realized that things were now falling into place in a way that I never could have predicted. As scheduled, I would have to see Levenberg first upstairs, then, somewhere around two-thirty, have my appointment for the rest of the night with Bert.

But meanwhile, there was no telling what might happen.

Chapter 18

The top two floors of Club Xanadu had been partitioned into private cubicles. They were actually regular bedrooms—much larger than those usually seen in bathhouses—and had wall-to-wall carpeting, nice beds, real decor, even reading lamps. Each had a small shower attached, with of course a private john and sink. It was indeed like a private gentleman's club. The kind that at one time suburban New Yorkers would stay in, when they could not get home to . . . well, usually the wives they'd been cheating on all along.

All those patrons who had signed up for private lessons were assigned a room, and down in the boys' dressing room, we were given sheets with the room number, customer name, and approximately how much time to spend with him. Steve handed them out. He never cracked a smile, while he gave orders. "Carlos, Mr. Roberts, remember him? He wants another lesson. This time, he told me, he wants to get his cock sucked a bit before you fuck him. And use only a tiny bit of Lube when you do dat; he don't like sloshing around, he said."

"*Sheet*," Carlos said sullenly. "You know I ain't no *maricon* dicksucker."

"Listen up, Evita Macho," Steve ordered. "For dis kinda money, you better learn. He wants two lessons; dat's double time. Your next lesson is . . ."

Ernie had three appointments, but they were quick and not going to be as lucrative as he had hoped. One man just wanted to grope him and be jerked off. Another wanted to be blindfolded while he sucked Ernie's big black dick. And the third was a voyeur who only wanted to look at Ernie while he jerked off. Siegfried and Roy did better because they could work either together (double fees) or alone. They hooted and petted each other, did high-fives, and kissed while Steve read out their assignments.

We had to wear a club uniform: black pants and tight black polo shirts, while working as "instructors." I was told that if, in the course of the evening, the uniform got dirty or soiled in any way, to go back to the dressing room and get another, since customers were never to see us looking any-

thing but perfect. It was expected we'd arrive at each room well-groomed and in good order, too. So, if you got paid to get fucked and things got kind of (well) loose up there, anyway, there was a private douching facility in the dressing room, too.

When he was finished, Steve, in his refrigerated Addams Family voice, ended with: "Good luck, boys. Remember, you can make a lotta money here for yaself and for da club; or you can screw up. It's jus', we don't like screw-ups. Okay?"

Then he left us, and soon enough Carlos and the two blonds left as well. Ernie dawdled for a moment next to me, while I brushed my hair. Suddenly a light went on in his face.

"Now I remember who you are," he said. "You're blond, not dark, right, and the mustache, it's . . . ?" I did not say a word. "What's gonna happen here? I'm getting kind of freaked out."

"Nothing that will hurt you," I said, and kissed him. "I mean it. I made sure of it."

"You think these guys are really . . . ?"

"*Evil?*" I said. "I'll be in room eight. If you get scared, just come in there. But make sure you're by yourself. And, remember, like Hubris says, nothing you see here can ever leave this place."

I'm not sure how Gil Levenberg managed to keep his eyes open by the time I got to his room. He was waiting for me with his white shirt and tacky gold tie off, his pinstriped jacket rumpled up and tossed to one side of the bed, and his shoes and socks kicked off to the other side. "Gosh-eree, you're hot!" he said, squinting at me.

"Thanks. So how can I make you happy, Mr. Levenberg?"

He smiled at me, and dove into my chest, pulling my black polo off, right over my head. He started slurping all over me, barely able to stand up. "Y'know, thash a *good* question. I wish more pipple asked me thash question."

I smiled. "Like who?" I started to unbuckle my belt, and slowly let my black pants slide down to the floor of the room. There was a small pink table lamp on. The room was nicely done: framed gay erotic photos on the walls—vintage Mapplethorpe leather; a few well-hung North African boys from Baron von Gloeden. A little bureau stood by the bed, topped with a generous gift basket filled with rubbers, Lube, even a fresh bottle of "room odorizer." At least Hubris gave you your money's worth, considering that a lot of money was changing hands here.

Levenberg looked at me like he had forgotten what "thash question" was. He got on the bed, unhitched his belt, and looked like he expected me to get him out of his pants. "Like who?" I repeated. "Who'd you like to ask, 'What can I do to make you happy?'"

He looked at me like he was trying to clear his mind; be a bit more sober. "Gee, you know. The Mayor for one. He needs to get all the damn freeloadin' Commie rent-regulation people outta New York. Like somma my tenants. There's a pain-in-the-ass gay couple in one of my buildings. He runs a magazine, maybe you heard—*InQuire*?"

"What's the other do?"

"Dunno. Cute. You kinda remind me of him, but he'sh a blond." He smiled. "I shore whish I could get in hish pants."

"Now you're in mine," I said, and drew his face up to my white Calvin briefs. He sniffed around them. I eased them down to the right, just enough so that he could lick the base of my cock. He took some of the hairs in his mouth and sucked at them, moistening the dyed roots of my pubic hair with his saliva.

"Tastes good," he said. I wondered: instead of blood, had he developed a taste for metalic chemicals—salts of mercury, silver—years ago? His eyes closed for a moment, then he slowly opened them. "I'm not sush a bad guy. I mean, I evicted a couple of people jush f'r money. So, I'm a greedy little bastard, but . . . but Hubris is big-time worsh. He's always bad. He'sh evil. I mean it. Maybe thash why we get along. He makes me look good!"

"We all have our problems," I said sympathetically. Mine was to get out of Gil Levenberg's room as fast as I could, and go see what Bert was up to. At that moment, I had no idea: I would leave some of this story to him. After leaving the dressing room, I had stopped off briefly at room eight. I did a double knock twice. Bert met me at the door. He had tossed his suit jacket, shirt, and tie off, and had on only a white T-shirt with the dark pants. "Get in here quick," he ordered. I did, and saw Niko and Billy waiting behind him. Before I could ask, "How did you get in here?" Billy told me as much of the scoop as he could on the place.

"It use t' be a cool bathhouse," he said. "Before it got all dolled up. It went straight for a while. Oriental massage. That sorta stuff. I know it like the back o' my hand, so I remembered this room eight. I had a good time in here before!"

"I'm going to try to get them up into the office," Bert told me. "But I guess you got your date with Gil first."

I told him I did, and so here I was, watching a very drunk Gil Levenberg trying to wriggle his fat butt, like so much wobbly Jell-O, out of his gray pants. "Need some help?" I asked. He nodded, and I grabbed the cuffs and jerked them off him, like I was doing a kid's magic trick—you know, yanking a tablecloth off a table. One with the silverware and plates already set on it. "Hey," he cried. "Not like that!"

I apologized and told him I could be a lot more gentle. It seemed like this was a good time to get to know Mr. Levenberg in a more intimate manner. 201

Now that he had his pants off, I started working around what was left, playing with his little dick inside his briefs, making him smile, kissing him lightly on his neck, his old droopy nipples, and then down towards his ballooning stomach.

"Thash feelsh great," he moaned softly. "I don' know who you are, but you shore know how t' do it." I thanked him, and then got him more comfy on the bed. I peeled down his briefs and his dick started to get a bit harder. I pulled out the lubricant jar, and eased some onto the palms of my hands. I began with his balls and perineum area, that sweet place just between the testicles and the asshole that men forget about too often. He sighed, started drooling a bit, and begged, "Don'sh shtop. Come on, don'sh shtop."

I wouldn't, I told him. Then I decided that this degree of intimacy required some personal questions, too. I began with: "Gee, Gil, I know nothing about this kind of thing, but"—I hesitated. Took my hands off his sexual parts for a moment, then said: "Could you tell me just how much money you're making off that building? You know, the one where that pain-in-the-ass gay couple live?"

He squinted at me, swallowed hard, then directed my fingers back towards his cock and asshole. "I shlike you t' touch me there, if you don' mind," he said. I nodded, wiggling, wriggling, and tickling him lightly. He smiled, then stuck out his bottom lip. "Gee, thash . . . big question. I make a lot. Shore, why not? I make a lotta money off my houses. Real estate's the only biz where anybody can get rich quick. You jus' gotta have enough balls, and you gotta know how to get real *mean*. I got th' balls, right?" He grinned at me, like he expected an answer. I told him he did have them. He smiled again.

Next question: "Do you know anything about that guy Chuck Knoedel, the one who worked for Alan?"

"Oh, thash a bad one," he said. "I'm not sh'posed to talk. Nobody is. Not even the Mayor."

"Why not?" I asked, placing one of my hands softly on his tender scrotum, just resting it there, while the other quietly started to explore the hilly, gelatinous badlands of his ass.

He sighed. "You're a pro, ya know?" I nodded quietly. "Why nosh?" he said. "Why nosh? 'Cause I don't want t' be killed, jush like Chuck, thash why."

I decided that the direction of this conversation needed a little chemical assistance. I left him, dried my hands on a hand towel, and then reached into the host's gift basket that my boss had generously provided. I pulled out the small vial of "room odorizer," with its specially printed label that said, "Eau d'Xanadu," and brought it back to him. Gil shook his head. "I don' like that shtuff. Does crazy thingsh t' me."

202   "Does good stuff to me," I said, and I slowly unscrewed the small cap.

The smell filled the room. It was good: I had to admit that. This stuff was strong enough to "odorize" Madison Square Garden. I took a tiny sniff of it, then placed it under Gil's nostrils. He rejected it at first, but I started fooling around with him in a very affectionate way. Sucking his tiny tired cock; going up to his navel and rimming that; then stroking him all over with my hands, until he gave in and I rammed the small bottle, forcefully, up his nose.

He tried to jump away, but I forced him to inhale from it until, I do believe, his eyes crossed. His cock snapped to attention like I had stuck an electric cattle prod up his ass. I sucked him a bit more, then stroked his dick with my hand until he was panting. Then I asked him once more if he knew anything about Chuck Knoedel's death. "Shore," he answered. "I know. But I don't know everything Knoedel knowed. Thash why he's dead and I'm alive. I wanna cum now. Can you make me cum?"

I told him "shore" to that, too; but first made sure that he took another good whiff from Madame Xanadu's flask of delights, and this time I thought his heart was going to explode. Every muscle in him tensed. His eyes bugged out. His teeth and fist started clinching at the same time, and then . . . I heard two knocks at the door.

"Whosh that?" Gil asked. "Whoshever it ish, tell 'em I payed at the office. And I'm a friend of the sh-owner."

I suggested to Levenberg that maybe we needed to shut off the lights, just in case it was a raid. "The Mayor wuddn't sh-dare!" he cried. "He comesh here himself, ya know?"

I cut off all the lights, then went, completely naked, to the door, where I let Bert in. This time, he had pulled the T-shirt off and was wearing just the dark pants. I put my index finger to his lips, and he tiptoed through the small dark room, right into the bath. Then I said, in a loud voice, "Mr. Hubris, everything's going fine. He's enjoying himself!" I popped the door closed.

I went back to Levenberg on the bed. "Who'sh that?"

"Hubris."

"Alan—whash he doin' here?"

"He wanted to make sure that since I'm new here, I know how to take care of you. And—" I paused, then said, "And he wanted to know if you had told me anything about Chuck Knoedel."

Levenberg's eyes bolted out of his head. "Why? Why'sh he ask you that?"

"Naw," I said. "I'm just joking. He didn't ask that. But I guess all that's supposed to be hush-hush, right?"

He nodded his head. "Ya wanna get me killed? Geesh. Jush the thought makes me shick. I could puke up thinkin' about it."

I told him that maybe he needed some water. He nodded. "Shore," he said. "I could use that."

"Maybe you need some water, too, on your face," I suggested. "You're a

bit drunk, right?"

"Naw," he protested. "But those poppers—they do make me kind of . . ." He got up, and I realized that the room was starting to spin for him. He could barely make it onto his feet, and I guided him into the dark bathroom, where Bert waited. A moment later, I gently placed Gil Levenberg's head in the small sink ("This'll make you feel much better," I said softly. "Just a little water"), as Bert held him down and we filled the basin completely.

Levenberg bucked and struggled to get away from us, but Bert held him down until most of the struggle left his body. Then I pulled him up by the back of his neck, and knocked him to his knees, placing his head into the toilet.

Bert flushed it a couple of times as Levenberg choked, gagged, and came close to dying, with his arms and feet flailing about weakly and hopelessly. Bert became enraged at the sight of him—he had tried to evict us so many times and had used every standard, illegal New York landlord trick in the book (setting fires in our hallway, throwing away three months' rent checks and then taking us to court, moving in junkies below us, knocking out our electricity, no heat in the winter)—and I was sure Bert was ready to kill him. But I did not want to. It seemed silly to kill someone as small as Gil Levenberg—even though the thought was delightful—when Hubris himself waited. "What'll we do?" I asked Bert, after we had stuffed a wet wash rag into Levenberg's mouth, and I decided that I'd had enough of the mustache. It itched. I took some warm water, and eased it off my face.

Suddenly Gil, like a cornered rat, looked up at me. "I guess you know who I am," I said. He stared at both of us, then a look came into his face. It was both furious and embarrassed at the same time.

"I should just kill him," Bert said. "Just rid the world of him!"

"No," I said. "But I think he knows what could happen to him if he doesn't leave us alone."

Bert shook his head. Despite being an angel and one of the world's great daddies, he had no patience for greedy little bastards, no matter what form they took. "What should we do?" he asked.

I shrugged my shoulders. I really had no idea. Then Bert decided to take matters into his own hands. He rammed Levenberg's head up against a tile towel rack, until our landlord passed out. Then we dragged Levenberg back over to the bed, bound him up as best we could with his gold tie and some extension cords that we found in a dresser drawer, and, after that, approached the door.

"Niko and Billy are already in the office, looking for clues," Bert whispered to me.

"Good," I said. "What do you think they'll find?"

"Everything," Bert answered. "But the question is, what'll we do with it, once we find it?"

204

Chapter 19

"We found it all!" Billy said, with that funny horse laugh of his, in the back room of Hubris's office. "Two ledgers, one with the real money in it, the other for the IRS, and a list of places they were going to close—with the Mayor's consent—and even backers. The list of backers is amazing. I think they're all Republicans. The kinda people who never give gays a chance, but who line up to take our money."

"I dunno how Billy did it," Niko said, "but he knew exactly where to look. I just flipped through the pages for him."

"Has Hubris or Steve showed up?" I asked.

"Naw," Billy answered. "They ain't been around. I think they're too busy supervisin' the dancin' lessons. Steve let us in. I used to know him from the old days, back at the St. Mark's Baths. He worked there—he's not as bad as he looks. Just creepy." Billy O'Geech went into his laugh again. "I told him I had to look up an old friend here, and as soon as I used the name Knight, the doors opened for us."

"Yeah," Bert said. "Now I'm a big operator from San Francisco. I kind of like the idea."

"That is the other end of the mountain, isn't it?" I said to Bert. He gave me a quick, disapproving glance. We would not talk about things like that in front of . . . well, almost anyone. "The only thing is, have we found anything that proves Hubris either murdered Chuck Knoedel—or had him murdered?"

"Nuttin' so far," Billy said. "But that don't mean nuttin', either. All we have to do is just get the IRS on Hubris's tail."

Bert's face fell. "Nothing? Not even Knoedel's signature on anything?" Billy shook his head. "I just can't imagine," Bert continued, "that with things the way they are here in New York—a corrupt police department, the property lords and corporations running the show instead of the people—that anyone's going to pin anything on Hubris. I feel like we're back at zero again."

"Or ten-seventy-seven," I said. "What are we going to do?"

"You guys are givin' up too fast," Niko put in. "Lissen, Tommy. You got me to do things I ain't never done—at least, never admitted to doin'. I bet you can do the same thing with this Hubris dude. He likes a good blow job as much anyone else, right?"

That I could attest to in any court. But we needed a witness—some real witnesses. I could see Billy reading my mind. "Y' know," he said, "This office's got everything. There's even one of them digital tape recorders for messages. It ain't that big. We'll bring it back to room eight—Niko and I'll stay under the bed, and listen to what's going on. It'll be dark anyway. You and Bert can get Hubris in there, and when he starts to sing, we'll make sure we have a record of it."

"Everything shipshape?" Hubris asked, back in the leather room. Bert, wearing only his underwear, had gone out looking for him, under the pretext that he had no towels—and at those rates, he expected the works. He found Steve, and demanded that Hubris personally bring them in. Hubris, his jacket neatly buttoned, arrived quickly with a fluffy stack of fresh terry cloth towels. He squeezed open the door, and complete darkness hit him after the bright hallway.

Bert closed the door behind him. It took Hubris a moment to get used to it. "It is now," Bert said smiling, taking the towels. "Why don't you get more comfortable, Alan? Take off your jacket, your tie. Your shirt, maybe. Why not mix some pleasure with your business? I like to do that."

"I don't usually do that." Hubris's arctic voice answered. "But," he paused, then said: "At times, I can."

Then, in that room that was starting to seem almost ruby red in the dark, he untied his tie and dropped his jacket. Soon after, his shirt cascaded to his feet. "That's better," Bert said, and he unhitched Hubris's belt and felt inside his briefs until he had Hubris's already hard dick in his hands. I could see a guarded, strange smile on Alan's face as his hands guided Bert's bearded face down to his cock.

Bert agreeably sucked him for a moment, then got back up. "That's nice," Bert said. "But why don't we use some of the equipment here?" He pointed to the array of restraints, slings, and ladders that came with the leather room.

"Sounds good," Hubris agreed. "Should we two tops tie Tommy up?"

"Sure," Bert agreed. I put my hands behind my back. Hubris must have forgotten about my mustache, or in the dark did not notice it was gone. Bert pretended to take a rope and some handcuffs to me, but instead snapped the cuffs onto Hubris.

"Wait a second!" Hubris protested. "Nobody does that to me. I'm always the *top* here."

206

Bert shook his head. "Sorry, Alan. It's time for you to enjoy yourself. Chill out. Tommy and I'll service you like you've never been done. I love to make my *bottoms* feel in command. Have you ever felt that way?"

"No," Hubris answered. "I've always been too—" He stopped talking. I could not tell if it were just shame, or some revelation he could not deal with.

"Sure," Bert said. "You've always been too much in command. Now, let us take over. We'll show you—"

He kissed Hubris warmly on the mouth, and, strangely enough, Hubris opened his mouth up to him, and they kissed like I could not imagine Hubris, with all of his reptilian cunning, kissing. It was as if he had opened up his whole *being* to Bert. He had capitulated: given himself up. Or was I being crazy, and foolish—and Alan Hubris had simply wanted to at the moment?

But I could admit that Hubris, then, in that complete, surrendering kiss with Bert, had made some contact with his own soul, his own aura, the very thing that in order to kill him, finally, for good, we needed to steal. Of course, Hubris had a soul—everyone does, whether they know it or not; even as worm-eaten as Hubris's might be. Still, that surrender of his aura surprised me; though, who, even momentarily, could not surrender to Bert?

We stripped Hubris completely naked and tied him up to a ladder by a wall. His legs were very darkly hairy—no wonder he had not wanted to take his pants off. They reminded me of the lower extremities of some cloven-footed creature; a goat, perhaps. His body, though, had no hair on it at all. His smooth chest, remarkably boyish, with almost no visible muscle in sight, was marked by a tattoo of a long, skullish face looking right at you, the lips curled up archly, the large teeth bared. Its horns—a goat, again?—curled around each of Hubris's dark extended soft nipples.

Bert kissed each of Hubris's nipples. Sucking on them. Licking them at first, then carefully biting them, with just the right amount of pressure. Hubris began to whimper, from a mixture of pleasure and pain. His cock started to twitch. The balls under them bounced from the pressure. Bert's mouth went to Hubris's balls. He sucked them so hard that Hubris started to cry out. He used no words. Just this long moaning cry.

I turned the lights up a bit. I really wanted to see what was going on. We were all now naked, and I enjoyed brushing up against Hubris's restrained body. He looked at me, knowingly, and did not complain at all, but suddenly squeezed his eyes closed, blinding himself. Then, without warning, Alan started screaming. "You must punish me! You have me now!" Tears streamed from his eyes. "Punish me, please . . . please . . . PLEASE!"

The words rocked back and forth in our ears. They were like the boom-box car in the storm, that night when I rode back with Niko to his house. They had thunder, lightning, rain in them. *You have me now! Please . . . please . . . please.* He was pleading, but why? What was the punishment for . . .

this time?

I wanted to stay right there in the moment. I wanted to find out what this . . . odious character was about: Hubris . . . Odred. But I could not: I was being thrown back with Bert . . . over the Bridge. I tried to keep it from happening. I grabbed hold of Hubris's body, and found myself locked to his slick, naked chest, as if he were holding me, though in fact he was not. Although, as he said, I "had" him, I could not let go. Even with his aura, his will and soul, now in my hands, *I* was the one sealed to him.

I could not let go. And neither could Bert. He had his tongue now on one of Hubris's nipples, and the nipple was holding him, as if an iron hand were pressed to Bert's face. Time swirled around us, giddy, extreme, like a merry-go-round attached to a rocket. We were hurled, propelled, centrifugally, out to the edge—where the words I heard were, "Please . . . *please* . . .

"Please," said Baron Odred de Campe graciously. "Come in!" We were both back in the dark chapel of the Baron's keep. Three years had passed since that morning when we had said good-bye to Neatsfoot—and I was now as close to manhood as I would be. We had experienced many adventures in this life, and I had known more than I would ever venture to dream. I could now read, and even write my own name in script. I had followed Sir Bertrand back to Provençe and we had gone all the way to the Holy Land together.

We had fought many battles, and in many ways I had grown up. I was no longer so frightened; I saw the world from a different viewpoint, no longer that of the unlettered churl. Still, as he had promised, Sir Bertrand had protected me *toujour*, always. When we had traveled through rich Burgundy, as spies for Sir Garet, and I had been captured and lashed to a stake, Bertrand had swept in on Fire. He cut my bounds, and rode away with me. When Akmet Bey, the Saracen lord of Jerusalem, had set a clever trap to capture me for his slave, Bertrand had disguised himself as an old Arab woman to come for me. Such valor! But never had we forgotten the Baron Odred—and our hatred for him. A hatred that forged a link with him that we could not cut without blood.

So again, in disguise, this time as merchants with excellent horses and an array of goods, but concealing daggers and swords in our robes, we had come in stealth at vespers time to the Baron's ugly keep. A multitude of eyes looked at us in the waning afternoon, smiling warily. With humility, we inquired where we might find the worthy *seigneur* of the castle.

"Baron Odred de Campe is in private chapel in prayer, good sirs," a young handsome archer told us. "Let us show thee," and he pointed the way. Thus, we entered once more this room with its evil pictures, goblets, and wealth. There, in its dark reaches, we found the Baron alone.

"Please," the Baron repeated, once the doors were closed on us and the three of us were alone in the chapel. "Do come in . . . I have been attending

for you."

"*Pourquoi*?" Bertrand asked, shrugging his broad shoulders. "We are only merchants, we . . . "

The Baron smiled. "*Pas*! Why lie, sir knight? I kouth your nature and that you would return. I commanded my men not to harm you, so we might be alone here—again—in the Demon Beast's own chamber. Remember this place? We will now have a service for him, the dark brother of our Lord."

"We shall have a service with your throat!" Bertrand said, raising a dagger from his rich cloak.

The Baron laughed. "Please . . . please, you are such a fool, Sir Bertrand. Do you so much desire that you and your sweet friend die? Is death as delicious to you as *he* is?"

"Its taste does not frighten me," Bertrand said. "I have tasted death before—"

"Then why be so arrogant, sir knight? I have a bargain for you; allow me to present it. I request your presence at a service we will here do in memory of Captain Turlow. Remember? My commander, whom you murdered as you would have murdered me?"

"You placed him in my hands," Bertrand said. "I deemst thou did not love him."

"I love no one," Odred answered wearily. "I kouth all. And wish only to know you two, if thou wilst, in the honest ways of the Demon. If so, I promise, I shalt give myself up, surrender, and be brought to trial. For, you see, the Demon, I fear, is up with me." He looked straight at us. "This I kouth, as he gives me no more favor. I plead then: please me, good knight, and I shalt please you."

I looked on, again speechless in the presence of the Baron. The Baron requested our blasphemy at the altar of the Demon, yet in the service of good . . . what is bad?

Bertrand looked seriously at him and nodded. For the first time, it seemed possible to look into the Baron's eyes and see human surrender—to see the Baron's very soul. We promised, then, that we would do as he pleaded and we would worship the Demon with him. He directed us: the three of us would strip ourselves naked. This we did, and he began the service, passing red wine to us in our mouths from a chalice. "Now," Odred directed softly. "Kiss me upon my lips, my nipples, and my tarse. Spill this wine from your warm mouths there upon these places, and then lick it. Show fealty to me, and I shalt be good to thee."

This we did, both of us, solemnly in this dark place, until there was no wine left in our mouths. At that, the Baron directed that we bind him, as he wished, to the altar table. In doing this, as he commanded, we observed closely a new sinister depiction on his smooth, bare chest: that of the long-

faced, horned Goat Man, the Demon Beast himself, who resembled in every way and feature none other than Odred.

Once bound, Odred directed my lord Bertrand to suck him on his pointed, hard nipples as if Bertrand were a wee child sucking on his mother's teats. Sir Bertrand leaned over and knew exactly how to please Odred, and they mingled with one another there; with Bertrand performing warily as Odred, on the altar table, moaned in pleasure in his own confinement, and I, willingly, sucking at Odred's erect tarse, giving myself to it, as it was shorn of all hair, though his legs were as hairy as a ram's.

"Yea!" Odred screamed, "Take my tarse into thy mouth, and my great balls, too. Suck on my balls, make them hot with your sweet mouth. Then suck my tarse again! Make my cock hard as that of a young ram, or a wild bull!"

As part of Bertrand's agreement, I did as he instructed. I took his cock into my mouth, and made him as hard as a bull's huge member, though it seemed foolish to compare him thus. His male shaft was nowhere near so big, though it was not small, either. But it became bigger as his excitement grew and grew. His cock throbbed with heat and power; then he begged to be unloosed from the table.

"Bugger me, Sir Bertrand!" he screamed. "Stick thy young, strong tarse up my bungshute! Do with me as thou wouldst any maiden. Take my maiden cunt head—and I shalt be thine for all time!"

And Sir Bertrand, because of his promise, honestly did this. He did not fuck the Baron from mere lust—for he had no lust for the awful Odred. But he untied the Baron, then bent him upon the altar table and applied his beautiful cock right up the Baron's hairy hot arsehole, whilst the Baron twisted and screamed from boundless animal lust, screamed for Bertrand to please him and to punish him at once.

The Baron's words froze in my ears like an arctic breeze, returning me quicker than I was prepared for to room eight at the club. I felt dizzy, slightly nauseated. Where was I? My head felt like it had been slammed. I opened my eyes to see Hubris's wet cock in front of me; emptied of all spirit and glued to Hubris's skin, my body, alone, with none of my soul in it, had been sucking it.

Now I was back in that body, while he screamed again that we must punish him. "Fuck me!" he cried. "Turn me around, Bert Knight, and give it to me!" Bert and I looked at one another, as two angels who had crossed Time and come back again. And although I felt strangely distant, Bert was as hard as a tire iron; and I knew that something had to happen, even while Niko and Billy listened.

210   "I'll be happy to fuck you," Bert said. "Let's take you down, and tie you

up on the bed. But first, Alan, I want you to answer a question for us."

"Anything," Hubris cried. "I'll do anything. Never have I felt so liberated. So joined completely with everything that I indeed am!"

Bert tried to phrase everything right. "Did you have Chuck Knoedel killed? Do you know anything about it?"

"I know everything!" Hubris answered. "I know it all. Fuck me now and I'll tell you."

We untied him and took him down from the ladder. He knelt at our feet, and wished only to be fucked by Bert. He kept calling him Bertrand. "Bertrand," he said. "I know you're Bertrand. Do you think I'm so stupid that I don't know who you both are—and have always been?"

We tied him back up and put him on the bed, then Niko and Billy came out from under it and watched in the dark, while Bert fucked him. He wore a rubber and used lots of Lube, then went at it slowly, getting first only the head of his cock in there, then all the way down he went, until he was right on top of Hubris's ass, which, unlike his smooth chest, was as hairy as his goatish legs and all animal muscle as well.

Hubris cried, sighed, and whimpered with pleasure and release. "You want to know everything?" he said as we listened. "Then I'll tell you. But it'll do you no good at all; because if I'm not here, then what was begun will only go on without me."

"And what's that?" Bert asked, working up a sweat, his hairy, graying chest now dripping with perspiration. It was very warm in room eight. But the sweat also dripped because Bert had become so involved with fucking Alan Hubris—slowly and deeply—and, at the same time, holding back his own struggling orgasm, as Hubris began to talk.

"I know what happened," Hubris announced. "And I know what happened to you, Thomas." He looked over at me.

"Me?"

"True!" Hubris announced. "You, Thomas Jebson. I know of your past life in that time. Just as I also know that even angels in the handsome form you two take have only *one* purpose on this earth at any time. The purpose is to serve, to bring comfort, to make well. And the purpose is the truth. But that purpose says you cannot serve angelic *lust* and human *truth* at the same time."

"You are the Devil," Bert cried. "You are the Demon truly."

"Oh, no," Alan Hubris answered. "Even I am not so arrogant as to say that, Bertrand. Even I know whom I *choose* to serve. That is why, my good knight, even if I confessed to you the death of Chuck Knoedel, it will do you no good. Because you cannot be here, doing what you are doing, and where I shall take you at the same time."

"I won't let you do it!" I screamed. "Bert, stop fucking him! Stop now!"

Bert looked at me. "I can't," he cried, tears coming down his face as his body jerked back and forth into Hubris's tight haunches. Perspiration poured from him, but he could not stop.

"Thou are most excellent . . . Bert . . . Bertrand. Now the three of us, ready or not, shall take this last trip back."

A deep shrill noise, like wind speeding through a tunnel, entered room eight, sliding us back into the dark chapel of the Demon. There Sir Bertrand was fucking Odred, who screamed with release with every stroke of my handsome lord's goodly member. The Baron had commanded me to bring my mouth to his tarse, and I, as part of our promise with him, was sucking him good, lavishing my tongue and lips with detail and service to him. Then, with a crash, the doors of the chapel stormed open.

Odred's whole army of men came in, armed in Norman mail and iron plate, swords drawn. "Take them!" Odred screamed. "They are the perverts of the Devil! Look in what positions you have found them!"

Only another scheme! Another trick! My anger raged within me. I became boiling angry—this Baron was indeed Evil-made-Human, the fallen angel of the Devil himself. And this "service" was only to serve him; and destroy ourselves. Now I knew it was all true: that my lord Bertrand's goodness would always stand in the way of his killing the Baron. Forever so.

Raging violently, my teeth bit into the Baron's still hard cock. He screamed and tore at me, pulling at my hair and throat, even as my mouth became filled with this monster's blood.

"Thou pervert! Thou witch!" Odred screamed and closed his hands around my neck to strangle me. I jumped up. I attempted with all my life to spring from his grasp, but could not as the Baron had snatched a fistful of my blond hair, latching his hand to my scalp with it. Though naked, Bertrand grabbed his sword from his robe and raised it to cut off the Baron's head. But Odred had maneuvered his own wicked face close enough to mine that Bertrand could not strike him without killing me.

All I felt then was the Baron's iron grip around my neck, and a slow, slow seeping in of light. . . . Light, silvery, fluttering about me. Even in that dark chamber—filled with silence—with the Baron's army frozen in disbelief, as the Baron, using all his might, rammed my almost lifeless body directly onto the gleaming point of the sword Bertrand held.

Thomas Jebson, the churl youth who had followed his knight, was dead. And Sir Bertrand, now older than any of his years, his heart broken, collapsed and cried only to be taken.

"I am done!" Bertrand sobbed. "You have us now, Odred. You may take me and do as you wish! Kill me that I may join Thomas. Kill me, I beg of you."

"Why?" the Baron smiled. "To do so would only anger righteous Garet

du Fontayne and his friends. They are *bon* knights, but of too much folly. *Pas*, we shall meet again, Sir Bertrand. Perhaps at the Court of William, King and Conqueror, sometimes himself called 'the Beast,' you know. It is the Year of Our Lord, 1077, and history will change England. Men like I will take this island kingdom. Only might, power, and wealth will reign. It will stay in the hands of a few men pledged to the King and his corporates. All else is foolishness, kouth that, Sir Bertrand. Kouth that *toujour*."

Bertrand shook his head. He got up and began to reclothe himself, as the Baron's army watched in silence. "God will punish thee, Odred de Campe, always. Thou will know no love, truth, friendship, nor happiness, no matter how much power and wealth thou possess. And I shall ride after thee forever, I promise."

Odred smiled. "Keep thy promise, and thy young friend!" He chuckled. "My men will permit you to leave. There is no more fear in me of you. My soul is intact." He spat at Bertrand's feet, on the polished floor of the dark chapel. "I shall vanquish thee at every try!"

After clothing himself, Sir Bertrand took my naked corpse with him and rode out slowly alone from the Baron's keep. It was now fully dark, and he entered the forest where he was met by Richard Smart and the other foresters who cried with him when they saw me. Bertrand cried over me all night, sobbing with loss, and Richard came and kissed him and sat with him, and tried to console him, but could not.

Then on the morrow, before the first light of the sun had kissed the earth, Sir Bertrand asked Richard Smart and his friends to leave. Then, as naked as I, he carried me, slung over the back of his horse, Fire, a short way off, up to a small knoll at the edge of the forest. This he remembered, as it resembled in its privacy that first place where Sir Bertrand of the Land at the End of the Mountain had met Thomas Jebson. And there, he met the sun's earliest rays.

He placed my body on a bed of ferns and herbs, and placed himself directly over it. His chapped lips were upon my lips and then upon my brow. The sun passed over him, gilding him, turning his dark long locks to molten gold, his eyes to silver, his tears to white wine.

"I cannot bring thee back, Thomas, as I did Neatsfoot," the knight said sobbing. "For to do so would mean to lose you forever. It is our law: we cannot keep eternally what we do. So I had hoped that we would both die together, that is why I had put us both into such danger; but it was not to be so. I cannot join you at this time on earth. But I shalt never leave thee, Thomas, and in a great pouring forth of Light we shall meet."

At this, I felt myself being lifted up, weightless, without care or fear, as if Jesus Himself had kissed me. Though my body remained with the forest men whom I loved, I was brought to the simple glowing Heights of the Everlasting and was taken into the calm Substance of God. There I waited for

my knight from the Land at the End of the Mountain, who rode off, once more alone, only to die in five years of wounds and fever, and then join me.

The wind stopped. I felt warm again, and at home, if only for being Tommy Angelo, in that body once more. "So," Bert said, looking at me. "We meet the Baron once more—he is an evil bastard! I should have killed him."

"You couldn't," I said. "That's the problem with good. Evil always does just pop back up. Then it tries to put the blame on lust or vice—just to throw us off its trail."

"Speaking of trail," Billy said, "Where's this Hubris guy? For a while, you guys looked like you weren't even here. I keep tellin' Tommy he's gotta stay in the moment, but Bert, you were fucking Hubris, and then . . . he just disappeared. How'd he do that?"

We looked around. Alan Hubris wasn't any place. We had come so close to taking his aura, and now he had it back. How could we explain any more to Niko or Billy? I'd been able to revive Niko; I was happy for that, but it meant that his coming back to me was purely on his own: I would never be able to keep him with me, as Neatsfoot would have wanted. So I could not explain Niko's revival, or Hubris's strange disappearance.

The situation was hallucinatory enough; soon Niko and Billy would think that we were all ready for a looney bin. The four of us were now alone in room eight, and even having the goods on Hubris—his books; the numbers—what good would that do? Bert and I hurried to put our clothes back on; it was already morning and more than time to leave.

But some commotion was going on outside. Doors knocked on. Loud voices. I popped my head out into the hallway and the first person I saw was Ernie.

"I been looking for you," he said. "Man, you better get your ass outta here! Your first dance lesson of the night—that Gil guy—"

"What?"

"He's dead, man. Somebody strangled him. He's over! And the cops are here!"

Hubris, perfectly dressed in his dark suit, appeared with three cops. "It's an awful situation," he said to one detective. "But I can vouch for all my boys. Hey, Tommy, you did not see Mr. Levenberg all night, did you?"

Bert, Niko, and Billy looked on dumbfounded. "No, sir," I said. "Not all night."

"This is his first night here," Hubris explained. "He's one of our best hosts. We run a private club for visiting businessmen. It's the host's duty to make them comfortable. Everything is above board here—even the Mayor can vouch for that. Personally, I think Mr. Levenberg killed himself. He was getting older and having a hard time in business lately. Some of his build-

ings, you know, are greatly undervalued; even now with the real estate boom. Taxes. Debt. He seemed kind of depressed to me." The detective, a short Hispanic man, wrote everything down in a small notebook.

Hubris excused himself, then turned to Ernie. "Ernie," he said, putting his arm around Ernie's shoulder, "I think your shift here has ended. In fact, all your shifts here have ended. We'll give you some severance and everything we owe you, but, frankly, you're just not bringing in the kind of requests we used to have for you."

Ernie's face fell. He looked at me and I smiled at him, because I knew that neither of us would ever come back again to Club Xanadu.

The good part of this story is that now we don't have to worry about Gil Levenberg—at least for a while. His estate is deep in probate, and we'll get some relief from him trying to evict us. Ray Lang, the photographer, laughed when he heard about it. "I just hope he got choked by a big dick!" Ray said to Bert on the phone from Florida. "You guys just don't know what you're missing down here. The boys! More sunshine, less attitude!"

"Yeah, and the hurricanes," Bert said, and then wished Ray a good night. Bert was tired. He had finally got *InQuire* out. In it was a big story about Alan Hubris, the Club Xanadu, and the rest of Hubris's gay empire—with some mention about the politics behind it. *InQuire* was the only newspaper in New York with any story about this. Bert had hoped that the *Times* might pick it up, but they never breathed a word about what really went on.

The investigation about the death of Chuck Knoedel literally disappeared, as quickly and mysteriously as he did. It was business as usual; politics as usual. And the city grinding on in its own way.

"There's so much for us to do here," Bert said to me that night, after the *InQuire* issue came out. (Lead story: ALAN HUBRIS'S EVIL EMPIRE. WHAT ALL OF US NEED TO KNOW.) We were in bed, finally, back in the loft. Bert was sticking his tongue in my ear. He had his hand on my cock. "A lot of gay men need our help. They need an angel on this earth."

A few feet away, Niko was calling his son. He had moved in with us— "Just to get my head together. I think I need to be away from my family for a while." I was glad for that. I couldn't hold on to him, but at least he'd be there for a time. I was trying hard not to fall in love with him: even angels do that, you know. In a short while, he'd be in bed with us. I was looking forward to that. Unlike Sir Bertrand, Bert was not possessive. I guess you can't stay together, on and off, for close to a thousand years and be that way. Anyway, Niko was crazy about him. He called him Daddy Bert and loved it when Bert fucked him, while I sucked his cock.

"What do you think Hubris is up to now?" I asked Bert.

He shook his head. "I don't know. But we've got to find a way to stop   215

him, even if we have to sink to his level."

Niko, naked, hairy, and very hard, appeared. "It sure is nice to get in bed with the both o' you guys." He climbed in and we rolled around together, the three of us enjoying every moment of each other. I could hardly believe how much heat three men could generate, but it was nice to feel it. Bert climbed on top of Niko, and with a well-lubed rubber fucked him. Niko moaned with pleasure. "You sure know what you're doin'," he said.

A moment later, of course, I was sucking this beautiful Greek's dick, when Gregory Nikolas, once called Neatsfoot, appeared. I realized he was now kissing me, and Niko's cock had become Gregory's tongue as it found its way into my mouth. I was in a complete angelic trance brought on by sex and the wonder of Nikolas (as well as Niko) himself. "I've missed you, Nikolas, my secret lover," I said.

"And I, thou," he answered. "Yea, I spent my life thinking about thee," he confessed. "I lived to be an old man of forty-three years. But an evil humor took me, perhaps the plague, I kouth it not. I have no complaints. I could not be with thee, Thomas, because of my promise to Bertrand, but thought of thee much."

"You are wise, Gregory," I said. "Tell me, what shall we do about the evil in the world, of the Baron Odreds, the Alan Hubrises, and their kind?"

"Pursue them," Gregory Nikolas answered. "Do not give up. Evil will not triumph in the end. And I pray you, remember one thing—no matter what form thou takes on the plane of this earth."

"What Gregory?"

"Create some bit of happiness for yourself, then bring others to it. After all, Thomas Jebson, my love—now Tommy Angelo—that is all we can do."

With those words and that wise smile, Gregory Nikolas disappeared; I knew then that Niko, sighing, hard and throbbing, was ready to come in my mouth. With this, all disappeared into darkness, with only the distant lights of the city fluttering, like silvery angel wings, into the loft.

The end.

Although Perry Brass's roots start slowly in his native Savannah, Georgia, he has lived in the exhilarating (and exasperating!) pace of New York City for most of his adult life. He edited *Come Out!*, the first gay liberation newspaper in the world, published by New York's Gay Liberation Front. With two friends, he founded the East Coast's first health clinic for gay men. His work has been included in *The Male Muse, Angels of the Lyre, The Penguin Book of Homosexual Verse, Gay Roots, Gay Liberation* (from Rolling Stone Press), *Out of the Closets, The Bad Boy Book of Erotic Poetry, Grave Passions: Tales of the Gay Supernatural,* and *The Columbia Anthology of Gay Literature.*

His 1985 play, *Night Chills*, one of the first to deal with the AIDS crisis, won the Jane Chambers International Gay Playwriting Contest. He has collaborated with many composers, including the late Chris DeBlasio, who set *All the Way Through Evening*, a song cycle based on five poems from which "Walt Whitman in 1989" was spotlighted in the groundbreaking *AIDS Quilt Songbook*; Ricky Ian Gordon, who set Brass's "The Angel Voices of Men" for the New York City Gay Men's Chorus's "Stonewall 25" Carnegie Hall appearance; and Craig Carnahan, who set "Waltzes for Men," also for the NYCGMC, under a commission from the Dick Cable Musical Trust.

His first two books, *Sex-charge*, a collection of poems, and *Mirage*, a gay science fiction thriller, were both published in 1991 and were both chosen as finalists for Lambda Literary Awards for that year. *Circles*, the even wilder sequal to Mirage, was described by *San Francisco Bay Times* as "a shot of adrenaline to the creative centers of the brain." *Albert or The Book of Man*, the third novel in this series, was described in *Men's Style Magazine* as "part of a saga, comparable to Tolkien's *Lord of the Rings* . . . a rich and complete imagining of a whole world." His novel, *The Harvest*, a gay "science/politico" thriller and a 1997 finalist for a "Lammy" in Science Fiction/Fantasy, deals with the coming brave new world of cloning and the market in body parts. His second book of poetry, *The Lover of My Soul*, published in 1998, was favorably compared by gay activist Jack Nichols to two of Brass's forerunners in the gay tribe, Whitman and Ginsberg. His first nonfiction book, *How to Survive Your Own Gay Life* was a finalist for a 1999 Lambda Literary Award in Religion and Spirituality.

Perry Brass currently lives in the Riverdale section of New York City. An accomplished public reader and speaker on gender and gay-related topics, he is available for public appearances.

Other Books by Perry Brass

SEX-CHARGE

" . . . poetry at it's highest voltage . . ." Marv. Shaw in **Bay Area Reporter**.

Sex-charge. 76 pages. $6.95. With male photos by Joe Ziolkowski.
ISBN 0-9627123-0-2

MIRAGE

ELECTRIFYING SCIENCE FICTION

A gay science fiction classic! An original "coming out" and coming of age saga, set in a distant place where gay sexuality and romance is a norm, but with a life-or-death price on it. On the tribal planet *Ki*, two men have been promised to each other for a lifetime. But a savage attack and a blood-chilling murder break this promise and force them to seek another world, where imbalance and lies form Reality. This is the planet known as Earth, a world they will use and escape. Finalist, 1991 Lambda Literary Award for Gay Men's Science Fiction/Fantasy.

"Intelligent and intriguing." Bob Satuloff in **The New York Native**.

Mirage. 224 pages. $10.95
ISBN 0-9627123-1-0

CIRCLES

AN AMAZING SEQUEL TO *MIRAGE*

"The world Brass has created with *Mirage* and its sequel rivals, in complexity and wonder, such greats as C.S. Lewis and Ursula LeGuin." **Mandate Magazine**, New York.

Circles. 224 pages. $11.95
ISBN 0-9627123-3-7

OUT THERE
STORIES OF PRIVATE DESIRES. HORROR.
AND THE AFTERLIFE.

". . . we have come to associate [horror] with slick and trashy chiller-thrillers. Perry Brass is neither. He writes very well in an elegant and easy prose that carries the reader forward pleasurably. I found this selection to be excellent." **The Gay Review**, Canada.

Out There. 196 pages. $10.95
ISBN 0-9627123-4-5

ALBERT
or THE BOOK OF MAN

Third in the *Mirage* trilogy. In 2025, the White Christian Party has taken over America. Albert, son of Enkidu and Greeland, must find the male Earth mate who will claim his heart and allow him to return to leadership on Ki. " Brass gives us a book where lesser writers would have only a premise." **Men's Style,** New York

"If you take away the plot, it has political underpinnings that are chillingly true. Brass has a genius for the future." **Science Fiction Galaxies**, Columbus, OH. "Erotic suspense and action…a pleasurable read." **Screaming Hyena Review**, Melbourne, Australia.

Albert. 210 pages. $11.95
ISBN 0-9627123-5-3

Works
AND OTHER 'SMOKY GEORGE' STORIES
EXPANDED EDITION

"Classic Brass," these stories—many of them set in the long-gone 70s, when, as the author says, "Gay men cruised more and networked less"—have recharged gay erotica. This expanded edition contains a selection of Brass's steamy often poems, as well as his essay, "Maybe We Should Keep the 'Porn' in Pornography."

Works and other 'Smoky George' Stories 184 pages. $9.95
ISBN 0-9627123-6-1

THE HARVEST
A "SCIENCE/POLITICO" NOVEL

From today's headlines predicting human cloning comes the emergence of "vaccos"—living "corporate cadavers"—raised to be sources of human organ and tissue transplants. One exceptional vacco will escape. His survival will depend upon Chris Turner, a sexual renegade who will love him and kill to keep him alive. "One of the Ten Best Books of 1997," **Lavender Magazine**, Minneapolis. "In George Nader's *Chrome*, the hero dared to fall in love with a robot. In **The Harvest**—a vastly superior novel, Chris Turner falls in love with a vacco, Hart 256043." Jesse Monteagudo, **The Weekly News**, Miami, Florida. Finalist, 1997 Lambda Literary Award, Gay and Lesbian Science Fiction.

The Harvest. 216 pages. $11.95
ISBN 0-9627123-7-X

THE LOVER OF MY SOUL
A SEARCH FOR ECSTASY AND WISDOM

Brass's first book of poetry since *Sex-charge* is worth the wait. Flagrantly erotic and just plain flagrant—with poems like "I Shoot the Sonovabitch Who Fires Me," "Sucking Dick Instead of Kissing," and the notorious "MTV Ab(*solutely*) Vac(*uous*) Awards." **The Lover of My Soul** again proves Brass's feeling that poetry must tell, astonish, and delight. "An amazingly powerful book of poetry and prose," **The Loving Brotherhood**, Plainfield, NJ.

The Lover of My Soul. 100 pages. $8.95
ISBN 0-9627123-8-8

At your bookstore, or from:
Belhue Press
2501 Palisade Ave., Suite A1
Bronx, NY 10463
E-mail: belhuepress@earthlink.net

Please add $2.50 shipping the first book, and $1.00 for each book thereafter. New York State residents please add 8.25% sales tax. Foreign orders in U.S. currency only.

How to survive your *own* gay life
AN ADULT GUIDE TO LOVE, SE,X AND RELATIONSHIPS

The book for ADULT gay men. About sex and love, and coming out of repression; about surviving homophobic violence; about your place in a community, a relationship, and a culture. About the important psychic "gay work" and the gay tribe. About dealing with conflicts and crises, personal, professional, and financial. And, finally, about being more alive, happier, and stronger.

"Wise . . . a book that looks forward, not back." **Lambda Book Report**. Finalist, 1999 Lambda Literary Award in <u>Gay and Lesbian Religion and Spirituality</u>.

How to Survive Your Own Gay Lifel. 224 pages. $11.95
ISBN 0-9627123-9-6

Warlock
A NOVEL OF POSSESSION

Allen Barrow, a shy bank clerk, dresses out of discount stores and has a small penis that embarrasses him. One night at a bathhouse he meets Destry Powars—commanding, vulgar, seductive—who pulls Allen into his orbit and won't let go. Destry lives in a closed, moneyed world that Allen can only glimpse through the pages of tabloids. From generations of drifters, Powars has been chosen to learn a secret language based on force, deception, and nerve. But who chose him—and what does he really want from Allen? What *are* Mr. Powars' dark powers? These are the mysteries that Allen will uncover in *Warlock*, a novel that is as paralyzing in its suspense as it is voluptuously erotic.

Warlock. 224 pages. $12.95
ISBN 1-892149-03-6